BORROWED JUDGES

ꟼP

BORROWED JUDGES

Visitors in the U.S. Courts of Appeals

by

STEPHEN L. WASBY

QUID PRO BOOKS

New Orleans, Louisiana

Published in 2018 by Quid Pro Books.

ISBN 978-1-61027-385-5 (hbk.)
ISBN 978-1-61027-386-2 (pbk.)
ISBN 978-1-61027-388-6 (ebk.)

QUID PRO BOOKS
Quid Pro, LLC
5860 Citrus Blvd., Suite D-101
New Orleans, Louisiana 70123
www.quidprobooks.com

Publisher's Cataloging-in-Publication

Wasby, Stephen L.
    Borrowed Judges: Visitors in the U.S. Courts of Appeals / Stephen L. Wasby.
        p. cm. — (Contemporary society)
    Includes bibliographical references and index.

1. Wasby, Stephen L., 1937–. 2. Judicial process—United States. 2. Appellate courts—United States. 3. Judges—United States. 4. Courts—U.S. courts of appeals. I. Title. II. Series.

KF775 .W86 2018
Library of Congress Control Number: 2018938812

TABLE OF CONTENTS

LIST OF TABLES (Appendix A)

PREFACE

Yes, another book on the U.S. (or if you will, federal or circuit) courts of appeals. But please don't run away, at least not yet. This is a different book. I know we all say that—and mean it. Excellent books on how the courts of appeals function have added substantially to our knowledge of these courts, which are crucial components of our federal judicial system not only for developing cases that do reach the Supreme Court of the United States, but also, and perhaps more importantly given the small number of cases the Supreme Court decides, for providing the final ruling—or, if you will, the final step or resting-place—for most cases in that system. Yet scholarship has touched only tangentially on the use by courts of appeals of judges other than those appointed specifically to sit on that court.

Some circuit courts of appeals make substantial use of such "other" judges, both visiting judges from outside the circuit and district judges from inside the circuit, just as they make considerable use of their own senior judges, those who have opted to take the status best described as "semi-retired" and continue to hear cases. The courts of appeals' use of these types of judges is important because who makes the law of the circuit needs to be understood. Is that law made by a court's own judges or by others, and if the latter, to what extent are they used and what is their effect?

Use of visiting judges and district judges sitting by designation is thought essential in some circuits if the court of appeals' caseload is to be processed. In short, if the courts did not borrow judges from other circuits and from district courts within their own circuit, they would not come close to completing their work. A most important question, especially when these judges sit in cases that result in published opinions, is "Which judges make the law of the circuit?"—what is known as circuit precedent. A court's use of judges other than its own active-status judges cuts against the normative premise that only a court's own judges should write circuit precedent. Under this premise, even if caseload requires use of the court's senior judges and especially if it requires use of "other" judges, only a court of appeals' own judges should be writing the law of the circuit, to avoid the risk of having that law made, at least in part, by judges who are not regular members of the court.

i

The hope is that this volume, which, because of the absence of much prior research, is largely descriptive, will assist in answering several questions. They include:

- In how many cases do "other" judges participate?

- Do those cases result in published opinions or non-precedential dispositions?

- Do those judges write the panel's opinion?

- Does the presence of those judges prompt the court of appeals to rehear a case en banc?

- Does their presence also affect the Supreme Court's decision to review cases?

Presentation of material directed to questions like these may serve not only to expand our knowledge of the courts of appeals as a general matter but will also assist judges of the U.S. courts of appeals obtain a better understanding of a practice in which many courts engage and other courts abjure. That statement may seem presumptuous, but judges are busy people focusing on "getting cases out," so they lack the time, and often the opportunity, to look closely and consider their own workings,

Over more than the last decade, the literature on the U.S. courts of appeals has increased substantially. However, although some scholars have touched upon some aspects of the work of these "other" judges, none has focused in an extended manner, or in book form, on judges who sit in circuits other than their own or on district judges sitting in their own court of appeals. Courts of appeals' own senior judges, usually included with courts of appeals' own active-duty judges, have also received almost no separate attention, so that their contribution to their courts is not known. In addition, visiting judges, when studied, have been examined from the perspective of the circuit visited, so that the perspective of the visiting judges themselves is missing. The present volume hopes to remedy these matters with a focus on judges other than courts of appeals' own active-status judges, primarily through attention to visiting judges and in-circuit district judges who sit on the U.S. courts of appeals, and to a lesser extent on courts of appeals' own senior judges. While attention is given to concern, lasting over several decades, about use of such judges, this is not a history of their use but instead a picture of their use and possible effects in recent times.

This book had its origins in several sources. One was commentary by judges and observers of the supposedly deleterious effects of the courts of appeals' use of visiting judges. Another was the presence of many such judges on panels of the U.S. Court of Appeals for the Ninth Circuit, long at the center of the author's research. That was reinforced by exploration of immigration appeals in that court, which produced the finding that judges from other courts had voting patterns different from those of the Ninth Circuit's own appellate judges. That led to a desire to determine the actual extent to which these other judges were used and then to further exploration as to who really wrote the law of the circuit, not only in the Ninth Circuit but also in several other circuits which made considerable use of judges other than their own. This made something larger out of what had commenced as an interest in the Ninth Circuit, so, with an examination of "What was the situation elsewhere?," the reader will see attention to other U.S. courts of appeals as well as on the Ninth Circuit, although that court remains central.

So, what is this book, which grew from initial examination presented in several unpublished papers,[1] portions of which as updated are used here? For one thing, this volume provides an attempt to address the questions posed above, and others, through examination of several U.S. courts of appeals which make considerable use of "other" judges, including their own senior judges. Thus set aside, after an initial overall look, are those courts which, as a matter of policy or simply of practice, have made very little use of "other" judges. While, as just noted, the primary focus is on the nation's largest federal appellate court, the U.S. Court of Appeals for the Ninth Circuit, attention is also devoted to the First, Sixth, and Eleventh Circuits, and also, as to senior judges, the District of Columbia Circuit, which by policy does not use visiting and district judges. Thus, the smallest U.S. court of appeals and several mid-sized courts are included, which also serves to provide some variation in the types of non-regular judges used. Judges' views of visiting judges reaching back into the 1970s are presented, and data for judges' case participation is drawn from over a decade, starting in 2004. Appendix B provides greater detail on sources of the data.

Much of this volume is given over to extensive description of participation by various types of judges, in different types of cases, in a number of circuits. The result is a lot of numbers—not statistical tests but raw numbers and proportions. This was considered necessary both to provide

---

[1] Stephen L. Wasby, "Visiting Judges Revisited," presented to Midwest Political Science Association, Chicago, Illinois, April 2015; Wasby, "Who Makes Circuit Precedent for the Ninth Circuit," presented to Pacific Northwest Political Science Association, Boise, Idaho, October 2015; Wasby, "Who Makes the Law of the Circuit: The Role of Other Judges," presented to American Political Science Association, Philadelphia, Pennsylvania, September 1-4, 2016; Wasby, "Visiting Judges: Their Views," presented to Midwest Political Science Association, Chicago, Illinois, April 2017.

the accounting, not previously seen, of dimensions of participation and to provide the granular picture indicating change over time. To have provided only summaries of participation covering an extended period would have missed the variation that was discovered from examination of the data collected for this study, and that is a key finding. However, in connection with panel composition for cases reheard en banc or for those reviewed by the Supreme Court, more extended periods are used.

For the reader who wishes some "tabled" numbers, several tables have been placed in Appendix A, with attention called to them in the text. The author may update some of the data and such supplemental material can be found at http://quidprolaw.com/?p=7392. For the reader who finds extended recitation of numbers ("the judges of the First Circuit did this, while the judges in the Sixth Circuit did that"), it is suggested that scanning parts of the chapters with such material should suffice, and the reader may then turn to the considerable other material of a different character, for example, analysis of judges' views, from interviews and their memoranda.

The Layout of the Book. Chapter 1, the introduction, provides an overview of the courts of appeals' use of judges visiting from other circuits and in-circuit district judges and includes a review of the limited literature on their use. The purposes for which they are used—to handle growing caseload and, in the case of district judges, to socialize them to the work of the court of appeals—will be discussed, as will basic concerns posed by their use and the role of senior circuit judges.

As a backdrop for the subsequent examination of visiting judges' actual participation, Chapter 2 presents the views expressed by judges on *visited* courts about using visitors; these views are drawn largely from earlier interviews of Ninth Circuit judges, including their reaction to a judge who regularly visited with them but who criticized the court. By contrast, based on a recent limited survey of most frequent visitors to other circuits, Chapter 3, beginning with the selection of *visiting* judges, provides their views, supplemented by a senior Ninth Circuit judge's extensive experience in several other circuits.

Chapter 4 turns to actual use of visiting judges and in-circuit district judges by presenting the extent of that use by the various courts of appeals, with attention given to the considerable variation across circuits both in general use and in their relative use of types of judges. Discussion is presented of courts which make little, moderate, and heavy use of "other" judges, with identification of the latter providing the basis for later more intensive examination of those courts. The use of "un-

published," that is, non-precedential, dispositions, which overall constitute over four-fifths of courts of appeals' disposition, is introduced.

Chapter 5 is a look at who the visiting judges are, with some focus on
individual judges, especially those who visit most frequently; also discussed is which circuits "give" and which "usc" (borrow) these judges. The
frequency of participation by individual judges is explored, with identification of what might be considered a "cadre" of those judges who visit
frequently and in several circuits.

If visiting judges are one major category of "other" judges used by the
court of appeals, the other is in-circuit district judges sitting by designation. They are examined in Chapter 6, where attention is given to the
districts which supply such judges to the court of appeals and to the
individual judges who sit by designation. Also included is a study of the
Second Circuit Court of Appeals, which, in a practice disavowed by other
circuits, has often allowed district judges to hear cases appealed from
their own districts.

Chapter 7 presents what is likely the most important part of the story,
at least in terms of normative concerns about use of "other" judges. The
chapter addresses "Who Makes the Law of the Circuit?," a question with
direct normative implications because of the view that the law of the
circuit is to be made only by a court of appeals' own judges. The chapter's
focus is thus on cases resolved by published opinions, which are "circuit
precedent" unless displaced by the court sitting en banc. Attention is
focused on the extent to which "other" judges write opinions and whether
their presence "make a difference," that is, whether their presence is
determinative, as when they cast dispositive votes when a three-judge
panel divides 2-1 or contains two "other" judges. To provide a view of how
"other" judges affect law in a specific policy area, information about their
role in immigration appeals in the Second and Ninth Circuits is provided.

In Chapter 8, attention shifts to courts of appeals' use of their own
senior judges. Judges' views of senior judges' presence on panels are
reported, followed by examination of the extent of senior judges' participation in cases with published opinions and in non-precedential dispositions in several circuits. Also reported are senior judges' authorship of
published opinions and their casting of determinative votes.

With attention thus far devoted to composition of and activity in
three-judge panels, Chapter 9 turns to an exploration, at least for those
courts of appeals which make considerable use of "other" judges, of
whether the participation on panels by visiting judges, district judges
sitting by designation, and senior circuit judges might be a prompt for a

court of appeals to rehear cases en banc or for the U.S. Supreme Court to accept cases for review.

Chapter 10 provides a brief conclusion.

Appendix A presents tables of data for those who wish to see the numbers, and Appendix B describes the sources of the data used in this study.

Acknowledgments. In the course of this project, from the papers presenting initial data through the completion of this book, one person has been of particular help—Jeff Budziak, my colleague at Western Kentucky University. We have never been co-authors, but we regularly interacted as colleagues in the best sense. Jeff and one of his assistants undertook important coding of case data, although remaining data-coding was my responsibility. More importantly, Jeff became a regular reader of papers and segments of papers, and he helped immensely by discussing how this project should develop into this book, all the while not interfering with his own, separate interests in visiting judges. His advice and nudging about some matters (he knows what they are, and I decline on advice of counsel to say) have been most helpful. He was also masterful in helping to construct the tables in Appendix A.

For certain parts of this book, conducting WESTLAW searches for cases was crucial. The best of all "law librarians," Dick Irving of the University at Albany, helped immensely by undertaking the challenge those searches provided. At much earlier stages of my research on the Ninth Circuit, resulting in an 1982 article on that court's use of "extra" judges, data-gathering and tabulating were performed by Becky Colford Murphy, Don Frazier, Susan Hickman, John Rink, and Michael Wepsiec.

As the book project came into being, my west coast colleague and sometime sounding board, Carolyn Long of Washington State University–Vancouver, was invariably helpful. Also quite helpful were the detailed comments by Justin Wedeking, University of Kentucky, on a paper about visiting judges' views of their experience. Very helpful in providing some intelligence about federal courts has been Gary Wente, former Circuit Executive of the First Circuit.

My work on the courts of appeals has long benefited from past conversations with "Woody," the late J. Woodford Howard, and with Richard Richardson. And my late father, Milton C. Wasby, a consummate contract-writer with a sharp eye for editorial "goofs," made substantive and stylistic comments on one of my first ventures into the present subject matter.

Others whose comments and questions were helpful include those who heard presentations of papers at the meetings of the American

Political Science Association, Midwest Political Science Association, and Pacific Northwest Political Science Association, and who attended a presentation to the Legal Studies Program, University of Massachusetts–Amherst.

I am grateful to others for materials about the judges' views. In particular, I thank Senior Judge Alfred T. Goodwin, for whom I served as archivist, for access to his papers, which provided further perspectives on his and his colleagues' views of use of visiting judges, and for access to his case files, which provided evidence of his experience sitting in several other circuits. I also want to thank the many judges who allowed themselves to be interviewed in person or by telephone or who responded in writing to my surveys, most recently about their experiences as visitors in other circuits and, earlier, about a wide range of subjects about their court, including their views on the use of visiting judges, district judges, and senior judges to assist in deciding cases. They deserve especial thanks for talking to "the [then much younger] professor." Assistance with construction of the earlier survey was provided by Dorothy Robyn and Professor Thomas Kerr.

Financial assistance for the very earliest stages of the research reported here came from the Office of Research Development and Administration, Southern Illinois University at Carbondale, and from the Penrose Fund of the American Philosophical Society.

I cannot conclude these acknowledgments without expressing my deep appreciation for the contributions of my publisher for this work, Alan Childress, and the excellent copy-editor Lee Scheingold. Lee's precise, careful work not only saved me from many minor errors but has led to a much cleaner book. Without Alan's enthusiasm for the project, this book would not have happened, and he could not have been more helpful. His meticulous attention to all phrases of the manuscript process is something now seldom found in publishing. It has been a pleasure to communicate with someone who is more like a colleague than someone "just doing his job."

STEPHEN L. WASBY

Eastham, Massachusetts
December, 2017

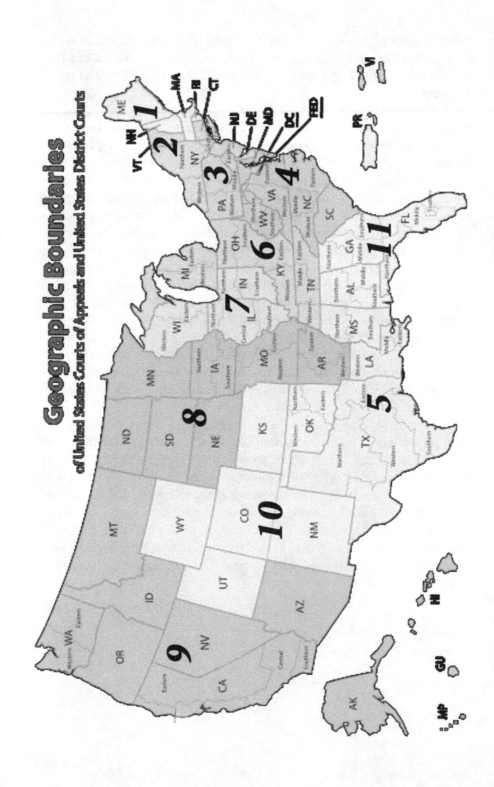

Geographic Boundaries
of United States Courts of Appeals and United States District Courts

1
INTRODUCTION

Overview

Over time, there have been significant transformations in the federal judicial system, which did not appear full-blown in its present form in the Judiciary Act of 1789. The Evarts Act of 1891, which created the U.S. courts of appeals basically as we now know them, was one such transformation, although at the time there were far fewer judges and some changes in the alignments of the circuits were to come. Another such transformation was the shift of the Supreme Court of the United States into a discretionary jurisdiction court, a transition begun before 1925 but happening in the most major way through the Judges Bill of that year with greater use of review by certiorari petition. Another transformation, although certainly of lower visibility, resulted from the problems courts encountered in processing their dockets when faced with significantly increased caseload without new judgeships. This situation was what led the U.S. courts of appeals to move to the use of what were initially called "unpublished" dispositions, which decide the appeal but are non-precedential.

Also of low visibility, but nonetheless significant, is the courts of appeals' increased borrowing from outside their own ranks, their drawing on judges from other circuits and district judges from within the circuit, who come to sit with the court of appeals "by designation," to help decide (dispose of) cases. The need for such assistance results from heavy, and growing, caseloads, which the courts of appeals, as mandatory jurisdiction courts, cannot turn away, unlike the Supreme Court, with its discretionary jurisdiction which allows it to select the cases to be reviewed. The out-of-circuit visitors brought to assist a court of appeals are quite likely to be senior judges. To sit outside their circuits, active-status judges not only must deal with their home court caseloads but must also obtain permission from the U.S. Judicial Conference's Inter-circuit Assignment Committee, but these strictures do not constrain senior judges who wish to travel. In-circuit district judges are also asked to sit with the court of appeals for another reason—to socialize them so that they understand what their appellate colleagues expect of them—and district judges are often brought to sit with the court of appeals within a short time of their appointment to the district bench.

1

One can speak of judges being "borrowed" because a court of appeals bringing judges from outside the circuit or from districts within the circuit has "borrowed" them from their own regular places of doing business to which they will return. The notion that these judges are "borrowed" is perhaps most apt when the judges who come to sit with a court not their own are on active status, because the time they spend in the visited court is time not available to the home court—nor, given the visited court's need for their assistance, is it likely to be repaid once the visitors return home, so it may be like the tool the neighbor "borrowed" but was later found in the neighbor's garage. Even when the visiting judges are senior judges, as they are most likely to be, with more flexible schedules and a desire to visit elsewhere in addition to whatever caseload they continue to handle at home, they have been "borrowed," as can be seen in the senior circuit judge who had served as a visitor but who ceased doing so because he knew there was work to be done at home for which his court would have to borrow. When courts of appeals use district judges from their own circuits (and especially when this is done early in their tenure when they certainly are in active status), there is no question that these judges are "borrowed." This is because not only are they temporarily unavailable in the home district, but on returning from the court of appeals, they must undertake all their regular district work *and* must meet their opinion-writing and reviewing responsibilities to the court of appeals.

* * *

The use of visiting judges and district judges sitting by designation along with use of a court's own senior judges—courts of appeals' borrowing of judges not on their own courts—is the subject of this book. While the picture many hold—or their unstated assumption—may be that panels of the courts of appeals are composed of three active-status judges, those panels are composed not only of those judges and the courts' own senior judges but also of judges borrowed from elsewhere: district judges from within the circuit and "visiting judges," that is, other circuits' district and appeals court judges. In the absence of a court of appeals' declaration of a "judicial emergency" because of a considerable number of vacancies, each panel is to contain at least one active circuit judge, who presides, and there is an expectation that a panel will contain two "judges of the court," which includes both active and senior circuit judges. Panels thus usually have no more than one non-regular judge, but instances do occur in which two judges on a panel are non-regular judges. The types of non-regular judges who sit on a court of appeals panel vary with the circuit because of courts' differing preferences. Very rarely, when all of a court's judges are recused, a panel may be composed entirely of out-of-circuit judges designated by the Chief Justice.[1]

Judges other than a court of appeals' own judges are borrowed to cope with a caseload that has grown regularly in the face of an absence of new judgeships, and considerable utilization by a court of appeals of its own senior judges is for the same purpose. The category "visiting judges" is not, however, unitary, because circuits differ in their relative use of visiting *circuit* judges and visiting *district* judges. Differences across circuits in the relative use of out-of-circuit visitors and in-circuit district judges further reinforces the need to keep those two categories separate.

In-circuit district judges, in addition to assisting with caseload, are brought to sit with the appeals court, usually shortly after their appointment to the district bench, to socialize them to its ways so they can understand what the appellate judges expect of them. The increased use of senior judges results not only from judges' increased availability through increased longevity after taking senior status, but also because no new judgeships have been created for quite some time—the last major judgeship bill was in 1991—and the number of court of appeals vacancies has remained large because of conflict between the President and the Senate over judicial nominations, especially to the courts of appeals, or the failure to make nominations in a timely fashion. Because a court's senior judges have long been part of its fabric, their participation in cases is not likely to cause the problems allegedly created by the presence of non-regular judges, although substantial participation by senior judges may constrain change that might be infused by newly-appointed judges.[2]

Circuit precedent is usually produced by three-judge panels of the courts of appeals. The law of the circuit is what a panel says unless it is overturned by the court of appeals sitting en banc or is displaced by a U.S. Supreme Court decision. As en banc rehearings are relatively rare, panel decisions are thus almost invariably the circuit's precedent. That is, those rulings are precedent when issued in opinions published in the *Federal Reporter*. Those rulings receive the judges' greatest attention, especially

---

[1] A recent example is DeMasters v. Carilion Clinic, 796 F.3d 400 (4th Cir. 2015), decided by a panel of three *Third* Circuit judges (Ambro, Barry, and Krause), on the recusal of all Fourth Circuit judges, perhaps because the CEO of one of the parties was the spouse of a Fourth Circuit judge.

[2] It must be remembered that senior judges cannot participate in their courts' rehearing of cases en banc, which most obviously establishes the circuit's precedent. If a senior judge was a member of the panel whose decision is reheard en banc, that senior judge may elect to participate in the en banc court, or in the Ninth Circuit's limited en banc (LEB) procedure, to be in the pool from which the en banc panel's members are drawn.

in the careful crafting of those opinions, while at the same time the vast bulk of court of appeals dispositions—over 80 percent in some circuits—are issued as non-precedential rulings (with a number of names, such as "memorandum decisions" in the Ninth Circuit and "summary dispositions" elsewhere). These were initially called "unpublished" rulings because they did not appear in the published case reports, but they now appear in the *Federal Appendix.*

Attention to the use of judges borrowed by one circuit from another is also warranted because of implications for a national judiciary. The federal judicial system has never formally developed a "flying squadron" of judges, unattached to a particular circuit, who could be moved where needed to assist with caseload. Yet the willingness of judges to cross circuit lines, and the ability of senior judges to do so with little difficulty, has perhaps created an informal cadre which serves the same purpose, and their traveling *does* serve to tie the regional courts of appeals together. Visiting judges can be cross-pollenators as they bring back to their own courts knowledge of other circuits' different procedures.[3] This assists in creating a more national judiciary, of which the U.S. courts of appeals are regional components. Many out-of-circuit visiting judges sit only in one circuit, perhaps attracted there by such family matters as wanting to visit their grandchildren, but among those who visit in other courts, there are some who travel from circuit to circuit.[4] One might, however, question the extent to which such traveling judges share, beyond their own chambers or in informal conversations with colleagues, what they have learned, and visiting district judges, on returning home, are not likely be in routine contact with their circuits' appellate judges.

* * *

To determine the accuracy of the mythic picture of a court of appeals panel of three active-duty circuit judges, it seems appropriate—even necessary—to engage in systematic examination of the recent actual use of non-regular judges. Is the panel of three active-status judges the norm, or do many additional faces appear on the appellate bench? And do those

---

[3] For example, Ninth Circuit Judge Alfred T. Goodwin, shortly before he became that circuit's chief judge, was sent by his chief judge to sit in other circuits specifically so he could learn about those differences in operation.

[4] Examples are the late Donald Lay of the Eighth Circuit; former state appellate judge and now Senior District Judge Richard Mills (C.D. Ill.), and Judge Jane Restani of the Court of International Trade. Retired Justice Sandra O'Connor has sat in all circuits but that for the District of Columbia, and the late Justice Tom Clark did sit in all the circuits. See Stephen L. Wasby, "Retired Supreme Court Justices in the Courts of Appeals," 39 Journal of Supreme Court History 146 (2014).

faces belong to a court's own senior judges, long familiar with the court's work, or are they "strangers"? How frequently are judges borrowed from elsewhere to sit on panels? And, beyond their simple presence, do those other judges provide the determinative (or "casting") vote when a panel divides 2-1? And do visitors simply fill a panel's third chair or do they write the opinions for the court and separate concurring and dissenting opinions?

While the U.S. courts of appeals' use of visiting judges and in-circuit district judges has long been a problem in the eyes of lawyers and judges, going back at least fifty years, it is a subject to which not much scholarly attention has been given. To remedy that deficit, this book attempts to provide some answers to questions related to "Who makes the circuit's precedent?" Is it the court's own judges, active or senior, or the circuit's district judges and out-of-circuit visitors? The answers—or at least the picture—provided will help the reader obtain a better understanding how the courts of appeals function. More importantly, however, the examination should assist in addressing the normative concern that the law of the circuit should be made only by a court's own judges. When a court of appeals makes use of many "other judges," concern about the viability of that premise are raised, undercutting it. On the other hand, if a circuit uses such "other" judges in only a small proportion of cases, their possible effect would be less, reducing concerns about violation of normative premises.

Beyond examination of the extent of other judges' participation in the work of certain courts of appeals, attention is also paid to the authorship of opinions by visiting judges and in-circuit district judges and to whether their votes are determinative in the cases in which they sit, as both constitute direct evidence of "other" judges making circuit precedent. While "other" judges' participation is a necessary condition for their effect on the law of the circuit, it is not always a sufficient one. More information about the courts' internal workings would be needed, and access required to additional materials, such as the judges' exchanges in their post-argument conferences and afterwards, in order to determine the part those judges play in developing the substantive content of court of appeals legal doctrine through suggested revision to proposed opinions. Thus, the picture provided here, while advancing knowledge of "who makes the law" in the courts of appeals, can provide only a partial answer to the questions posed.

If "other" judges' participation in cases decided with published opinions raises the question of their potential role in developing the law of the circuit, the use of such judges in the predominant mode of disposition in most courts of appeals—"unpublished," non-precedential dispositions—does not have the same normative edge, because these dispositions are not the law of the circuit and, while they may now be cited to the court, the judges themselves determine what value to be attached to them. (Until relatively recently, they could not even be cited to the court, which could also not cite them in its dispositions.) In short, participation by non-regular judges in cases decided by memorandum dispositions diminishes the possible effect these "other" judges may have on the circuit's law. This is true even if they are assisting greatly in disposing of caseload, although, as well, in-circuit district judges sitting by designation become socialized into how the court of appeals with which they are sitting by designation functions.

However, there is fluidity in the decision as to whether to publish a disposition or to issue it in non-precedential form. The panel in conference often decides on the form in which the disposition is to be written, with the assigned author having a say, and at times that decision is "author's choice," but what starts as non-precedential ruling may morph into a published opinion as the author works on it. Thus it is not as if either in-circuit district judges or out-of-circuit visitors are brought in and assigned to a set of cases designated to be decided in non-precedential form. And, after release of a non-precedential memorandum disposition, one of the parties may ask for publication—usually because the ruling is said to affect other cases—but these requests are not often granted. It should also be noted that court of appeals screening panels, which handle the "easiest" cases, the ones most likely to result in non-precedential dispositions, are composed solely of the court of appeals' regular active-duty and senior judges, not visitors or in-circuit district courts.

In this study of the borrowing of judges to conduct the court of appeals' work, not all circuits are examined, a direct result of variation across the circuits in use of non-regular judges. In some circuits, decisions are made almost entirely by the court of appeals' own circuit judges, both active-duty and senior. Indeed, since 1994, the Court of Appeals for the District of Columbia Circuit has had a policy not to use out-of-circuit visiting judges, and it could not use its own district judges because, as the circuit has only one district, they would be reviewing their own colleagues' rulings. Until quite recently, the Seventh Circuit, also by policy, used no in-circuit district judges, and it continues a policy of not using out-of-circuit visitors. Even without a formal policy of exclusions, a court of appeals' may make only minimal use of "other" judges. By contrast, other courts of appeals, particularly the First, Second, Sixth, Ninth, and Eleventh Circuits, have made significant use of visitors and/or in-circuit district judges in some combination. Because of its considerable use of "other" judges, the Ninth Circuit, the nation's largest, receives particular attention in this book. Several Ninth Circuit judges have noted that use. One stated that "[i]n the year ending June 30, 2012, these judges [visitors and in-circuit district judges] participated in 4.9% of the appeals our circuit resolved on the merits"; two years earlier, "visiting judges participated in more than 1,100 cases that were decided on the merits"; and in 2010, the court "had 185 visiting judges—district judges from the Ninth Circuit and district and circuit judges from elsewhere—helping us by sitting on panels."[5]

What We Know

The three-judge panels deciding U.S. court of appeals cases have received some attention, with greatest focus on their ideological mix, usually based on which president appointed the judges.[6] However, the composition of panels has received only limited and incomplete attention.[7] Yet there are some matters we have learned. The most recent contribution comes from work by Jennifer Bowie and her colleagues, based on some 60 interviews and use of the Court of Appeals Database. Among other matters, they investigated whether visiting judges affect procedural questions such as the decision to hold oral argument, which they found more likely when a designated judge was present;[8] who is assigned the opinion of the court, with district judges less likely to receive the assignment;[9] how long the court's opinion will be: longer when

---

5 Morgan Christen, "Introduction" (to Ninth Circuit Survey), 43 Golden Gate University Law Review 1, 3 (2013); Susan Graber, "Introduction," 42 Golden Gate University Law Review 1, 2 (2011); Marsha Berzon, "Introduction," 4 Golden Gate University Law Review 287, 287 n.1 (2011).

6 See, for example, Joshua Fischman and David Law, "What is Judicial Ideology, and How Should We Measure It?," 29 Washington University Law & Policy Journal 170 (2009); Frank H. Cross and Emerson H. Tiller, "Judicial Partisanship and Obedience to Legal Doctrine: Whistleblowing on the Federal Courts of Appeals," 107 Yale Law Journal 2155 (1998); and Richard I. Revesz, "Environmental Regulation, Ideology and the D.C. Circuit," 83 Virginia Law Review 1717 (1992).

7 But see Stephen L. Wasby, "'Extra' Judges in a Federal Appellate Court: The Ninth Circuit," 15 Law & Society Review 369 (1980-81), and Jeffrey Budziak, "The Strategic Designation of Visiting Judges in the U.S. Courts of Appeals," 36 Justice System Journal 233 (2015).

8 Jennifer Barnes Bowie, Donald R. Songer, and John Szmer, *The View from the Bench and Chambers: Examining Judicial Process and Decision Making on the U.S. Courts of Appeals* (Charlottesville: University of Virginia Press, 2014), p. 47.

9 Id., p. 83.

written by a district judge;[10] how long it will take for the court's opinion to be released, which is longer when the author is a district judge;[11] and, replicating a finding from other studies, who, if anyone, will write separate opinions.[12]

In addition, on the matter of what type of non-regular judges a court of appeals might prefer to use, Marin Levy has written that in-circuit district judges are preferred by some as "the ones most familiar with circuit law," who thus "can be most helpful in identifying a published opinion." Others prefer circuit judges from outside the circuit "on the ground that those judges feel like 'colleagues'" and "are used to the job and have the time needed to do the work required of a sitting," while district judges "can be overly deferential to the other judges on the panel." Still others wish to utilize judges who are in neither category and "do not sit on district courts or ordinary courts of appeals, such as judges from the United States Court of International Trade" because "those judges do not have their own, competing body of law and . . . , given their relatively low workload, . . . are best positioned to accept a writing assignment and therefore serve as real members of the court."[13]

But what else have we learned about use of non-regular judges? In the oldest study, Justin Green and Burton Atkins examined 1965-1969 and found that almost half of court of appeals panels included at least one designated judge, with 5.7% including two; they also found considerable inter-circuit variation, ranging from a low of 25.3% (Eighth Circuit) to levels slightly exceeding 70% (Fifth and Ninth Circuits).[14] In a Research Note limited to the Ninth Circuit, Stephen Wasby provided a preliminary picture of what he called "extra" judges. Starting with the Green-Atkins study, Wasby noted an increase in such use in the Ninth Circuit.[15] In their reports on rates of participation by in-circuit district judges, Saphire and Solimine showed that rates ranged from 23% at the start of the 1984-1993

---

[10] Id., Table 9, p. 114. This finding was, however, not statistically significant.

[11] Id., p. 112.

[12] Id., Table 15, p. 148.

[13] Marin Levy, "Judge Justice on Appeal" (review of William M. Richman and William L. Reynolds, *Injustice on Appeal: The United States Courts of Appeals in Crisis* (2012)), 123 Yale Law Journal 2386, 2416 (2014). How visiting judges are selected is covered in Stephen L. Wasby, "Visiting Judges Revisited," paper presented to Midwest Political Science Association, Chicago, April 2015, and in Chapter 3 below.

[14] Justin J. Green and Burton M. Atkins, "Designated Judges: How Well Do They Perform?," 61 Judicature 355, 363-64 and Table 4 (1978). See also Burton M. Atkins and Justin J. Green, "Consensus on the United States Courts of Appeals: Illusion or Reality?" 20 American Journal of Political Science735 (1976).

[15] Wasby, "'Extra' Judges in a Federal Appellate Court," 371.

period (1984, 1985) but decreased to 14.6% in 1993.[16] Such participation, while 16.4% overall for Statistical Year (SY) 1991 (September 30 1991-September 30 1992), ranged from the Eleventh Circuit's 8% to the Tenth Circuit's 35% and the Sixth Circuit's 36%, with above-average usage of district judges also occurring in the First (20.3%) and Fourth (25%) Circuits.[17]

Also explored have been problems involved in including "extra" judges on the court's panels, something "dictated by caseload pressures."[18] The presence of "extra" judges meant resident judges had to interact with more (different) judges; the force of precedent was diminished by their presence in a panel's majority;[19] and district judges had difficulties getting out opinions for which they were responsible. Interviews revealed a question whether judges visiting from other circuits brought more benefit to the visited court or the visitor's court, and judges noted the problem of visitors' lack of knowledge of the procedure of the circuit they were visiting.

Saphire and Solimine also noted that the presence of district judges sitting by designation could increase the difficulty of maintaining collegiality and consistency in circuit precedent. The judges whose views Jonathan Cohen presented also indicated that use of non-regular judges affects collegiality; judges expressed concern that the presence of a visitor meant that the law may be made by someone not a member of the court.[20] Also noted by those judges Cohen interviewed were visiting judges' "unhealthy tendency to defer to the circuit judges on a panel" and concerns that visitors' presence "skews the work on a panel onto the active judges," as the latter wish to retain important cases "because they perceive that it would weaken the authority of an important rule if it were written by a visiting judge";[21] that resident judges had to provide addi-

---

[16] Richard P. Saphire and Michael E. Solimine, "Diluting Justice on Appeal? An Examination of the Use of District Court Judges Sitting by Designation on the United States Courts of Appeals," 28 University of Michigan Journal of Law Reform 353, 365 (Table 1) (1995).

[17] Id., p. 367 (Table 2).

[18] Wasby, "'Extra' Judges in a Federal Appellate Court," 376.

[19] Id., 374-75.

[20] Jonathan M. Cohen, *Inside Appellate Courts: The Impact of Court Organization on Judicial Decision-Making in the United States Courts of Appeals* (Ann Arbor: University of Michigan Press, 2002), p. 192.

[21] Id., pp. 193, 196.

tional help to visitors who did not know the visited court's procedure; and that visitors caused delay because they were busy with their own work.[22]

Two additional studies, while limited to single circuits, depict a relatively passive role for non-regular judges. Examining participation of non-regular judges in Ninth Circuit decisions, Benesh found that they wrote somewhat less than their proportion of opinions and particularly that they were quite a bit less likely than the court's active judges to issue dissents or concurring opinions.[23] Examining the District of Columbia Circuit, Black and Owens found visiting judges less likely to make suggestions about "home" judges' opinions; visitors' opinions were also more likely to be the subject of requests for change.[24]

The Saphire-Solimine study and two others were limited to district judges sitting with their own circuit's court of appeals. Examination of published and unpublished dispositions in labor law cases from 1986-1993 by Brudney and Ditslear produced the basic finding that these district judges were "significantly less likely to author signed majority opinions, or to dissent from majority opinions, than are their appellate colleagues."[25] Peppers et al. found reason to believe that chief circuit judges' selection of district judges to sit with the court of appeals was motivated by policy considerations, with chief judges choosing those with similar ideologies.[26] A like finding by Budziak, based on 1997-2009 data, was that circuit chief judges were more likely to select visitors sharing the chief judges' policy preferences, but the visitor's presence did not change the voting behavior of the visited circuit's judges. In addition, cases decided by panels containing a visiting judge have been cited differently from those cases decided without a visitor.[27]

---

[22] Id., pp. 193, 196, 197.

[23] Sara Benesh, "The Contribution of Extra Judges," 48 Arizona Law Review 301, 311, 313 (2006).

[24] Ryan C. Black and Ryan Owens, "Bargaining and Legal Development in the United States Courts of Appeals," 41 American Politics Review 1071, 1086 (2013).

[25] James J. Brudney and Corey Ditslear, "Designated Difference: District Court Judges in the Court of Appeals," 34 Law & Society Review 565, 581 (2001).

[26] Todd C. Peppers, Katherine Vigilante, and Christopher Zorn, "Random Choice or Loaded Dice: The Politics of Judicial Designation," 10 University of New Hampshire Law Review 62, 80, 88 (2012).

[27] Jeffrey Budziak, "Fungible Justice: The Use of Visiting Judges in the United States Courts of Appeals," Ph.D. dissertation, Ohio State University, 2011, and Budziak, "The Effect of Visiting Judges on the Treatment of Legal Policy in the U.S. Courts of Appeals," 38 Justice System Journal 348 (2017).

2
WHAT THE JUDGES SAY I:
ABOUT VISITING JUDGES

Prior to examining actual participation by visiting and in-circuit district judges, it is important to know judges' views about the presence of these judges. The views of 21st-century judges and other observers are reported after examination of earlier views of members of the Hruska Commission and of Ninth Circuit judges in 1977 and 1986. These views of judges of an oft-visited court demonstrate that more recent concerns are quite similar to those previously expressed, thus indicating that not much has changed in observers' views of the situation.

Views expressed by *visited* judges are not necessarily shared by those who visit, which are presented in the next chapter.

Among assorted general observations from the legal community about the presence of visitors to the courts of appeals to assist with caseload is the 1995 publication in a legal newspaper of "Pinch-Hit Justice at the 9th Circuit: Biggest U.S. appeals court relies more than ever on designated judges." It was pointed out that published opinions by non-Ninth Circuit judges had "more than tripled" from 1991 to late 1995, and the writer related this use of visiting judges to calls to split the Ninth Circuit because this use made the circuit actually bigger than people thought.[1] Five years later, an article, "Guests Doing the Cooking," carried a subtitle which read in part, "Visiting Judges Are Doing More Work Than Usual, Some of It of Great Consequence."[2] Cited were numerous instances in which an out-of-circuit visitor or Ninth Circuit district judge wrote the panel's opinion, including when the panel was split, and an observer was quoted as to erosion of an earlier rule on not having out-of-circuit judges write for the court in major matters.

Despite the negative tone about the practice that those accounts exhibited, reaction in visited circuits to visiting judges' presence could be quite positive. One could see this in the thanks sent to a visitor for sitting. Although this might have been a matter of simple courtesy, it was coupled

[1] Howard Mintz, "Pinch-Hit Justice at the 9th Circuit," The Recorder, November 11, 1995, pp. 1, 12.

[2] Pamela A. MacLean, "Guests Doing the Cooking," San Francisco Daily Journal, July 18, 2000, pp. 1, 8.

with wishes for that visitor's return. Comments by a visited court's judges have also been often highly positive when they were asked for feedback about visitors. In measured, not slapdash, reactions, Ninth Circuit judges made numerous positive remarks. One judge "endorse[d] with enthusiasm" two out-of-circuit judges with whom he had sat and noted "very positive experience" with two others.[3] A regular visitor was said to be "hard-working and entirely collegial."[4] In one of the strongest encomiums, another visitor was said to be "an absolute pleasure to have ... sit with us the entire week. He fully cooperated in the bench memorandum exchange process. He was well engaged during oral argument. His participation at conference was extremely valuable and he has willingly accepted writing assignments in his share of cases."[5] The advantage of having a particular visitor sit with the court is seen in the remark, "We benefit from his good judgment and can learn something from his broad experience."[6] Likewise, some district judges received high praise. A Ninth Circuit judge said that Judge Samuel King (D. Hawai'i), held in high regard, "defies the aging process" and was "[p]ractical, very well prepared and chock full of wisdom. This guy could teach judges how to judge."[7]

Judges also perceived problems with visiting judges, and their feedback contained negative marks about individuals,[8] but concerns and negative comments were expressed more frequently about in-circuit district judges than about out-of-circuit visitors. One visiting judge was said to be "both smart and quick, but his work is hasty and not very thorough or careful";[9] however, that did not appear to disqualify the visitor, who returned regularly. Another senior circuit judge was said to be "maybe a bit too 'retired' to be a good visiting judge," as unavailability of a law clerk to prepare memos resulted in the judge's own "very brief, off the cuff" memos in which an important point was missed, leading to additional work. (An in-circuit district judge was likewise said to be

---

3 Stephen Reinhardt, memorandum to Clerk of Court Cathy Catterson and other judges, June 26, 2000.

4 Michael Daly Hawkins, memorandum to Catterson, July 10, 2000, re: Judge Donald Lay (8th Cir.).

5 Diarmuid O'Scannlain, memorandum to Catterson, re: Judge Walter Stapleton (3d Cir.).

6 Ronald Gould to Catterson, June 5, 2003, re: Richard Cudahy (7th Cir.).

7 Michael Daly Hawkins, memorandum to Catterson, June 2, 2003.

8 For an especially serious problem created when a very frequent visitor to the Ninth Circuit, residing in the circuit because of health issues, criticized the Ninth Circuit in an opinion in the judge's home circuit, see the last section of this chapter.

9 William Fletcher, memorandum to Catterson, May 30, 2003.

"a little slow in grasping the issues.") In addition, positive reaction was accompanied by mention of health issues which had slowed down judges who had regularly visited the circuit; there was also deafness, which interfered with their functioning at argument and conference. It is clear that the circuit's judges gave careful attention to whether the balance had tipped against these judges' continued return.

Perceived problems went beyond individual idiosyncrasies to the systemic, as when a court sought to limit use of visitors and there was talk of "term limits," restrictions on where visitors may sit, a policy not to use out-of-circuit district judges, and not inviting judges from the "specialty courts because they do not have the wide experience we need."[10] (To fill the court's needs, this judge would have placed Ninth Circuit senior district judges ahead of visitors.) Some problems were said to result from visiting judges' lack of familiarity with the visited court's procedures, particularly as to what to do in advance of argument, although some concerns related to post-argument disposition of cases. While the matter might be as minor as pointing out that circuit practice was to list judges in order of seniority,[11] judges felt that time and effort had to be expended in telling visitors how the court did things. To reduce visitors' problems, some host judges did make accommodations for them, for example, preparing a draft order on denial of rehearing[12] or asking, "Would Judge Sessions like my chambers to file the memorandum disposition on his behalf?"[13]

One difference in procedures that has particularly affected judges visiting the Ninth Circuit is its use of shared bench memos, in which a judge's chambers prepares a bench memo for all three judges on a panel in one-third of the cases on a calendar rather than having each judge prepare internal chambers memos in all cases. Some noted the quality of such memos from visitors or district judges, and there were complaints of having received bench memos without citations or some "not up to our standards." One judge "would not look forward to sitting again" with either of two district judges because "[t]heir chambers work-up of cases

---

[10] J. Clifford Wallace, memorandum to Catterson, June 29, 2000.

[11] "I reiterate only for the sake of thoroughness that in preparing the caption, the Ninth Circuit's convention is to list circuit judges in order of seniority." Alfred T. Goodwin, memorandum to panel containing Judge Jack Zouhary (N.D. Ohio), Oct. 18, 2012, *re*: King v. Astrue, 497 Fed. Appx. 758 (9th Cir. 2012).

[12] "I have prepared the attached draft order granting the extension as a courtesy to Judge Zouhary." Diarmuid O'Scannlain, memorandum to panel, January 18, 2013, *re*: Karpetyan v. Holder, 500 Fed. Appx. 597 (9th Cir. 2012).

[13] Kim McLane Wardlaw, memorandum to Judge William Sessions (D. Vt.), November 14, 2011, *re*: Singh v. Holder, No. 07-72100, 2011 WL 5833172 (9th Cir. Nov. 21, 2011).

was thin and the work they produced was sub-par."[14] However, even a critical judge said that those memos were still important because they "ensure at least a minimum level of preparation by visitors," who, "without them, might be quite unprepared."[15]

The flip-side of this concern is what a Ninth Circuit judge accustomed to shared bench memos does when serving as a visiting judge, as shifting one's method of operation was necessary. Thus one had "to decide early on how best to utilize law clerks," with "only two practical alternatives— short, targeted bench memos in all or most cases, or full memos in fewer, selected cases, or gradations in between." This judge felt the absence of shared bench memos made a visiting Ninth Circuit judge's work harder: "Preparing for an argument calendar in a circuit with a comparably-weighted calendar as ours without the aid of shared or pooled bench memos is significantly more work for both my law clerks and me than preparing for a calendar here at home."[16]

Other problems were said to take place in the writing and circulation of dispositions. District judges sitting with the court of appeals may have particular difficulty in getting out their appellate opinions because they must return to their own caseloads, with the result that their assigned court of appeals opinions are pushed to the back burner. (Of course, some appellate judges are also hardly swift in circulating opinions.) A district judge may even have to turn back an assignment, as when one wrote to the circuit's chief judge to state he was "full of remorse for the extra load placed on you for taking over my writing assignment" and said "there isn't any good excuse except an overload of work." Replied the chief judge, himself a former district judge, "No apologies needed. I have been trying cases in the district court lately and I know how hard you guys work."[17] Of another district judge, it was said the judge "takes a long time to get his dispositions into circulation and, when they arrive, they aren't very satisfactory," perhaps because that judge "overextended himself with non-judicial duties."[18] As if that were not enough, there are also logistical problems that result from "other" judges sitting in the Ninth Circuit.[19]

---

[14] David Thompson, memorandum to Visiting Judge Committee, June 27, 2000.

[15] Marsha Berzon, memorandum to Associates, January 5, 2009.

[16] A. Wallace Tashima, memorandum to Associates, January 5, 2009.

[17] Judge Harry Hupp (C.D. Cal.), letter to Alfred T. Goodwin, Dec. 9, 1991; Goodwin, letter to Hupp, December 12, 1991.

[18] A. Wallace Tashima, memorandum to Catterson, May 30, 2003.

[19] See discussion below in this chapter.

Earlier Concerns

Courts of appeals' use of visiting judges has long been a matter of concern, particularly when substantial use was made of any judges other than the court's own. Expressions of such concern can be found in the materials of the Commission on Revision of the Federal Court Appellate System (the Hruska Commission) in the early 1970s. Such a source may seem outdated, but concerns raised at that time have set the tone for much subsequent discussion. This is also true of the interviews of Ninth Circuit judges in 1977 and 1986 reported below. In addition to judges' views, those of knowledgeable external observers were important because the question of use of "other" judges is in part a perceptual one—of how their presence is seen by those who interact with the courts.

Shortly before the Hruska Commission's creation, judges from several circuits testified to Congress against use of "other" judges. Chief Judge John Brown of the (old) Fifth Circuit reported that his court's use of 45 visiting judges in 1966-1967 proved "it was impossible to effectively assimilate that many visiting judges."[20] Third Circuit Chief Judge Collins J. Seitz asserted that, while his court had used district judges from districts behind in their work, they did not like doing so. He also reported that his court "tr[ied] not to schedule [district judges] when a senior judge is sitting because we don't really want a senior judge and a district judge to sit together because generally in the assignment of the opinions, you don't assign as many to a district judge because he has to go back to his own full-time job," thus "delay[ing] the disposition of the court of appeals work and the senior judges frequently aren't able to take as many cases."[21]

Further concerns were stated at the Hruska Commission's hearings. Fifth Circuit Judge John C. Godbold observed that "the visiting or district judge is not a part of the ongoing institution and can make no contribution to the court's collegiality."[22] And Harvard Law School Dean Erwin Griswold opined:

> You get a visiting District Judge from X Circuit visiting a Court of Appeals from X Circuit and a District Judge from somewhere and maybe a judge from the Court of Appeals, and they are all fine, conscientious, able people, but the notion of stability, the

---

[20] Hearings, "Revision of Appellate Courts," Subcommittee on Improvements in Judicial Machinery, Senate Committee on the Judiciary, May 9-11, 1972, p. 55.

[21] Id., p. 41.

[22] Judge John Godbold, Statement, *Hearings: First Phase*, pp. 376-77 (New Orleans, August 22, 1973).

notion of knowing the tribunal you are dealing with is very widely missing. . . .[23]

These comments are not unlike the later broader statement of concern by a committee of the Association of the Bar of the City of New York, which "believed that the use of . . . visiting circuit judges or district judges sitting by designation . . . is preferable to docket delays which result from unfilled judgeships" but viewed their use as "a generally unsatisfactory substitute for a full complement of active judges in the circuit because of the recurring problem that circuit decisions by divided panels are substantially diminished if not emasculated as precedent in the circuit when decided by a majority consisting of one or two visiting [including district] judges."[24] This view echoed a decade-old complaint about Second Circuit practice: "Consistent use of trial judges on appellate panels may be thought to make the decisions of the courts of appeals less authoritative in the eyes of the bar and public."[25] Some evidence, if indirect, of this possible effect can be seen in the observation by a circuit judge who, as a district judge, had visited in another circuit: that almost every time he had sat as a visitor, his opinions had resulted in requests for rehearing, which he said stemmed from his being a "visitor" rather than a district judge.

Nor was it only lawyers who felt this way. Similar views were expressed by some judges interviewed in the 1970s. One Ninth Circuit Court of Appeals judge said that "litigants frequently wonder whether the result would have been different" had there not been a district judge on the panel: "If the case is important and it is assigned to the district judge to write the opinion, the case has an unavoidable asterisk by it which impairs it." He was joined in this view by a colleague who wrote that a district judge "should not write where there is division on the panel," which could affect assignment of cases. These views have found some support in recent research, based on Shepardizing, on how other circuits treat cases decided by panels containing visitors or in-circuit district

---

[23] Erwin Griswold, Statement to Commission on Revision of the Federal Court Appellate System, *Hearings: First Phase*, Washington, D.C., August 2 1973, p. 16. For an instance of the panel composition to which Griswold referred, see the panel in the somewhat-later case of Meloon v. Helgemore, 564 F.2d 602 (1st Cir. 1977): First Circuit Chief Judge Frank Coffin, Fifth Circuit Senior Judge Elbert Tuttle, and Senior District Judge Albert Wollenberg of the Northern District of California.

[24] Alvin K. Hellerstein (Chairman, Committee on Federal Courts, Association of the Bar of the City of New York), Statement, Commission on Revision of the Federal Court Appellate System, *Hearings: Second Phase,* pp. 1123-24 (Washington, D.C. April 29 1975).

[25] Note, "The Second Circuit: Federal Judicial Administration in Microcosm," 63 Columbia Law Review 874, 879 (1963).

judges. The presence of visiting judges results in more negative treatments by other circuits but the presence of in-circuit district judges does not have the same effect.[26]

In the Commission's hearings, considerable attention was paid to the Ninth Circuit. Judges' testimony indicated the dimensions of that court's use of "other" judges. Chief Judge James R. Browning said that use of such judges provided the court of appeals with the equivalent of four additional judges in addition to its then 13 active judgeships, but in obtaining that assistance, the court used "80 different people . . . our own 12, . . . five of our senior judges, and . . . five to 10 Court of Appeals judges from other Courts of Appeal [sic], and . . .between 50 and 60 active and senior District Court judges"; he conceded that this was "more district judge assignments, or nearly as many, as in all of the other circuits . . . combined."[27] Browning's predecessor, Chief Judge Richard Chambers, said the court was "doing the best we can" through its use of district judges, who were used "as the third judge on the panel on about 80 percent of our cases," with some but "not too significant" out-of-circuit help. In any year, the court brought in "for short periods of time 40 to 45 of the 59 active, and the dozen or more retired district judges," many of whom could "ill afford to leave their districts."[28] Ninth Circuit Judge Charles M. Merrill observed that, with "[o]ne third or 30 percent of our work . . . being done by judges who are not members of our court, . . . the communication and contact between the judges is lost to a very substantial degree."[29]

Others from within Ninth Circuit's territory did not hesitate to state their concerns about this heavy use of "other" judges, although Chief Judge Walter Early Craig (D. Arizona) found it "a good experience for District Court judges to occasionally sit on the Court of Appeals."[30] A critical position that was more typical was the comment by U.S. Attorney Stanley Pitkin (W.D. Washington) that this use meant that "the effective number of judges in the Ninth Circuit is far greater than the 13 authorized," but more importantly, "it increases the potential for inconsistencies in the rulings of the various panels of the court."[31] More blunt was the

---

[26] Budziak, "The Effect of Visiting Judges on the Development of Legal Policy in the U.S. Courts of Appeals."

[27] James R. Browning, Statement, *Hearings: First Phase*, pp. 908, 910 (San Francisco, August 30, 1973).

[28] Richard Chambers, Statement, id., p. 662 (Seattle, Washington, August 28, 1973).

[29] Charles M. Merrill, Statement, id., p. 904 (San Francisco, August 30, 1973).

[30] Walter E. Craig, Statement, id., p. 841 (Portland, Oregon, August 29, 1973).

[31] Stanley Pitkin, Statement, id., p. 752 (Seattle, Washington, August 28, 1973).

Portland attorney who called the court of appeals "a poor school to train trial judges" and opposed their use because "[t]he work is entirely different ... many district judges who are excellent trial judges are not qualified for the Circuit Court of Appeals. You need writers up there," and claimed many district judges "never give written decisions." Thus "to confront them with cases over there where they go over a trial record and write decisions, they just agonize [about] them."[32]

Such criticisms of use of so many "extra" judges appear to have played a part in the Commission's recommendation that the Ninth Circuit be split, as one could see from its statement that "[t]he size of the court ... and the extensive reliance it has been required to place on the assistance of district and visiting judges have threatened its institutional unity."[33] Several Hruska Commission members, interviewed in 1977 shortly after the Commission completed its work, added to those concerns. A state trial judge stressed that district judges think differently from appellate judges and did not like sitting with the court of appeals because they fell behind in their own work and were likely to "expedite" (read: rush) their court of appeals assignments.[34] An attorney member said that among the disadvantages of having district judges sit was that they were not continuous members of the appellate court.[35]

Another member, an appellate judge from another circuit who had sat with the Ninth Circuit, was more positive about district judges sitting by designation, which, in addition to providing variety in their work, would familiarize them with circuit judges' work and they would learn the importance of making adequate findings. He would have district judges continue to sit with the court of appeals, but he thought it should be only if the district judge could sit with two active-duty circuit judges.[36] A district judge from a busy district with many criminal cases subject to the Speedy Trial Act would experience undue work pressure, he believed, and there was the risk that they would be unwilling to reverse other district

---

[32] William H. Morrison, Response to question from Judge Alfred Sulmonetti, id., p. 782 (Portland, Oregon, August 29 1973).

[33] Excerpts from report of Commission of Revision of Federal Court Appellate System, at 60 ABAJ 209, 210 (1974). The quoted statement was immediately followed by observations about intra-circuit inconsistency engendered by the large number of panels the court used.

[34] Interview of Judge Alfred Sulmonetti (Circuit Court, Multnomah County), by author, February 8, 1977, Portland, Oregon.

[35] Interview of Francis P. Kirkham (Pillsbury, Madison & Sutro), by author, March 30 1977, San Francisco, California.

[36] Interview with Judge J. Edward Lumbard (Second Circuit), by author, May 2, 1977, Portland, Oregon.

judges, so they should not be put in the position of writing an opinion when they reverse their own district.[37]

While not exactly thrilled about having judges visit from other circuits, these Commission members seemed more positive about their presence than they were about having in-circuit district judges sit. The state trial judge thought that the experience would move visiting judges away from provincialism and they would bring ideas with them, but he was concerned that they not be selected to hear specific issues or to slant a case result. The attorney member, the most negative generally, said that visiting judges did not follow Ninth Circuit decisions because they read only their own cases. (However, at the time, ease of retrieval of caselaw from any jurisdiction had not yet developed.) Use of visiting judges was acceptable in an emergency, said the federal appellate judge, who found a limited advantage in that by sitting, they might obtain ideas to use in the administration of their own courts. He also suggested that some of the best help came from senior district judges, who had a more flexible docket. He also felt that, just as district judges had to deal with their own caseloads, visiting judges had work in their own circuits and had some tendency to put their own circuit's work first. And, echoing his fellow Commission member, he thought them not as familiar with the law of the visited circuit.

Ninth Circuit Judges' Views, 1977 and 1986

In addition to their comments on specific advantages and disadvantages of the court's use of visitors and of district judges (discussed immediately below), Ninth Circuit judges interviewed in 1977 and 1986 made two types of general statements worthy of attention. (See Appendix B for information about those interviews.) One type bears directly on "who writes the law of the circuit?" and is most evident in the remark that when a district judge sat on the court of appeals, "Someone not on the court was making the law of the circuit," and in the statement, "Some feel circuit law should be written by circuit judges."[38] The matter was put most directly by the judge who said, "If you have a senior circuit judge from the Second Circuit and a senior district judge from Des Moines with one active judge from the Ninth Circuit,' it isn't right to have two strangers

---

37 Interestingly, this problem persists in his own circuit, the Second, and not in a trivial way. This is discussed in Chapter 6 on the use of district judges.

38 Interview with Judge Arthur Alarcon, Los Angeles, March 26, 1986; Interview with Judge Jerome Farris, San Francisco, April 18, 1986.

making law,"[39] and the matter would be worse in the occasional instance when two senior judges and a district judge or a visitor sat together, so that the panel did not have even a single active judge. A Ninth Circuit district judge who sat on a panel with a circuit judge and a visiting judge said this led the circuit judge to say he "felt the Ninth Circuit wasn't sitting."[40] It is not that judges are unlikely to be interchangeable (or fungible) or that a visiting judge's ideology might vary from that of a resident circuit judge who might otherwise have sat (although that is possible), so much as that visitors might bring with them adherence to different lines of circuit precedent, coupled with lawyers' perception that they do so. These comments make clear that, even when visitors don't import their own circuits' jurisprudence, they serve to *displace* the home court's own judges—even if, without their service, fewer cases would be resolved in a given time period.

It might be that district judges from other circuits would be less likely than visiting circuit judges to import other circuits' law, because the former would not have been involved in making precedent in their own circuits—unless they sat by designation with those courts. After all, they would be familiar with their own circuit's precedent from having applied it.

These views by insiders of their own court was reinforced by the views of those outside the court: "If lawyers continually saw appellate court opinions written by district judges," a Ninth Circuit judge said, there would be a "perceptual problem," particularly for the lawyers.[41] Another said that "in principle, it's dead wrong to have them [district judges] sit, and asserted that "lawyers want judges from this court."[42] Taking the point a bit further, another judge observed that "litigants frequently wonder whether the result would have been different" if a circuit judge rather than a district judge had sat. He added, "If the case is important and is assigned to a district judge to write, the case has an unavoidable asterisk which impairs it."[43] Other judges spoke to this point by focusing on their responsibility to make circuit precedent, as when one said, "We should do our own work—the law of the circuit is our responsibility."[44]

---

[39] Interview with Judge Ozell Trask, San Francisco, April 11, 1977.

[40] Interview with Judge Spencer Williams (N.D. Cal.), San Francisco, February 16, 1977.

[41] Interview with Judge Melvin Brunetti, San Francisco, April 15, 1986.

[42] Interview with Judge Stephen Reinhardt, Los Angeles, June 20, 1986.

[43] Interview with Judge Joseph Sneed, San Francisco, March 3, 1977.

[44] Interview with Judge William Norris, Los Angeles, April 24, 1986.

Another stated, "We sit as a circuit court and circuit judges should sit as circuit judges; district judges should sit as district judges." In emphasizing the virtue of circuit judges sitting together, the then-chief judge put a different twist on the matter by saying that "the law should be developed by people with whom they work constantly."[45] Another problem lawyers had with non-regular judges sitting on panels is that "not only did the lawyers have to figure out 28 judges (the court's regular members) but all these other participants as well.[46]

Another set of general comments about use of non-regular judges might be called "structural" because the comments bore on how the judicial system as a whole would be better tied together. More than one judge referred to the "cross-fertilization" that occurred when other judges sat with a court of appeals;[47] from visitors' presence, the receiving court acquired broadened philosophy, offsetting judges' tendency to become provincial.[48] This could happen when judges from other circuits visited a court of appeals, creating horizontal glue, while Ninth Circuit judges focused their attention on the consolidating effect of having the circuit's own district judges sit with the court of appeals. To them, this "seems to make for a more cohesive court system, instead of a fractured system, [as it] ties it together," and another judge said it gives the district judges "a sense of belonging to this legal community,"[49] something this judge had felt when he had been a district judge. Having district judges sit with the court of appeals shows them, as one put it, that they are "part of one system instead of one system overseeing another" and, according to another, allows them to learn that "we are working in a system, not isolated territorial pads."[50] The circuit was "vertically integrated from the circuit down to magistrates," said one judge, making it "important to get to know each other and get to know what each other's problems are."[51] "Diplomatic problems inherent in structural relations between district and circuit courts" could thus be avoided, as the court of appeals didn't "want to antagonize [district judges] or have things happen like mandates

45 Interview with Chief Judge James R. Browning, San Francisco, February 2 and 23, 1977.

46 From interview with Judge Cynthia Holcomb Hall, Pasadena, May 2, 1986.

47 Interview with Judge Thomas Tang, Pasadena, Cal., June 3, 1986; interview with Judge Charles Wiggins, San Francisco, April 16, 1986.

48 Interview with Judge Walter Ely, Los Angeles, March 1, 1977.

49 Interview with Judge J. Blaine Anderson, San Francisco, April 16, 1986.

50 Anderson 1986 interview; interview with Judge Shirley Hufstedler, Los Angeles, February 28, 1977.

51 Interview with Judge J. Blaine Anderson, San Francisco, February 10, 1977.

being evaded."[52] A former district judge also observed that one could have judges know each other without having them sit on panels, by having more frequent meetings between circuit and district judges.

About Visiting Judges. Ninth Circuit court of appeals judges had mixed views about judges visiting from outside the circuit. They placed somewhat more emphasis on problems than on advantages beyond helping with caseload. On the whole, they did not see problems as especially difficult, although one judge was clear in not wanting visitors "unless the judge is a superstar who can bring an insight we may have missed," a point a colleague echoed in saying that "the only good thing about the original program [of having visiting judges sit] was the out-standing ones" like the Fifth Circuit's Judge Elbert Tuttle or "outstanding judges from all over the country." This judge went on to say that this good exchange was undermined when Chief Justice Burger "made a decision that a court couldn't be both a borrower and a lender if judges were sitting elsewhere, a court couldn't have anyone from outside."

Some problems were "mechanical" and stemmed from visitors' lack of familiarity with the procedures of the visited court, because they "don't have the background and experience in procedure . . . of the circuit." The visitors would not know the process for circulating opinions or whether dispositions should be published or unpublished. In general, "They're used to their circuit rules and have to learn ours,"[53] with the result that visitors "require special handling." "Courtesy requires," said a judge who made particular efforts to facilitate visiting judges' work for the court, "that we communicate well in advance" of the visitors' arrival for their panels,[54] and a colleague observed that visitors' "lack of knowledge about our procedure" could be "overcome with a manual."[55] Although saying that it was a problem but "not a real problem," a judge on a receiving court observed, "There is time and effort in telling them how we do things: how you manage cases, including non-argued ones." One visiting circuit judge raised questions about "how do I know that a case will not be argued?" and wished to learn about the Ninth Circuit's process for

---

[52] Interview with Judge William Canby, Pasadena, Cal., June 4, 1986.

[53] Interview with Judge Charles Merrill, San Francisco, February 11, 1977.

[54] Interview with Judge Eugene A. Wright, San Francisco, April 12, 1977. He mentioned the "perplexing problems" faced by a visiting senior district judge with whom no one had communicated and thus "didn't know what to do." The Ninth Circuit judge "visited" with the visiting judge even though not on a panel with him.

[55] Interview with Judge J. Clifford Wallace, San Francisco, March 1, 1977; by telephone, March 9, 1977.

deciding to submit cases on the briefs.[56] Another visitor did not realize that a case in the Ninth Circuit's *pro bono* program could not be submitted on the briefs.[57] The matter might be as minor as pointing out that circuit practice was to list judges in order of seniority.[58]

It should be noted that courts other than the Ninth Circuit also experience the difficulties caused by visitors' presence. The chief judge of the Second Circuit called attention to such a problem in writing that visiting judges' presence hindered his court's practice in which each judge submitted a voting memorandum, which were "often simply overlooked and their value lost" as visiting judges often came without a secretary, or district judges sitting by designation were "interrupting busy trial schedules." With "[t]he distances that have to be traveled, the workload, and . . . other factors . . . [,] for the most part . . . conferences are held during a sitting week and . . . voting memoranda for Thursday and Friday are apt to be few and far between or, where visiting judges are concerned, nonexistent," which was "unfortunate."[59]

Potentially more serious than familiarizing visiting judges with minor aspects of the procedure of the court they are visiting is a logistical problem that can result when an out-of-circuit visitor or in-circuit district judge has served on a panel and the case returns as an appeal after a remand to the district court (a "comeback" case), as it can be difficult to arrange argument on the new appeal. Video-conferencing could be used in such circumstances, with the visiting judge participating from home chambers, but that process may be sub-optimal because of distracting technological problems such as quality of video, a few-seconds time lag, echo on the audio, and the need for presence of technical staff to make things run smoothly, which is thought inappropriate during conference.[60]

---

[56] Morton Greenberg (Third Circuit), memorandum to panel, March 26, 2001. A Ninth Circuit judge with whom he was to sit responded with an answer. Johnnie Rawlinson, memorandum to Greenberg, March 26, 2001.

[57] See Jack Zouhary (N.D. Ohio), memorandum to panel, September 23, 2012, recommending submission on briefs, and the response of Diarmuid O'Scannlain, memorandum to panel, September 24, 2012, *re*: Karapetyan v. Holder, 500 Fed. Appx. 597 (9th Cir. 2012).

[58] "I reiterate only for the sake of thoroughness that in preparing the caption, the Ninth Circuit's convention is to list circuit judges in order of seniority." Alfred T. Goodwin, memorandum to panel containing Jack Zouhary (N.D. Ohio), Oct. 18, 2012, *re*: King v. Astrue, 497 Fed. Appx. 758 (2012).

[59] James L. Oakes, "Grace Notes on 'Grace Under Pressure,'" 50 Ohio State Law Journal 702, 704 (1989).

[60] These matters were discussed in an exchange involving Judges Alex Kozinski and Raymond Fisher, who had participated in such a teleconference with Judge Frederick Block (E.D.N.Y.), who had served on the panel. See Kozinski, memorandum to all

Assigning opinions to visiting judges posed a separate problem. For one Ninth Circuit judge, concern about visitors' workload led to dividing a panel's work 45-45-10 by giving the visitor the simplest, non-controversial cases, especially when the visitor was a senior district judge with only one law clerk. Of far greater concern than visitors' workload were their views and the precedent they allegedly brought with them. The concern that visitors relied on their own circuit's law was raised by more than one Ninth Circuit judge. One stressed that the visitors "bring in *interesting* ideas," quickly adding "but they are non-circuit ideas" and that "it doesn't help to have other circuit's ideas when your circuit has [its] own way." Even a judge who was enthusiastic about their presence, saying that "[t]hey bring all of the learning and none of their precedents" and thus were "tremendously beneficial," saw a "problem in assigning a case where the rule of the [visitor's] circuit was involved (because the lawyer wanted it applied in the Ninth Circuit).[61] Going further, one judge argued that visitors had "a kind of free-booting mentality; they won't be here long, will shake things up, but then they leave the circuit with their result and are not around to defend it."

One judge singled out the approach brought by judges of specialized courts. In an argument applicable to present use of judges of the Court of International Trade, he named Claims Court judges as examples of those who operate under different rules and "want blind adherence to specialists' expertise."[62] (Tax Court judges were also mentioned, but, as non-Article III judges, they didn't sit with the U.S. courts of appeals.) These concerns about inconsistency that visitors might introduce into the law of the visited circuit illustrate the tension between using such visitors to assist with burgeoning caselaw and maintaining stability of the visited circuit's precedent.[63]

Along with concerns that visiting judges import law inconsistent with that of the visited circuit was praise for useful administrative ideas they brought. One judge, critical of the legal ideas visiting judges brought with them, said that as to judicial administration, "one gets to know more about other circuits and how they operate," something more [valuable] than with other cases," and another Ninth Circuit judge observed that when one sat with visiting judges, one "picked up tricks of the trade." A senior district judge who had sat in other circuits had a similar view: "I

---

judges, May 3, 2007, and Fisher to all judges, May 4, 2007.

[61] Interview with Judge Anthony Kennedy, San Francisco, March 7, 1977.

[62] Interview with Judge Stanley Barnes, Los Angeles, March 2, 1977.

[63] I thank Justin Wedeking for raising the "tension" issue.

see an incredible number of *procedural* differences in this unified system (customs of practice and procedure)."[64]

About District Judges. Beyond the general proposition that the presence of the circuit's district judges helps deal with appellate caseload, the Ninth Circuit's court of appeals judges' extensive comments about them can be gathered under several rubrics. The appellate judges see a major advantage in district judges' being able to understand how the court of appeals functions, which is why, as part of their socialization, newly-appointed judges are brought to sit with the court of appeals. However, often-raised concern about problems leads even those who would continue having district judges sit on court of appeals panels to suggest limiting such use, perhaps by having them sit initially, shortly after appointment, as they usually do, but then bringing them back only every few years.

In general, the use of in-circuit district judges is perceived as more a procedural than a jurisprudential problem. District judges sitting by designation are accustomed to applying their own circuit's law, so they would be less likely than out-of-circuit visitors to draw on out-of-circuit precedents. So the greater concerns are, for example, about their unfamiliarity with appellate procedure and their own heavy district court workloads.

A district judge who sits with the court of appeals "gets the perspective of our job, which makes his job better" and gets to learn the problems appellate judges face, although a judge who said it was helpful to learn each other's problems did not know that the appellate judges learned the district judges' problems but "they certainly learn ours." The district judge also develops "personal acquaintances with circuit judges that broaden perspectives" and, more important, gets "to understand the appellate process [and how to] review findings," which "assists the district judge in knowing the importance of the record" and teaches "how to make an appropriate record"; that "makes an appellate court's job easier." This is part of district judges' reaction that their sitting with the court of appeals makes one "a better trial court judge as a result,"[65] or, another stated it, "I'm a better district judge for the rather substantial experience I've had as a circuit judge." Coming at the record with a perspective different from that of an appellate judge, a district judge might find something there,[66] and a district judge who sat regularly with the Ninth Circuit suggested that the district judge also gets to "look at other judges' trial record." In

---

64 Interview with Judge Robert J. Kelleher (C.D. Cal.), Los Angeles, March 2, 1977.

65 Interview with Judge Howard Turrentine (S.D. Cal.), San Diego, March 21, 1977.

66 Interview with Judge Anthony Kennedy, Pasadena, Cal., April 4, 1986.

the same vein, a senior district judge stated, "District court judges—and circuit judges who were district judges—read the record differently from one who has not been one"; they "have different reactions to the printed word."

District judges will also remind circuit judges about the problems of "being on the firing line" with "decisions made under pressure,"[67] so that, as a district judge put it, "concepts like 'harmless error' take on different meanings": "No one can know the burdens of a district judge without having been there." The district judge will also remind the court of appeals that language at the end of an appellate opinion like that directing the district court to take action "not inconsistent with this decision" is not helpful to them. One district judge went so far as to say that when he sat with the court of appeals, it "provides an opportunity for missionary work about trial court problems." District judges "can communicate experiences, things not immediately [evident] from the record." An appellate judge found it interesting to sit on a panel with a judge who says, "I've tried this type of case." Another circuit judge observed that some district judges have a "unique savvy on some points" more than do the court of appeals' own former district judges or judges who had been trial lawyers. Those court of appeals judges get "a certain appreciation of trial judges' problems we should keep in mind."[68] As stated by a district judge who sat regularly with the Ninth Circuit, district judges' presence helps circuit judges "get information about district judges' attitudes, which is particularly important when a circuit judge has never sat on the district court,"[69] although, as a former district judge observed, district judges remind even former district judges of "some things we lost sight of after a while."[70]

Given the inherent tension between district judges and the appellate judges who "grade their papers," the former, by seeing how the appellate court operates, can be "convinced that we fully consider questions in a fair review of decisions." As a senior district judge put it, sitting with the court of appeals allowed district judges to "see reasons for reversals," with a Ninth Circuit judge adding that it "tends to break incipient paranoia on a district judge's part," so that "they don't feel a conspiracy when reversed." Thus, the court of appeals "might make a friend of a potential critic if that judge were to experience and understand the [appellate] court's prob-

---

[67] Interview with Judge Dorothy W. Nelson, Los Angeles, May 18, 1986.

[68] Interview with Judge Robert Boochever, March 27, 1986, Pasadena, Calif.

[69] Interview with Judge Gus Solomon (D. Or.), May 3, 1977, Portland, Ore.

[70] Interview with Judge Otto Skopil, Portland, Ore., June 25, 1986.

lems," thus "mak[ing] that judge more receptive to suggestions and more willing to accept than fight."

Not surprisingly, Ninth Circuit judges also identified problems accompanying the court's use of district judges. While their presence "enables us to get that much more work done," and "we couldn't get our work done without them,"[71] a basic problem is that, just as with out-of-circuit visitors, court of appeals judges have to deal with people who are not in the continuing flow of the court's law-development, judges who are among "the more people you have to deal with that you don't deal with regularly."[72] As one judge put it simply, "Bringing in other people changes the balance already there." Stating it more extensively, another judge (at the time a district judge who sat regularly with the court, of which he later became a member) said, "The bigger the court, the more difficult it is to reach consensus. It is desirable to have predictability. When you are drawing on large numbers of individuals for panels, there is no way of predicting the predilection of the panel."[73] Part of this is that use of district judges "delays how long before we [court of appeals judges] sit with each other." With the greater number of judges with whom home-court judges must deal when district judges are added to the judge-mix comes having to deal with the idiosyncrasies of particular judges. That is no different from a court of appeals' judges having to adjust to each other's habits or quirks, but that it involves visitors means there are *more* such idiosyncrasies with which to become familiar and to which to adjust. Also, while appellate judges can become familiar with those district judges who sit regularly with them and can do so far more easily than with those who pop in for only a few cases and then do not return, even the more-frequently-sitting district judges increase the need for home court judges to learn about, and adjust to, more people.

A specific problem is that district judges "are not as familiar with how we get things done," so using them is thought to be inefficient. They may need assistance when first writing appellate opinions. Although they have applied circuit precedent in the district court, they are said to be "not aware of trends of the circuit" and thus, as another judge stated it, "may be out of step" or "not know of cases we have developed."[74] In particular, they don't understand issues relating to whether certain matters need to

---

71 Interview with former Chief Judge Richard Chambers, May 20, 1977, San Francisco; Barnes interview.

72 Interview with Judge Mary Schroeder, April 8, 1986, Pasadena, Calif.

73 Interview with Judge Harry Pregerson (then Central District of California), Los Angeles, March 1, 1977.

74 Interview with Judge Procter Hug, Jr., Pasadena, April 10, 1986.

be taken en banc; they are not familiar with memoranda relating to en bancs, and their presence on a panel which must respond to en banc calls disrupts the flow of that activity. Further, the presence of a district judge on a panel that finds itself in an en banc situation means that the circuit judges on the panel "have lost the input of one-third of the panel" in a situation where "we need all the input one can get."

More than all of this, however, as several judges pointed out, is the mind-set district judges are said to have, one different from appellate judges' and one tied to the fact that they were confirmed to a different court. As some circuit judges observed, "Just because Congress confirmed a district judge doesn't mean he's eligible to be an appellate judge," and "All trial judges are not appellate judges." With a different mind-set, when district judges sit on the court of appeals, they "have to switch hats to become an appellate judge." It was "impossible on an instantaneous basis to change their focus" and to reverse their loyalties; moreover, district judges, who acted alone, were "not accustomed to accommodating to others' reviews and were unwilling to do so." Indeed, if someone "has been a district judge for many years, that judge is "absolutely disabled" from functioning at the appellate level." Conversely, one judge didn't know how, if a district judge sat regularly on the appellate court, that judge, having become an appellate judge, could go back and sit on the district court.

Compounding matters is what many court of appeals judges see as district judges' unwillingness to reverse their fellow district judges. If the possibility that out-of-circuit visitors will bring their own circuits' law with them is seen as a major problem, so, too, is the belief that district judges are unwilling to reverse. Ninth Circuit judges' comments extend from the relatively gentle one that district judges "can have an overly sympathetic attitude" toward rulings under review to the stronger "they could be biased toward district judges" or that there is a "built-in skewing toward affirmance." One Ninth Circuit judge said district judges are more likely to affirm "because his brethren won't like being reversed," and a colleague observed, "Some district judges don't like to be asked to review acts of brother district judges," with "some feel[ing] no one of them should be reversed"; said the latter judge, such judges "are not asked back." District judges were also said to "uniformly lean to affirm on anything which can be called an issue of fact." This "natural dislike of reversing their brethren" led some to prefer not to write opinions reversing or even to join such opinions by circuit judge.

Beyond the matter of district judges' supposed unwillingness to reverse, they are also thought to be predisposed to "go along" with their appellate "superiors," the court of appeals judges with whom they are sitting, because those judges will later review the district judge's cases.[75] And this deference to the appellate judges might be particularly evident when the district judges are new to the bench and they are brought to sit with the court of appeals to see how that court operates; perhaps this deference would diminish over time, so that when the district judges returned to the court of appeals after some further experience, they would be less likely to be deferential to the judges with whom they sat. It must, however, be remembered that many district judges come to the bench from positions in which they were not reluctant to "speak out" and "talk back." And it is clear that district judges do dissent from circuit judge panel majorities, indicating a willingness to disagree and a likelihood that they may have brought a different perspective to their appellate task. Because the rate of disagreement in the U.S. courts of appeals in cases decided by three-judge panels is quite low, with dissents having to be written in addition to regularly-assigned panel majority opinions, even an occasional dissent on a panel is worthy of note. Thus it should not be expected that district judges, and visiting judges, particularly when the former sit with the court of appeals early in their district court tenure, would dissent often. (Whether a dissent contributes to the likelihood of en banc rehearing or to the Supreme Court's granting review in a case will be discussed later.)

To return to whether district judges sitting on the appeals court adopted a critical stance, a Ninth Circuit judge who was a former district judge thought it was a myth that district judges sitting on court of appeals panels did not examine other district judges' work as critically or objectively; it did happen occasionally, he said, but it was not substantial.[76] Moreover, some judges said that district judges sitting with the court of appeals by designation were not under pressure from their appellate colleagues. When some Oregon lawyers had argued to the Hruska Commission that mixing appellate and district judges to decide appellate cases was unwise both because circuit judges' objectivity was impaired by

---

75 See Maxwell Mak and Andrew Sidman, "Collegiality on Trial: Three-Judge Panels and the Voting Rights Act," paper presented to Midwest Political Science Association, Chicago, Illinois, April 2017.

76 Interview with Judge John Kilkenny, Portland, Ore., May 3, 1977. Judge Kilkenny was long on the district court (D. Oregon) before being elevated to the Ninth Circuit. On the matter of district judges sitting on the court of appeals showing deference to their district judge colleagues, Budziak has produced evidence that district judges promoted to the court of appeals are less likely to reverse the district court, although this effect fades with increased tenure on the appellate court. Jeffrey Budziak, "Promotion, Social Identity, and Decision Making in the U.S. Courts of Appeals," 4 Journal of Law and Courts 267 (2015).

frequent contact with district judges when the latter served as appellate judges, Ninth Circuit Judge John Kilkenny, a former District of Oregon judge who had sat in that capacity with the Ninth Circuit, disagreed: "Other than a feeling of due respect and friendship, I never felt pressure when sitting with the circuit as a district judge," he said, and he called attention to his own dissents from the court of appeals and to the dissents by the late Judge William Byrne (C.D. California), adding, "I do not believe that the association between the circuit and district judges is in any way objectionable and certainly not coercive."[77]

Some other specific problems caused by the use of district judges relate to constructing panels and, more importantly, to opinion-assignment within panels, problems exacerbated by the fact that district judges usually sit only with the court for a couple of days during a court week. Their participating is also related to their ability to complete their assigned court of appeals tasks, something they must do in the face of dealing with the district court work to which they return from sitting with the appeals court. However, one judge who had been through that experience, while acknowledging that "preparation is intense" and "the additional writing responsibility can be substantial," said that nonetheless the experience was worth those pressures.[78] It was also suggested that having to be "in and out" was also difficult for the district judges. Yet, on the other hand, use of district judges was thought valuable if the court wanted to have panels sit for a five-day week, with flexibility for judges to take a month off. District judges' availability means they can be used to fill out panels, although that may make them seem, and feel, as if they are simply a "third wheel." If, in looking at the composition of a court's panels, one sees several panels each of which contains resident circuit judges Jones and Smith but with different district judges in the "third slot," it becomes clear that they—just like visiting judges—are in some ways there to be "filler."

Further complicating assignment of opinions is the norm that a district judge sitting by designation should not be on a panel considering cases from that judge's district. This norm is strongly adhered to in panel construction.[79] A judge from Montana noted that when he sat on the court's Portland-Seattle calendar, he couldn't sit on any Montana cases, so he and a district judge from Idaho who also sat with the Ninth Circuit

---

[77] Hruska Commission, Hearings: First Phase, p. 814 (Portland, August 29, 1973). As to Judge Byrne, he added, "We could write a book on [his] dissents . . . in the past two or three years."

[78] Personal communication, e-mail to Stephen L. Wasby, November 28, 2016.

[79] But, for the Second Circuit, see Chapter 6.

had an "arrangement," in which the Idaho judge "would sit on the panel with the Montana cases and I'd sit on the panel with the Idaho cases."[80] One judge noted, "When clerical error has produced that, I have informed them and they have changed judges,"[81] and another judge told of a case in which an order had been written by a district court colleague but the case was listed under the name of its original judge, something not discovered until later, and the district court colleague, Judge Gus Solomon, "was not happy" about being reversed.

Beyond that norm about assignment, district judges' presence further constrains the court of appeals' work. A repeated theme was that district judges' own workload hinders their work for the court of appeals. As stated by a judge from another circuit, "A problem is district judges who have huge dockets and can't get their stuff done for the court of appeals," something this judge thought "a worse problem than with visitors" from other circuits. One Ninth Circuit judge stated strongly that district judges "shouldn't be given an assignment in a heavy case that will get attention within the circuit or from other circuits."[82] Another judge, generally agreeing, said presiding judges on panels were "disinclined to give them as heavy assignments as we assume" because "they don't bring with them awareness of precedential or other considerations that arise from our daily dealing with cases of the circuit."[83] The district judge's "tremendous burden in trying cases" meant they were "not fairly well acquainted with the court of appeals' lines of case authority."

The most prominent reason for assigning less writing work to a panel's district judge was their home district court workload, with district judges given lighter assignments "know[ing] they will not give full attention because of their workload."[84] A senior judge thought this was the only real problem in the court's use of district judges, as "they are too busy at home to deal with what we drop on them,"[85] so it was "difficult" [for them] to devote time and attention to another court." As one judge stated directly, "There is difficulty in making assignments in giving district judges a fair share of the workload" because "the district judge goes home to new cases," so "we don't assign difficult cases to the district

80 Interview with Judge William Jameson (D. Mont.), Pasadena, April 11, 1986.

81 Interview with Judge Albert Wollenberg (N.D. Cal.), San Francisco, February 14, 1977.

82 Interview with Judge Betty B. Fletcher, Pasadena, April 7, 1986.

83 Interview with Judge Cecil Poole, San Francisco, May 15, 1986.

84 Interview with Judge J. Clifford Wallace, San Diego, California, April 29, 1986, and telephone, May 2, 1986.

85 Interview with Judge James Carter, San Diego, March 31, 1977.

judge on the panel." However, a chief judge, who acknowledged that district judges on returning to their own courts did not get to the preparation of their appellate opinions, said the matter could be corrected, and, moreover, "if they don't keep up, they don't get asked back."[86] And another circuit judge observed that, "once in a while," when the district judge "doesn't get work out" and "holds the opinion too long, the circuit judges on the panel will offer to take the district judge off the hook, they will say they were just about to get to it and will be given another couple of weeks; if they don't do it, we'll remove it."

District judges who sat with the court of appeals agreed that they faced a problem once they returned to their own chambers, and a district judge who agreed said that if a district judge was from a busy district and was assigned a difficult case, it "raises havoc with his own calendar."[87] Agreeing, another district judge spoke of the "additional work it puts on the district judge," as they "take cases as an overload," and he added, "It doesn't help our court."[88] Some circuit judges called it an "imposition" to give district judges appellate assignments: "We dump our work on top of theirs instead of replacing it"; the problem was that district court caseload was growing because of "the Speedy Trial Act and the increasing number of cases." Moreover, district judges coming to the court of appeals were not only losing the day in their own district when they were sitting with the Ninth Circuit but they also incurred travel time. This same consideration led another judge to say the use of district judges was inefficient because of costs in time and transportation for both the court of appeals and the district court and the "interruption in the rhythm of a trial."

The appeals court judges observed that district judges "must put aside their own work to come with us" and, because they "may hold up our disposition process, we may have to jog them to get a reaction." A district judge may feel he "must expedite his own work or put it aside," but either way, the disposition of the judge's court of appeals assignment is delayed. A district judge may be embarrassed to say the assignment should not have been given, and, as noted above, may even have to turn back that assignment. It was even suggested that some district judges are "not honest," as they say they'll dissent so they won't have to write an opinion, but then later they concur. However, when they *did* dissent, the appellate judges might be annoyed, with one district judge reporting his belief that

---

[86] Interview with former Chief Judge James R. Browning, San Francisco, April 17 and June 11, 1986. Earlier, he had said, "Those who go home and never write opinions are 'vetoed' as to their return." Browning 1977 interview.

[87] Interview with Judge Charles Renfrew (N.D. Cal.), San Francisco, February 17, 1977.

[88] Interview with Judge William Sweigert (N.D. Cal.), San Francisco, February 18, 1977.

the two circuit judges to whose ruling he dissented were "still irritated" with him.

If sitting on the court of appeals was "serious interference" with district judges' work and "a very serious drain" on their time, it was particularly so for those in active status if they were "going to pull their weight and not just come over and vote." It was even suggested that some of the "better" district judges felt that their calendars kept them too busy to sit with the court of appeals, making it "possible that some of the less competent district judges were available." One of the more acerbic comments was that there were "two kinds" of district judges—the "overworked," for whom sitting with the court of appeals was "an imposition" or who do not do enough work on a case, and the retired, who "come to see their children so they don't pay attention." A further negative view was that some will "come unprepared" or they will be "too dilatory in getting out the work we assigned to them." And among the others, "Some are me-tooers who don't dig in and do the work."

Certain advantages inure in the use of district judges, but senior district judges are seen in a much more favorable light. While some of these "seniors" continue to carry a nearly full load of cases, a number do not, or at least they are not involved in as many trials. However, although they "usually have more time," they also have "less energy"; nonetheless, as the judge saying this thought, some senior district judges "do excellent work for our court." As they "are separated from the trial process, they are more neutral as to affirming or reversing" and "think more like us and are less defensive." A further advantage of senior district judges is that, because of their greater availability, they can sit with the court of appeals for longer periods of time, and they also have "more time to study and get acquainted with the law [of the circuit]." Indeed, some "feel like any other member of the court," "are de facto members of the court," or are "almost entirely with us." Specifically mentioned in this regard were Judges Gus Solomon of the District of Oregon and Judge William Jameson of the District of Montana.

The Odd Case of Judge Aldisert[89]

Seldom do visiting judges seriously test the patience or equanimity of the host court. However, a particularly difficult problem arose when a senior circuit judge began to reside in another circuit and to sit there regularly and then spoke out about the visited court's allegedly inade-

---

[89] This section is based on a portion of Stephen L. Wasby, "Visiting Judges Revisited," paper presented to Midwest Political Science Association, Chicago, April 2015.

quate handling of its business. Not surprisingly, this caused major controversy in the visited court. The individual at the center of the controversy was Judge Ruggero Aldisert, who had been appointed to the Third Circuit in 1968, took senior status in 1988, and retired fully in mid-2014, shortly before his death later that year at age 95.[90]

Because of serious health problems, Judge Aldisert was advised to move from Pittsburgh, where he had his chambers. With the Third Circuit approving his change of duty station, he moved to Santa Barbara, California, with chambers in rented government space. He resolved his health problems and sought to sit with the Ninth Circuit, which certainly was in need of assistance, particularly from a judge who was well-respected and known for work on court administration. While Judge Aldisert continued to handle some Third Circuit cases, he began to sit with some regularity in the Ninth Circuit. And sit he did. As Aldisert was to write to Chief Justice Rehnquist, Ninth Circuit Chief Judge Alfred Goodwin "was a little concerned about the 'lender-borrower' rule, but we both felt that this rule would not apply to my sitting with the Ninth"—because he was now living there.[91]

Beginning with a case decided in February, 1988,[92] Aldisert participated in *over 500* Ninth Circuit cases, under one-third of which (30.8%) were resolved by published opinion, thus creating circuit precedent;[93] he wrote 55 opinions in those 155 cases and filed dissents in four others. The extent of his participation varied over the first several years: 34 cases in 1988 but then fewer—25 in 1989 and only 14 in 1990—before rebounding to 25 (1991) and increasing further into the lower 30s per year—30 (1992), 34 (1993), and 32 (1994). His highest participation was in 1995-1998, where he participated in over 40 cases per year (40 in 1997, 43 in each of the other years). After sitting in 38 cases decided in 1999 and 25 cases in 2000, he sat far less frequently, in only five cases in 2001 and none in 2002. His activity briefly rebounded to 24 cases in 2003 before dropping to only 11 in 2004 and declining to scattered numbers until reaching 11 in 2008, the year his last published opinion for the Ninth Circuit was filed;[94] the opinion in the last case in which he participated was filed on October 3, 2011.

---

[90] See Ruggero Aldisert, "A Nonagenarian Discusses Life as a Senior Circuit Judge," 14 Journal of Appellate Practice & Process 183 (2014).

[91] Ruggero Aldisert to Chief Justice William H. Rehnquist, September 3, 1987.

[92] White Mountain Apaches v. Hodel, 840 F.3d 675 (9th Cir. 1988).

[93] There was one case in which he was a member of the panel but recused in mid-case, with the case being decided by the remaining two judges, a valid quorum.

[94] Southwest Marine v. United States, 535 F.3d 1012 (9th Cir. 2008).

The decline in Judge Aldisert's Ninth Circuit participation from 2003 to 2004 is related to controversy the judge created. The difficulty arose when, in a 2003 opinion for the Third Circuit,[95] Judge Aldisert criticized the district court there for relying on a Ninth Circuit case. However, he also said that the Ninth Circuit ruling had departed from another ruling by that court.[96] Claiming that another court had decided two cases differently when they could not be distinguished *might* have been fair comment. Judge Aldisert did not, however, stop there, but in his slip opinion, he asserted that the Ninth Circuit, about which he claimed to know something, had not been paying attention to its own rulings. He stated that in that court, "it is not a rare event for one panel to overlook the reasoning of a previous panel on the same subject," with the second case's reasoning and decision "seem[ing] to fly squarely in the face of what should have been binding precedent in that court." This statement about the Ninth Circuit as a large court not being able to avoid inconsistence echoed what Judge Aldisert had stated shortly before in answers on a "Twenty Questions" segment of the *How Appealing* blog.

By the time of final publication of the opinion, the "offending" paragraph had been removed, leaving the language, "We accept *Cisneros* and reject *Prince* because we believe that these two cases cannot be reconciled ... the *Prince* panel ignored both the teachings of *Cisneros* and [a] definition...."[97] Yet the damage to the judge's relations with the Ninth Circuit had been done. Before judges in the Ninth Circuit learned of the revision, they had engaged in extended communication about the matter. Judges criticized Aldisert's reading of the Ninth Circuit's action in the two cases in question, saying that the second panel had carefully examined, not ignored, the prior decision before reaching its conclusion. But the judges went further, to consider whether Judge Aldisert should continue sit with the court. Some judges found him a good colleague, and others warned against using disagreement with what a visiting judge said as a reason for taking that judge off the visitors list, but a number of judges did want him removed from the list. Criticism of him went beyond the case in which he had been critical. He was said not to be able to disagree without being disagreeable; to be condescending, "arrogant, scornful and impolite to litigants," and "arrogant without the slightest reason for being so"; and to have made "no attempt at common courtesy." Further, one

---

[95] Donovan v. Punxatawny Area School Board, 336 F.3d 211 (3d Cir. 2003).

[96] The two cases were Prince v. Jacoby, 303 F.3d 1074 (9th Cir. 2002), the one on which the district court in the Third Circuit had relied, and Cisneros v. Board of Trustees of San Diego Unified School District, 106 F.3d 878 (9th Cir. 1987).

[97] *Donovan*, 331 F.3d at 223.

judge found his "work quick and sloppy and his manner sometimes difficult."

Yet, not surprisingly, it was not Judge Aldisert's style that was central. The judge's criticism of the way in which the Ninth Circuit dealt with its prior cases drew the most serious fire. One judge wrote that the Third Circuit opinion was "the first time I have seen an opinion criticizing the processes of another court."[98] For a colleague, the opinion "continues to tell the world that we do not know what we are doing, by insisting that the two opinions of our court are irreconcilable (which they certainly are not)."[99] Another judge reminded his colleagues that this was not the first time Judge Aldisert had criticized a Ninth Circuit ruling, having done so in a Ninth Circuit case dealing with "hazardous neutrality" in an asylum claim. The judge who had separately concurred in that case had written that Aldisert had "chosen to write an opinion that applies our law while casting doubt on its legitimacy" even though not frontally.[100] What was at issue there was not Judge Aldisert's views but criticism he leveled while sitting on the Ninth Circuit. As Judge Hawkins had put it:

> Our duty while writing opinions in this circuit is to apply the law, not to cast doubt on its viability. If an individual judge dislikes our precedent, he or she may so state in a separate opinion; it is inappropriate to express such individual concerns, however subtly, in an opinion that purports to speak for our court.[101]

By comparison, said Judge Hawkins, an example of how a visiting judge should handle disagreement was an Eleventh Circuit judge who had sat with the court when the panel on which the visitor sat "had occasion to deal with an issue where 9th Circuit law departed from an 11th Circuit opinion [the visiting judge] had written earlier." Judge Hawkins reported that the judge had "drafted an entirely respectful concurrence and circulated it to the panel for comment."[102]

---

[98] Procter Hug, Jr., to Associates, July 22, 2003.

[99] Marcia Berzon to Associates, August 12, 2003.

[100] Rivera-Moreno v. I.N.S., 213 F.3d 481, 487 (9th Cir. 2000) (Hawkins, J., specially concurring). Aldisert's opinion, said Hawkins, "suggests that our court's established law of 'hazardous neutrality' conflicts with the Supreme Court's decision in Elias-Zacarias," id., a view which Hawkins challenged. See INS v. Elias-Zacarias, 502 U.S. 478 (1992). Judge Aldisert had written, "We adhere to the precept notwithstanding the statements of the Supreme Court in 1992." 213 F.3d, at 483.

[101] 213 F.3d, at 487 (Hawkins, J.).

[102] Michael Daly Hawkins to Associates, July 21, 2003.

After hearing from colleagues, a judge who initially defended Judge Aldisert concluded that "being invited as a frequent guest does entail special responsibilities of reporting fairly on one's host," and he criticized Aldisert for holding himself out as an expert but then having "failed to live up to his responsibility of fairness to us."[103] As another judge then put the question, "In a nutshell should we keep inviting someone into our house who goes around the neighborhood bad-mouthing what a poor house we keep?"[104] The end result appears to have been that Judge Aldisert's invitation to sit with the court in 2004 would not be revoked, as he was already scheduled to sit then, but that he would not be invited further— although the earlier-cited numbers do suggest some minimal participation later.

---

[103] Alex Kozinski to Associates, July 22, 2003.

[104] A. Wallace Tashima to Associates, July 24, 2003.

3
WHAT THE JUDGES SAY II:
VISITING JUDGES' VIEWS

With the views of judges of *visited* courts having been explored, it is important to obtain the perspectives of the judges who did the actual *visiting*. Thus this chapter's primary focus is visiting judges' views, first their selection and then their experience. To provide a more in-depth examination of what visiting judges do and how they see that work, an extended view of one visiting judge's experiences is then provided from observations by Senior Ninth Circuit Judge Alfred T. Goodwin based on considerable visiting judge experience, both when he was sent to learn about other circuits' procedures in preparation for his service as Chief Judge and, as a senior judge, after he completed his service as Chief Judge in 1991.

Selection of Visiting Judges

One needs to know how judges become visiting judges. According to anecdotes from judges on visited courts, visitors invite themselves to serve in other circuits, perhaps because they wish to visit grandchildren. That leads not only to requests to sit with a particular circuit but to sit in a specific city. Such anecdotes perhaps derive from a visited court's less-than-positive experience with a self-inviting judge. However, as will be seen, matters are often otherwise.

The processes by which a circuit's judges come to sit in another circuit are not well known. We do not know, for example, whether, in inviting visiting judges, circuits are primarily concerned about obtaining "warm bodies" to fill panels and help with expanding dockets, whether they prefer circuit judges over district judges or vice-versa, or whether it is a matter of indifference. Budziak has suggested that the lack of firm policy and the use of informal methods of selecting visiting judges provides "space" within which circuit chief judges are able to select visitors on the basis of ideological affinity, so that selection of visitors who share the chief's policy preferences is more likely,[1] both initially and after their

---

[1] Jeffrey Budziak, "The Strategic Designation of Visiting Judges in the U.S. Courts of Appeals," 36 Justice System Journal 233 (2015).

initial sitting, the more so if the ideological affinity remains. This may be true even if, when a visitor is selected, it is not known what set of cases would be before the panel on which the visitor was to sit. Moreover, the fact that visitors do dissent and do write separate concurrences is some evidence that they are not selected because they "go along."

Selection processes clearly are different for active judges and for senior judges. For active circuit judges, the process is formalized. Their transfers must be approved by the Inter-circuit Assignment Committee of the Judicial Conference of the United States (JCUS), which operates under rules which speak of "borrowing" circuits and those from which judges have been borrowed. One visiting judge, who as an active district judge was subject to the rules, did note the "lending" and "borrowing" rules, in which a circuit which "borrowed" visiting judges could not "lend" its own judges, but the judge pointed out that the lending/borrowing rules did not apply to senior judges. One active district judge who did have to go through the formal process reported that the judge's circuit chief judge approved the request and there was no difficulty. Senior judges are not subject to the full range of rules, but the Inter-circuit Assignment Committee, having sent a questionnaire to senior judges, keeps a roster of judges willing to sit outside their home circuits.[2] When judges take senior status, they can indicate to the Administrative Office of the U.S. Courts (AO) that they are available for service elsewhere, what one judge called "the traditional thing."

The rules, while important, do not, however, control most judge-visiting, as active judges are sufficiently busy "at home" to be unavailable to serve elsewhere—unless, for example, as rarely happens, an entire panel of visiting judges must be sent to a court because all of its judges have recused, in which case the Chief Justice designates the visiting panel, the judges of which may be drawn from different circuits.[3] In addition, at least one circuit has a policy under which its own active judges may not sit in other circuits.[4] In one important exception to having visiting judges drawn from senior judge ranks, Ninth Circuit Chief Judge James R. Browning sent two judges—Alfred T. Goodwin and Eugene Wright—to sit in other circuits to learn the procedures used by those circuits, in order to

---

[2] Marion A. Ott (staff assistant, Administrative Office, U.S. Courts), memorandum to Judge Alfred T. Goodwin, September 6, 1991.

[3] See, e.g., Common Cause of Pennsylvania v. Pennsylvania, 558 F.3d 249 (3d Cir. 2009), in which the judges were from the Second (Leval), Seventh (Flaum), and Tenth (Ebel) Circuits, and United States v. Casellas-Turo, 807 F.3d 380 (1st Cir. 2015), a panel of Judges Sentelle, Jordan, and Benton, from, respectively, the D.C., Third, and Eighth Circuits.

[4] Personal communication to author, May 9, 2014.

bring back ideas to the Ninth Circuit; those contacts led to repeated later invitations to Judge Goodwin after he took senior status.

Overall, however, selection of visiting judges is not highly organized. Some elements of selection are somewhat haphazard. At least when the Ninth Circuit was smaller, one could find instances when the Chief Judge, traveling on court business to one of the cities where court was held, might arrange for the construction of a panel to hear some pending cases. For example, when Chief Judge Richard Chambers would go to Seattle, Washington, to see about space for bankruptcy referees, he would call the Clerk to ascertain where there were enough Seattle cases to be heard and then whether there were judges available; he would sit, find another circuit judge, and draw in a local district judge to be the panel's third member.[5] This type of situation reinforces the view that, at least to some extent, "other" judges become "filler" on panels on which two court of appeals judges have already been placed; one sees a series of judge-combinations in which two circuit judges remain constant while the third judge, a visitor or a by-designation district judge, varies. (Likewise, there are panels in which two active-duty circuit judges sit for a week while a series of "seniors" occupy the third spot).

There can, however, be some elements of organization in the process. In one circuit, when outside judges wrote letters saying they would like to serve, the circuit executive "kept an inventory and when a judge was needed would look in the file." In another circuit with "no policy," one judge has coordinated bringing visitors to the court. In still another circuit, a judge reported that his court had "no set policy. The Chief Judge is in charge."[6] Designation of visiting judges was "on an ad hoc basis" in yet another circuit.[7] The visitors selected tend to be judges "we have had before" and it "tends to be a buddy network."[8] In a circuit in which visitors were needed because of the "Clinton back-up" resulting from the delay in confirmation of nominations, "informal pleas were made to judges one knew to come sit," so "a small group come in on personal invitations."[9] One judge suggested inviting two judges from another

---

[5] From conversation with Alfred T. Goodwin, January 12, 1977.

[6] Personal communication to author, May 14, 2014.

[7] Personal communication to author, May 9, 2014.

[8] Personal communication to author, May 9, 2014.

[9] One judge spoke of another circuit's having solicited a visit once the judge had taken senior status, but arrangements couldn't be worked out.

circuit as "we could benefit from their perspectives"; both the prospective visitors were African-American.[10]

The courts of appeals appear to vary in the extent to which the process of selecting visitors is controlled. At least some circuits have internal policies about judge-visiting; some have considered whether a judge's visits to other courts should be counted against the number of calendars in which the judge is obligated to sit each year in the judge's home court or should be considered additional work "on the judge's own time" just like writing of separate opinions. One judge with experience in several circuits observed that "other circuits exercised greater quality control concerning the selection of visiting judges" than did his own circuit, with some having a judge committee "required to approve a visiting judge before he or she may sit."[11] Thus, where before 2000, "recruitment of visiting judges was largely left to the Circuit Executive's office," the court's discussion of this matter led to the creation of a Committee on Visiting Judges "to review the quality of visiting judges through a regular system of feedback from members of our Court."[12] The committee, with the aid of the Clerk of Court, obtained feedback about visitors from judges who had sat with them. A guide for the order of preference was also established, with the first category the not particularly precise "experienced and known out-of-circuit judges"; the second was within-circuit district judges appointed for at least a year. Only after those would out-of-circuit district judges be considered.[13]

In some instances, the Chief Judge of a circuit reached out and asked if a judge wished to come sit. Yet invitations from Chief Judges were not necessarily the Chief Judge's idea but were often prompted by someone else. Judges often had friends on the court they visited, from their pre-judicial careers, or at least they might know people on the court, and so, as one judge observed, there was no surprise when an invitation was made. In one instance, a senior judge on the visited circuit a judge knew "had a problem" because of the unavailability of a resident judge and

---

[10] Stephen Reinhardt, memorandum to Cathy Catterson [Clerk of Court] and other judges, June 26, 2000.

[11] The remarks were by Judge Alfred T. Goodwin, as reported by Judge Sidney Thomas, memorandum to [Ninth Circuit] Executive Committee, May 16, 2000, about potential action items from the court's Symposium.

[12] Judge Sidney Thomas, memorandum to Associates (Ninth Circuit), July 24, 2003.

[13] Examination of documents indicating which circuit judges were going to sit in what locations and when shows that out-of-circuit visiting judges are more likely to be identified early (the initial list of circuit judges' sittings comes in October or November), with many remaining slots designated as "vj1" or "vj2," etc., with those slots more likely to be filled by in-circuit district judges.

informed the circuit executive of the judge's availability, and the circuit executive contacted the judge, who did serve as a visitor.

In some if not all courts, the process is thought often to be a matter of a judge who wishes to visit another court alerting another judge (often a friend) in the court to be visited of their availability and wish to visit and then their being selected by that court. According to anecdotes, which might result from a less-than-positive experience with a visiting judge, would-be visiting judges self-invite. However, while some visiting judges have "let it be known" that they would like to receive an invitation from another court, other visitors report otherwise. For example, one judge had very specifically declined to do that but waited to be contacted, and another stressed, "I never initiated visits," because "[i]t is little intrusive to sit in a particular place," and doing so was "busybody activity." However, making one's availability known is not the same as seeking an invitation, and surveyed visiting judges primarily said they became visiting judges by invitation, not initiated by the visitor.

More than one judge had made contact with a judge on the visited court through service together on a committee of the Judicial Conference of the United States, with one remarking that the invitation happened "serendipitously" as a result of a conversation over dinner at a committee session, when the judge who was to become a visitor noted he was going to go to the visited circuit to help out in a district court. "Why don't you come sit with the court of appeals?" asked his dinner companion. A former district judge had known someone on the court he visited through their joint attendance at the Federal Judicial Center's "Baby Judges School." When the visited court asked if he wanted to sit in Atlanta in August or Miami in February, it was "the easiest decision I'd made all day," while another judge, invited to sit in Montgomery, Alabama in the summer, accepted ("The other judges wondered why I would do that."), as the judge had family ties to the city. In another instance, a judge who had been a visiting judge mentioned one of his colleagues to a judge there, and that led to an invitation to visit.

Judges who seek to sit elsewhere might not offer reasons why they want to visit, but at times they are quite explicit about wishing an assignment. In an instance in which a judge wished assignment to a district court, he wrote to the chief judge of the circuit containing that district, "Thank you ... for your considerable efforts in attempting to have me assigned to the Central District of California so that I might perform my son's wedding in Santa Monica."[14] At times, as in the instance just noted,

---

[14] Jim R. Corrigan (D. Colo.), letter to Alfred T. Goodwin, December 13, 1990.

prospective visitors indicate where they wish to sit and may even say they will not sit with certain other judges.[15] Visitors' geographic preferences can cause problems for the receiving court. An example is the Ninth Circuit, where "some visiting judges have displaced active judges from locales, particularly Seattle and Portland,"[16] so the court decided that its own judges should have priority, as they do for sittings at Honolulu and Anchorage.[17] When a former state court colleague suggested to the Ninth Circuit's judge who was about to become the Ninth Circuit's chief judge that it would be nice if a U.S. district judge could sit in Alaska because that judge liked to fish, the Ninth Circuit judge responded, "If I sent a district judge to Anchorage at any time I would have a mutiny on my hands by the circuit judges. Anchorage is such a desirable assignment that our judges go in rotation and no judge . . . can go back until every other judge in the court has had an Anchorage assignment."[18]

Another element of geography is the proximity of judges, particularly district judges, to the seat of the court of appeals. Thus, the Second Circuit has "so many great SDNY [Southern District of New York] judges that we use them a lot" as well as judges from the Court of International Trade, "located across Foley Square from us."[19] The risk of using "next door" judges, particularly when a district such as Southern New York generates many cases, is that district judges might sit on appeals from their own district. For many observers, this practice (discussed later) is distinctly to be avoided because either the district judge will hesitate to criticize (reverse) a district colleague or the result may lead to friction among the district judges.

At least some aspects of selection of district judges to sit with the court of appeals are different from selection of out-of-circuit visitors. Initially, district judges come to sit with the court very early in their tenure to be socialized to the ways of the appellate court. After this initial service, other factors are likely to govern whether they return. Ideological affinity might be one, but the concern of the chief judge and of the Clerk of Court to move cases may prevail, so a district judge who, on returning

---

[15] Personal confidential communication to author, January 5, 2015.

[16] Sidney Thomas to [Ninth Circuit] Executive Committee, May 16, 2000.

[17] Not only are the circuit's own circuit judges the only judges to sit in those two locations, but none, after sitting, may return until others have had their opportunity to go there.

[18] Alfred T. Goodwin, letter to Arno Denecke, May 3, 1988, responding to Denecke, letter to Goodwin, April 26, 1988. Judges Denecke and Goodwin had served together on the Oregon Supreme Court.

[19] Richard Wesley, e-mail to Stephen L. Wasby, May 12, 2014.

to chambers, does not "get out" the opinions for which the judge is responsible is not likely to be asked to return. And even if a district judge wishes to return, that decision might depend on the Chief Judge's judgment as to whether particular judges could be spared from their districts because of their caseload there, and at times the unavailability of district judges for this reason tilted the court toward use of visiting judges. For those who are invited back, it can be seen "as a credit to the reputation of the District Judge who is asked to serve" further.[20] Indeed, some judges return with sufficient frequency that they become "regulars," and what their primary "social identity" is might not even be clear—as a district judge or as an appellate judge. Certainly when district judges who have sat regularly with their own circuit's court of appeals are elevated to that court, their transition to appellate work has already taken place.[21]

Although not explored in detail here, the processes for the inter-circuit transfer of district judges to sit in the *district courts* operates in the same way as for appeals court judges. For active judges, the Inter-circuit Assignment Committee must be utilized, but matters are less formal for senior district judges, and each circuit has its own processes for inter-*district* transfer of judges. Thus, in the Ninth Circuit, surveys are first undertaken of district chief judges' need for judicial assistance and of district judges' willingness to serve elsewhere and their availability. A judge might sit in another district for a fixed period of time (a week for a month) to help handle the district's business or might be needed to try a particular case, either because of recusals[22] or because a case is long and complex.[23] When there is a need, there are priorities for the order in which invitations will be made, starting with senior district judges, in order of their last assignment, and then active district judges. A further rule is that unless borrowing was for a specific case, no active judge from a borrowing district may serve elsewhere.[24]

---

[20] Personal communication, e-mail to Stephen L. Wasby, November 28, 2016.

[21] Examples in the Ninth Circuit include Judges Warren Ferguson and Harry Pregerson, both on the Central District of California before their appointments by President Carter to the Ninth Circuit, and Judge Alfred T. Goodwin, of the District of Oregon before his elevation to the court of appeals.

[22] In one instance, a district judge from Oregon was sent to the Northern District of California to handle a case brought against a judge of that district, where all the Northern California judges had recused.

[23] There are also instances in which retired magistrate judges are "recalled" to service to aid in the districts in which they had served, and bankruptcy judges are also recalled for use in other districts.

[24] See, e.g., Greg Walters (Cir. Exec., Ninth Cir.), memorandum to Chief District Judges, Dec. 30, 1987.

Visiting Judges' Views

The visiting judges whose views are reported here were drawn from among those who served most frequently in that capacity (see Appendix B on Data Sources), although observations from some other sources are also included. One will see that judges, while noting some drawbacks, uniformly had positive views of being a visiting judge. The overall "positivity" may result in part from a selection effect. Judges willing to serve as visitors, and particularly if they seek to do so, are unlikely to be a random sample of judges or even of senior judges, who are the ones most likely to visit. Moreover, the judges who serve most frequently as visitors are highly likely to be positive, for, were they not, after less-than-positive initial experiences, they would cease serving as visitors.

Why visit? Why did judges wish to visit? Those who did recognized the basic reason a visited court used them was that they were wanted "to help out with their dockets," but why visitors had wished to sit in other circuits differed somewhat from judge to judge. Their reasons centered on variety—on wanting to see how other circuits functioned, to obtain ideas that might be useful for their own courts or in their own work, so it was, as one judge put it, "useful variety." Sometimes it was simply a matter of doing something new, "just something I hadn't done," "tourism in a way to see something." As active judges seldom could visit, the desire to do something new when a judge took senior status could be considerable. Variety could mean seeing differences in jurisdiction or in the mix of cases. For one judge, it was because his court lacked criminal jurisdiction which he could experience in other courts. For a district judge, it was wanting to learn about appellate work—which he also could learn from sitting with his own court of appeals. Other judges echoed the desire for "variety" in their practice, saying "how other circuits differed from ours" and "to see how other circuits operated."

Even when judges emphasized variety, as when a judge "was curious to see how other courts would be similar to or different from" sitting in his own court, they also talked of learning. One visitor thought it "would be interesting and instructional to see how other circuits conducted business." That judge spoke of "different circuits [having] different cultures—how the judges relate to each other and how they relate to the bar"; he said, "When you sit in one place, with the same judges, you think the way you do things is the only way, the best way. That can't be—and isn't." So through being a visiting judge, "You learn instructive differences and bring them back to one's own circuit to consider using." Thus, the desire for variety was often centered on bringing ideas back to their own court, as when one visiting judge had "wanted to look at how their court functions to see if we can find a better way of succeeding in our tasks" in his own court and another said, "What I would learn would be helpful to my own court."

Another reason for wanting to sit as a visitor was what might be called personal payoff, as when a judge said that serving as a visitor "is helpful to being a well-rounded judge" or, as another put it, "I might learn some things that would be helpful to me in my work." And one judge's desire to serve as a visiting judge had an interesting twist in that he wanted to be what amounted to be an ambassador from his court. While recognizing that his court was "one of the most misunderstood circuits," he thought it was "the best" and found it "good for the circuit to have others see us—not as extreme."

Expectations. What did visiting judges expect to derive from their experiences? Their expectations closely tracked the reasons they wished to visit in other circuits. Although some had no expectations or were not sure what to expect (or, as in one case, not sure that expectations would be met), the expectations held by most judges fell into two principal categories. One was that the judges would meet other colleagues. At times this was for personal benefit, as when a judge said he did not expect to get anything "professionally" out of visiting but expected "social contact with friends," and it included particular cities in which to sit, with New Orleans being a favorite. One judge said it "would be enriching to be with other colleagues," particularly after working with his regular colleagues on such a regular basis." Another "expected to get to know judges [with whom] I would not otherwise have had the opportunity to discuss our respective circuit courts." A special aspect of the personal facet is seen in remarks of an African-American judge who "wanted to help [judges in the visited circuits] understand what is or is not discrimination," as they "had not felt it" and he "had some special information to share on that."

The other principal expectation was to obtain "a fresh perspective on how they do their work." This included both institutional and personal aspects. One judge stated that he expected "to learn a substantial amount about how the judges process their work and how they function individually as a judge." Desiring "a better understanding of how the various circuits operate," judges who were to visit expected to obtain ideas for better case-processing that could be used in their home circuit. On this point, one judge stated an expectation to obtain "ideas on procedure of deciding cases in a more expeditious way."

Another judge expected to obtain ideas to apply to his own method of judging; he spoke of perhaps finding out "something done differently that could translate into an improvement of my work" on his home court. On this point, a judge who had visited in the Tenth Circuit contrasted it with his home circuit, with the Tenth having "an extraordinarily current docket," which he attributed to vacancies being filled. In three of six cases on a criminal appeals calendar, the reply briefs had been due only a week before. "That's a current docket," stated the judge. Not only docket-processing but different case-mixes were part of judges' expectations. The composition of the docket might be different from judges' home-circuit fare, as when a Ninth Circuit judge, noting the "slight differences" in the mix of cases, said that his circuit "has lots of immigration cases, and the other circuits don't get those"; however, the judge "wasn't trying to find certain kinds of cases."

The visiting judges were clear that, with minimal caveats, their expectations were met. One said his expectations were "completely met"; another judge put it this way: "There were no expectations not met, nor anything I did not like"; and a third said that in his experience, "They were always met." One judge who had expected to be treated "the same as in my own circuit" found that expectation "fully met." Another's expectations were met because his service in another circuit exposed him "to different jurisdiction and a different set of people." And one could also see that expectations were met about learning ideas to "take home" in a judge's comment of having "learn[ed] a number of helpful things useful to my work on my home circuit." A judge who had expected to obtain ideas for more expeditious handling of cases found that expectation met "by realizing that most of the other circuits do a lot of screening prior to oral argument, in order to thin out cases which were not of major concern." One relatively minimal reservation about expectations being met came from a judge's observation that "[t]here was insufficient time to really explore the function of the [visited] court and to be able to look more seriously at the data that would be helpful" in understanding that court.

Many judges would have agreed with the judge who said that being a visiting judge was "very comfortable—not new and different," or, in another judge's words, that the process was the same across circuits. Yet one judge did say that "there were some surprises" although these were not "disappointed expectations." The surprises related to how another circuit operated, such as much greater use of unpublished (non-precedential) dispositions, as the visiting judge's circuit used few while the circuit he visited made very high use of them. He observed that "in four days of sitting in the Ninth Circuit, I produced only one published opinion but I signed many memorandum dispositions," whereas in two other circuits he produced more published dispositions.

The one judge who had been unclear as to whether his expectations would be met was a district judge. His uncertainty stemmed from his having been aware that "[d]istrict judges have different views of sitting with the courts of appeals," with some "not cut out to sit on the appellate court" because "they want the autonomy they have as district judges." However, he "enjoyed the collaborative work" on the appellate court, to which was added his being able to sit with a number of judges—rather than a smaller number when he sat with the court of appeals in his home circuit—and particularly with judges of widely-divergent ideological positions. Another judge, now a member of a court of appeals but who spoke of his experience sitting as a district judge by designation, likewise spoke of the "very valuable experience" of sitting with the appellate court: "It gave a newly appointed District Judge insight into how the appellate judges approach decision-making counseled cases" and "how to question counsel during oral argument," as well as about "the process of circulating draft opinions for comments and suggestions." He said that, while the initial experience was "a bit intimidating to be in the presence of two brilliant jurists, it was also reaffirming for me."[25]

Like and Learn. Before turning to what the surveyed visiting judges said they liked and learned, it may be useful to inject observations by some offered at other times. One of the advantages of service as a visiting judge is that, by visiting other circuits, judges learn about different procedures and bring those procedures home. This can be seen when, at a meeting of the Ninth Circuit's appellate judges, judges who had been visitors in other circuits made presentations and one discussed at some length the Fifth and Eleventh Circuits' procedures as to staff attorney use and "serial screening" while noting "emerging differences" in procedure between the two circuits.[26] In another instance of a visiting judge taking a liking to a procedure not previously experienced, a senior Fifth Circuit judge speaking to a Ninth Circuit judge, "unprompted and with some enthusiasm, praised the [Ninth Circuit] bench memo system and its 'front-loading' and sharing of research."[27] Judges also come away with impressions of other courts' general atmospheres and compare them with that in their own court. A visitor to the First Circuit said it "managed a greater collegial congeniality in crafting opinions," perhaps because of its lesser dependence on law clerks. He found "an apparent greater willingness to respond and revise opinion in response to ideas that run against

---

25 Personal communication to Stephen L. Wasby, November 28, 2016.

26 The judge was Alfred T. Goodwin. See his memorandum to Carlos Bea and other judges, May 25, 2006.

27 Susan Graber, memorandum to Associates, September 12, 2012.

those of the author of the opinion" and suggested that the First Circuit judges' use of first names rather than "judge" contributed to this: "The mask 'Judge' was dropped."[28]

Just as judges' expectations often flowed from their reasons for wanting to serve as visiting judges, what they liked in their experience and what they said they learned were often a function of their expectations. Indeed, what they liked was often clear from their statements that their expectations had been met, as those expectations were not negative and neither were their reactions to serving as a visiting judge. The positive reaction is evident in a judge's remark that he "felt privileged to be able to work with" the judges of the court he visited, and in the remarks of another, who found that "sitting was wonderful" and said "they treat you well; they appreciate what you are doing," although he added, "Maybe Southerners are unnecessarily polite." Still another found the experience "an intellectual feast" in which one gets to sit with "brilliant minds." And yet another visitor found the judges of the court he visited to be "enormously accommodating," with the court he visited, one that used many visitors, "a well-oiled machine" that "set out matters well for the visitors." Another judge found that same court "highly efficient" and "welcoming of visiting judges," which "certainly [created] a satisfactory experience." One of these judges added that with e-mail, it was "easy to communicate," which addresses a concern stated in earlier years by a visited court's judges who found communication with a visiting judge difficult once that judge had returned to home chambers, a comment made before regular use of e-mail.

More specifically, one judge said what he liked was that being a visiting judge "provides a good means for judges to visit other courts to observe how they approach the decision-making process." He learned that the visiting judge experience was of value and that "it is very beneficial for circuits to have judges from outside their circuit to participate in resolving cases." This was similar to the reaction of the judge who thought "the greater benefit was for me in making my observations and, in some cases, pickup up new ideas which I attempted to pursue."

Experience as a visiting judge was also liked because it would broaden a judge's outlook. Some of this broadening came from "the variety of the cases in different circuits." Judges sitting outside their own circuit may also obtain a clearer picture of differences in caseload mix. A Ninth Circuit judge who had sat in five other circuits reported that "[t]he cases in other circuits vary somewhat as to the substantive matters presented."

---

[28] John Noonan, memorandum to Associates, November 30, 1987.

He added, "Many of those in the upper Midwest involve land problems and farming in the Dakotas" and in another circuit, "we didn't have the burden of criminal appeals and habeas cases with which I am most familiar." He also noted, "I don't believe I saw an immigration case in other circuits."[29] Another judge, who said that "one gets a sense of variety" and that "the cases are different," noted that his home circuit had few maritime cases, unlike the Fifth and Eleventh Circuits in which he had sat, and that as to immigration cases, most in the Ninth Circuit were about deportation but the smaller number in the judge's home circuit were about asylum.

However, another judge mentioned the benefit of "working with other judges on issues, many of which turned out to be issues common to" those on the judge's own court. Indeed, one judge said he had learned that "[t]he process of appellate judging is essentially the same in every circuit" in which he had sat. However, another judge took away the opposite lesson: "Different circuits have different cultures and customs, as well as different procedures." (A former court of appeals law clerk has commented that in meeting with clerks of visiting judges, "the clerks often exchanged stories about the ways in which our respective courts' procedures were similar and dissimilar," not unlike what the judges themselves were doing.[30])

Working with the judges in other circuits would provide new perspectives, something particularly important for district judges visiting out-of-circuit, as they were accustomed to operating solo; by sitting on an appellate panel, a district judge might learn about "compromising," not necessary in a district judge's usual work. Beyond that, there was the pleasure of getting to know judges in the visited circuits. One judge observed that he now "consider[s] many of them to be close friends," and another spoke of the benefit of "social contact with admired, respected people I liked" and of working with them. One judge pointed to the interaction with other judges while visiting their courts as "in many respects, more profitable than just meeting with Judges from other Circuits at conferences and seminars" because one was "dealing with specifics and discussing them."

Judges also liked the sightseeing that could accompany visiting another court. One judge said that "seeing the courthouses and the cities in which they are located has been a positive experience," and another spoke of the "cultural anthropology" side of visits to other courts, through which

---

[29] Eugene A. Wright, "Good Lawyers Before Appellate Courts," unpublished ms., 1981.
[30] Jonathan R. Nash, e-mail to Stephen L. Wasby, April 2, 2017.

one "learned differences in customs, political life, and cultural patterns, and that New Orleans was different from St. Louis and New York." Perhaps most generally, "there is a certain amount of refreshment of getting away from what you have been doing for decades in a particular Circuit and having a new experience."

Dislikes and Problems. Did the visiting judges find any downside to being a visiting judge? In evaluating their experiences as visitors, these judges certainly had far more good things than negatives to say. When asked specifically about dislikes and problems, one judge had "no criticisms," and most found nothing to dislike in their experience, with one saying there was "absolutely nothing" he didn't like and another saying that differences in operation of the courts "didn't bother me" and he found "nothing unpleasant." Another judge observed that he was "able to adjust to their system easily," a remark which somewhat echoed the observation by a Ninth Circuit judge who had been a visitor in several other circuits; he had found "minor differences in terminology, but no major procedural differences between the Ninth Circuit and the other big circuits."[31] One visitor even had "been able to persuade circuit judges about the view of the law." and he said there had been no "resentment" when he had dissented in a visible case. This is evidence for the more general point that visiting judges were treated on the same level as the home-court judges and shared equally in decision-making on cases.[32] This was put well by another judge, who had sat in six circuits outside his own and who had found "[a]ll of my experiences . . . positive": "I have been uniformly treated the same as one of their own judges and I have felt free to concur or dissent in various cases the same as I would in my own circuit."

The judges did, however, identify some problems, matters they did not like, but there was no consensus as to particular difficulties. It is interesting to note that one judge found the only thing he did not like was other courts *not* using visiting judges. He thought it a "mistake" not to utilize them, "for they might learn from visiting judges on how to resolve cases." Among the difficulties noted, one judge had experienced being "somewhat sensitive to filling in" for a judge of the visited court, something he had seen in visitors to his own court, with the result that he said he would "not be acting as I would in my own court." Part of "unstated

---

31 Alfred T. Goodwin, e-mail to Stephen L. Wasby, January 8, 2001.

32 This is parallel to the views expressed by the judges in the Bowie et al. study who spoke about their experience as visiting judges: "[N]one felt that either of the regular judges on the panel treated them any differently than they treated their other colleagues." Bowie, Songer, and Szmer, p. 53.

expectations" and "dimensions of the role that are not present when one is sitting in one's own circuit" was "pressure to go along" which a visiting judge might feel as an "inclination to be a bit more deferential than with [one's] own colleagues," something he definitely did not experience in his home court. This part of a visiting judge's general sense of situation is captured in remarks worth quoting:

> Each visiting judge has to feel his or her way how one is going to conduct oneself; you never lose sight of the fact that you are a visiting judge. That doesn't mean you cast votes contrary to principles. But short of that: one might be more insistent at home to get a colleague to insert certain changes—fussing about language—[there is] more of it with [one's] own colleagues.

While the judge felt it could be "appropriate to trim the sails," it was clear that "one can't lose one's status as an independent judge," but "short of that, [one] should be accommodating."

If visitors sensed an expectation to defer, it was possible that they brought that deference to the visited court with them. This can be seen in a judge's stated concern about some visiting judges who "would come into conference and say, 'Whatever you two want to do.'" His reaction was, "I *hate* that!" because "there should be conversation back-and-forth."[33] Another judge told a similar story, although he said it had happened only once when "a visiting judge said he didn't come for heavy lifting." Still another visiting judge put it politely in saying, "I get the sense that visiting judges had different attitudes about work; some come just looking for the trip, not looking for work." However, he thought that the visited court "tracked" visiting judges and "if they have a bad experience with one, let them know." (They are more likely not to receive another invitation.)

What about the effect of judge-visiting on judges' law clerks? One judge, who had sat with the court of appeals as a district judge, thought that returning to the appellate court after his initial sitting there would be valuable for his law clerks, even as it increased chambers workload. Another judge suggested that visiting another circuit "does change the rhythm in chambers," with clerks being affected. One aspect related to the number of clerks traveling with the judge. One judge spoke of taking only one clerk on travel, whether that clerk had worked on cases to be heard out-of-circuit and had prepared material for them. Where the traveling clerk had not been the one to have prepared a case, from time to time the

---

[33] The judge then read to me from a David Brooks' column on the importance of exchange among competing points of view.

clerk was concerned about stepping on other clerks' toes, but the judge felt that "was the clerk's problem not mine."

There was a particular effect on the chambers of judges either visiting from the Ninth Circuit or visiting that court that resulted from of the Ninth Circuit court's use of shared bench memoranda. Those documents were not prepared in other courts of appeals, where "[w]hatever is done by chambers, it's for our own use; we don't share." Bowie and her colleagues had noted that the only negative comments they heard in their interviews were from two visitors to the Ninth Circuit. Both "spontaneously mentioned their dislike of that circuit's practice of having one clerk write a memorandum of law that was distributed to all three judges on the panel," something with which these visitors "went along only because they thought it was not their places as outsiders to challenge what appeared to be established practice of their 'host' circuits."[34]

Judges in the present interviews who visited "out West" would find that the preparation of bench memos, which one called "pre-assignment,"[35] "shifts when work is done" in chambers from being most heavily post-argument to before argument.[36] The Ninth Circuit judge visiting elsewhere found work harder, as law clerks would have to prepare memos just for the judge on all cases, rather than for only some to be shared with other panel members. Thus a judge had "to decide early on how best to utilize law clerks," with "only two practical alternatives— short, targeted bench memos in all or most cases, or full memos in fewer, selected cases, or gradations in between." As another judge stated in communicating to colleagues, "Preparing for an argument calendar in a circuit with a comparably-weighted calendar as ours without the aid of shared or pooled bench memos is significantly more work for both my law clerks and me than preparing for a calendar here at home."[37]

---

[34] Bowie, Songer, and Szmer, p. 53.

[35] In the Ninth Circuit, it is regularly the case that the chambers that prepares the bench memo in a case is assigned the writing of the opinion or disposition in the case, unless that judge is not in the majority. The court does not use the term "pre-assignment," however, although such a term is used in some other appellate courts where a judge is assigned the writing of a draft opinion for the court. One judge stated that, when a chambers was preparing the bench memo in a case, that judge "then becomes the 'lead' judge on the case (and the presumptive author)."

[36] Two of the judges interviewed for the Bowie et al. study "spontaneously mentioned their dislike" of the shared bench memorandum practice and "indicated they went along only because they thought it was not their place as outsiders to challenge what appeared to be an established practice of their 'host' circuit." Bowie, Songer, and Szmer, p. 53.

[37] A. Wallace Tashima, memorandum to Associates, June 5, 2009.

Although judges had spoken of getting ideas from their visits, one judge found the experience of being a visiting judge "far too rushed," particularly to learn how the visited court functions: "In just a few days you cannot really make any in depth analysis." This concern is related to another judge's observation, "Visiting is different from being on one's own court: you are there only once a year, not in regular contact, and not [sitting] on en bancs," and you "don't see the judges regularly." However, another judge noted "differences" not only between visiting circuit judges and in-circuit district judges but also "as to whether they sit regularly or are there only on a 'one-shot' basis."

This concern about limited contact with visited judges is related to the dislike of travel, mentioned by several judges. One Ninth Circuit judge, while not being negative, noted that travel from the West Coast to Puerto Rico occupied a full day, but he found that no different from sitting in Alaska or Hawaii in his own circuit. Another visiting judge who had crossed the country in the other direction found it "a long run for a short slide," if one were sitting for only a couple of days and had not added some other activities to one's itinerary. Another, who had sat in several circuits, complained of airport security and the like, which "had become more intrusive, time-consuming, and tiresome." "No one," he said, "liked the travel part—congested, wasted time." Indeed, the travel was one reason a judge removed his name from the list of those interested in being visiting judges: "I don't like living out of a suitcase," he said, but he added the reason for ceasing to serve as a visiting judge was that his circuit used visitors and he felt he should stay there "so that we would not need to be so reliant on outside help."

Carrying Circuit Law. The judges were asked about one particular possible problem—whether there was any difficulty in following the law of the visited circuit—because of concerns, stated earlier by judges on visited courts, that visiting judges would bring the law of their home circuit "in their flightbag" and would be inclined to follow it rather than the law of the visited circuit they were expected to apply. The visiting judges surveyed, however, unanimously and clearly rejected the suggestion that there might be such a difficulty, with one judge responding, "Never."

Concerns about visiting judges importing their own law were first stated when finding the law of the visited circuit required a manual search rather than electronic data-retrieval. The availability of WESTLAW may help explain why today's visitors state, "One can find the law of the circuit easily, which is like finding the law of the state that one is applying" in diversity cases. Or, as another visitor put, "I had competent law clerks who researched based upon . . . whatever Circuit I sat in." To the extent that the concern continues, said one judge, it might be because the judges have "a cultural disposition against using visiting judges," which leads them to that concern. And they might be led to it after a bad experience with a visiting judge. In connection with this topic, one judge talked of sitting in his own circuit with "a judge who not only did not apply our law but wrote dissents against it."[38] We can also see it in the view of a judge of a court that used many visitors, who mentioned what he thought was over-use of "out-of-circuit senior district judges" and "[t]oo heavy a reliance on visiting judges." He said the use of "visitors who have no idea of Ninth Circuit law and very little idea of how a federal court of appeals develops circuit law . . . can have an adverse impact on the development of circuit law."

Visiting judges certainly understood the norm to be that they were to apply the law of the visited circuit. As one put it, "I tried to pay attention to that. I was sitting as a First Circuit or a Tenth Circuit judge." Another judge, with no real concern about use of visiting judges, said that visitors "try to fit their behavior to the judicial process." He then added, "The more conscientious and professional, the less likely [they are] to come with an agenda." Bringing an "agenda" is not the same as importing home-circuit caselaw, but the two are related in that a visiting judge's focus on an agenda could well interfere with applying visited circuits' law.

There might be tension when circuits' views on an issue were in conflict. One judge took the position that if he did not like the law of the visited circuit, he would raise the matter in conference and that court's judges would respond; as far as he was concerned, once it was established that it was the law of the circuit, that was the end of it, noting "That's why we have different circuits." However, a court of appeals judge who had visited in another circuit, discussing having views that differed from those of the court he was visiting, argued that the worst thing one could do in that situation was simply to go along.[39] Another judge spoke of a case in which he had participated where there was a pre-existing circuit split, with his home court on one side of the split and the visited circuit not having taken a position. The judge was uncomfortable about that situation when the opinion was assigned to him, so he said one of the resident judges should write the opinion and he would then deal with what it embodied. He claims that he "would have been OK" if the opinion had

---

[38] While this judge, from the Ninth Circuit, declined to say that the judge was the late Judge Ruggero Aldisert, the incident is known; indeed, it was worse than the judge stated, as Judge Aldisert complained about the Ninth Circuit in an opinion for his home Third Circuit. See Chapter 2 for exploration of this problem.

[39] From conversation with Judge John Noonan, Pasadena, Cal., February 3, 2004.

distinguished his circuit's case on the facts, but no problem developed, as the draft opinion came down on his circuit's side of the issue (perhaps because of his presence on the panel?). Yet if visitors were to bring their own circuits' jurisprudence which differed from that of the circuit they were visiting, and if they were to insinuate their home court's views into the visited circuit's law, it might serve to even out inter-circuit differences in positions on an issue, thus lessening the possibility of inter-circuit splits.[40]

What Do Differently? Would visiting judges who have visited circuits do anything differently, and would they, as judges, do anything differently as visitors? The judges' answers provide a further indication of their likes and dislikes. The judges mentioned few matters that, as visiting judges they would do differently. One, saying "Not really" would he do so, nonetheless observed, "I continue to refine my own practices in getting ready" so he could be "more effective in getting prepared"—although he admitted "I don't do it" as often as he should.

Nor did the visitors mention many matters that they would have the courts they visited do differently. This may be because visiting judges do not think it is in their remit to make such suggestions. As one with considerable visiting experience said, "I tried to avoid being a busybody." And another, who spoke in a way that indicated he felt there was a problem, did not put it in those terms; he simply commented that, while the court he had visited had "a pretty good system," he was "somewhat surprised that some cases go to the oral argument calendar," after which he observed, "The weighting is off. . . ."

One judge converted his satisfaction with his visiting experience into something his own court could do. After noting that he was "surprised by how hospitable they were," he followed with, "Maybe we are colder; we use visitors but don't make a fuss," which is a suggestion for his own court's better treatment of visitors. Another judge who could not find anything for the visited courts to do differently said that, "If anything, I drew insights that might be worth applying in my own circuit" and said he came away with a view that his own court could change its practices. In particular, concerning whether to issue opinions to be published or non-precedential ("unpublished") dispositions, he said that he and his colleagues "take a lot of pride that almost all of our cases result in published opinions," while "[o]ther circuits give summary treatment where we would have a published opinion to give fuller treatment to issues." Yet he felt that his own court "may overdo its use of published opinions." He

---

[40] I am indebted to Scott Ainsworth, University of Georgia, for this suggestion.

recognized its use of unpublished dispositions was "an act of survival," because if that court published as his did, "they couldn't do it [stay on top of caseload]," and he added that perhaps the visited circuit "can overdo the summary treatment approach." Another judge was, however, more positive about use of unpublished dispositions, which he thought was "smart," because in his circuit, "they make work to write long opinions on (too many) cases," in what he called "a case of work expanding to fit the time available."

Use of shared bench memos, earlier mentioned by some judges as a difference between circuits, with an effect on how their chambers pre-pared for cases, was something one judge from the Ninth Circuit suggest-ed could be used with benefit in other courts. He thought "it might be useful for some of the other circuits (the busier ones) to experiment with the pooled-bench memo, at least in a limited set of cases."

Differences Across the Circuits. It is quite clear that judges visiting another court almost invariably feel they learned about different modes of operation. Earlier, a senior district judge who had sat in other circuits said, "I see an incredible number of *procedural* differences in this unified system—customs of practice and procedure."[41] Although some differences among the courts of appeals have already been noted, there are other differences the surveyed judges felt sufficiently important to mention.

Although a number of judges observed that, in effect, judging was judging wherever one found it, they did note a number of differences, and those responses, even for this relatively small number of judges, serve to underscore not only procedural differences among courts of appeals but also what might be called "cultural" differences. Some of the differences noted are of the nitty-gritty variety, like "very minor differences in terminology" or that "[d]ifferent size fonts are used. The order of the judges' names on the first page are sometimes different. The numbering of lines or paragraphs in proposed opinions vary." These may seem picayune, but one must remember that "errors" by the visiting judge (just as by in-circuit district judges) may result in additional exchanges needed to transmit the rule and explanation to the visitor. Of greater import were differences in "[h]ow cases were chosen for oral argument or submission without argument" and "[h]ow cases are chosen for published, preceden-tial opinions," as well as "[h]ow and when writing responsibility is assigned."

Some inter-circuit differences which do not relate to mechanics might be called part of the "court culture." One is whether a three-judge panel

---

[41] Interview with Judge Robert J. Kelleher (C.D. Cal.), Los Angeles, March 2, 1977.

stays together for an entire calendar week or the panels are instead "shuffled" (or "churned") during an argument week. A judge who had visited in the Second Circuit "sat with everyone; the panels rotated so I got to sit with everyone." His explanation was that the court "wanted all to be exposed to someone who was visiting," but, even without visitors present, this court of appeals tends to "churn" its panels regularly. On the other hand, in the Eleventh Circuit, the same judge sat with the same panel for an entire week. These differences certainly would affect how many judges a visiting judge met. Also part of the differing cultures was what one might call "atmosphere." Certainly, visiting judges came away with impressions of the general atmosphere in a visited court and compared it with that in their own court.

Differences also included the earlier-mentioned one between the Ninth Circuit and other circuits in use of shared bench memos. Another important aspect is the extent to which judges of a court believe in panel autonomy from efforts to produce an overall court view on panel opinions, with the extent of that belief varying across circuits. One can see this in the difference in courts of appeals' use of rehearing en banc. A judge from a circuit whose judges valued panel autonomy and whose en banc procedure was "free-wheeling, and consequently more robust" did not like it that "[s]ome circuits use the en banc procedures, as well as other measures, to keep three-judge panels 'in line.'"

With respect to en bancs, in which, of course, visiting judges do not participate, another judge, sitting in a circuit which used en bancs more than in his own court, observed that "references were made that if an opinion were done a certain way, en banc will be raised." Related to the use of en banc rehearing is another difference one judge emphasized: the circulation of opinions within the (full) court before their release. This visiting judge came from a circuit which, like some others, does not circulate opinions outside the panel before filing them, but in two of the circuits in which he visited, there was such circulation "with a certain period in which to comment"—although he was told it did not happen often. This judge did report that in his own circuit, there would "occasionally" be an "informal en banc," but only when precedent was to be altered "when Supreme Court cases require it."

Related to the panel autonomy aspect of court culture is what a judge called a "strong difference" in the level of skepticism about opinions and the amount of editorial criticism made when the author of a disposition circulates a draft opinion within a panel. Where this judge saw other courts being deferential to the opinion author, in his court other judges "really go after draft opinions as to problematic law," although there is less concern about memorandum dispositions (as not precedential). This judge also found that in other circuits, one is less likely to come into court knowing what the other members of the panel will say, something he found a "big plus." His preference for a "cleaner" conference discussion of a case, without knowledge of other panel members' views, results in part from his reaction to the shared bench memos in his own circuit even though the judge whose chambers transmit a bench memo might disagree with the recommendations it might contain.

Visiting Judges' Role. To bring visiting judges back from specific likes and dislikes, they were asked finally whether, having been visiting judges, they had concerns about the visiting judge's role and whether their views had changed as a result of their experience. The responses are interesting. Some judges spoke, in one way or another, of the caseload assistance they provided, as when one said, "There is a need for their work—that's there." Another spoke of the "tremendous benefits" visiting judges were to the receiving court. However, some, while claiming that they had no concerns about visiting judges' role, then engaged in riffs, some incorporated above, that were quite illuminating.

As to whether their experience as visitors had led to a change in their views, some said their views were reinforced, but others said their views had not changed. One, a judge on a court that itself used visitors said, "I had greater appreciation of the considerations" visiting judges "brought to their role" and now was able to sense some of the behavior that other visitors had described. Another judge, who had held his skeptical views since his service as a district judge sitting by designation with his own court of appeals, found those views strengthened as a result of his experience: "I'm struck by that all the more now." Yet some did notice change beyond reinforcement of earlier-held views. A judge who visited in more than one circuit and was a member of a court that itself used visiting judges said he tried "to be more hospitable to the visiting judges to my home court," which, he said, "need[ed] to orient them on nuances which might prevail in our circuit but not in another."

A judge most skeptical about the use of visitors had a basic concern that what he called a district judge's "microschedule" was different. As it was going to be hard for a district judge to get his appellate work out, the judge sitting by designation would be "worried was my opinion going to be good enough?" He had an additional concern as a circuit judge visiting in another circuit, related to the stability of the law and about which he quoted Karl Llewellyn: "If I wrote for the [visited] Circuit, I would wonder how reliable would that opinion be as a statement of the circuit's law," particularly as he would not "be there on panels to apply the rule that I had developed in my opinion," so "the people there would wonder." This judge felt that, as in his own circuit, "[w]ith lots of visiting judges and a large court, one does not have reckonable law that can be applied by district judges and lawyers." (Imagining himself as a lawyer in Atlanta gave him pause.) That is difficult enough, but, he said, "Visiting judges water down reckonability even more."

* * *

The visiting judges who responded to this recent survey gave full recognition that visiting judges were needed. As one judge put it, "We have to have them," given the volume of cases facing the courts. Without them, it would take many years to get the court's work done—or, as the judge said after pausing, "we could turn it all over to the law clerks."[42] Beyond that recognition, however, these judges expressed strong support for the use of visitors. An example is a statement by a circuit judge who had been a district judge: "I think all courts, circuit and district, would benefit from using visiting judges on occasions. I think it would benefit individual judges to visit courts outside their district or circuit, to see how things differ." Another positive statement, although one made with a caveat, was the remark, "I think the practice of visiting judges is a useful practice," followed by "but all courts do not share the same views on the use of visiting judges," evident from those courts of appeals which make no use of them as a matter of policy and others which, as a practical matter, used few if any visitors.

Stronger was the statement by a judge who had often sat elsewhere: "The practice of judges visiting in other circuits should be encouraged." He added that because one had to be a senior judge to visit, "It is tragic that not all can do it." Another judge, likewise positive, noted that "[s]ome circuits will not utilize out of circuit judges," a position the judge called "a mistake, for they might learn from visiting judges on how to resolve cases." In considering these statements, the reader should keep in mind what was noted earlier: that those judges who visit, because they are engaging in a voluntary activity, are likely to be especially favorably disposed to having judges visit other circuits, with those who do not volunteer to participate, or who decline invitations, probably being less likely to be enthusiastic about the practice.

---

[42] A judge writing on a different matter and who knew of my interest in visiting judges added an observation from the perspective of the visited court: "We would fall hopelessly behind our case load about their valuable help. We are very glad to have them."

This evidence of support for the use of visiting judges by those who so served is strong, but there is an underlying—and competing—theme several judges expressed. One said, "Other than helping the Court with a needed Judge, I am not sure I was of any benefit to the Circuit where I visited." The position is, however, best represented by what was said by a judge who, while recognizing that "[v]isiting judges do perform extraordinary service and we learn much," nonetheless "wishes his court was in a position to sit only with its own judges" and asserted it would be "better if we sat with our own judges." This would, he said, "[a]void having a case with an important issue assigned to a panel with a district judge from Hoboken, a senior, and one active judge," something which he felt—with others mentioned above—weakened the effect of the ruling in the case.[43]

Thus, in reading all the "positives" stated by this small set of visiting judges, one should keep in mind that there is underlying discomfort—if not stronger negative feelings—about visiting judges, voiced here by visitors but more frequent among judges on visiting courts. The use of visiting judges, one might say in concluding, remains problematic for many judges.

Judge Goodwin as a Visitor

As noted at the beginning of the chapter, Judge Goodwin was a visitor both prior to becoming the Ninth Circuit's Chief Judge and then after he took senior status. He had single stints in the Second, Seventh, Eighth, and Tenth Circuits, two visits to the Fifth Circuit, and many "return engagements" in the Eleventh Circuit over a number of years. His comments cast light on issues that different procedures create for visiting judges and on whether they "import" their own circuit's law.

When he sat in the Second Circuit, Judge Goodwin discovered that the procedures of another court of appeals varied from those he knew in the Ninth Circuit. Each Second Circuit chambers prepared a "voting memorandum" for each case and each judge signed a "tab" and sent it to the Clerk's office, a process which somewhat confused Judge Goodwin.[44] He also asked whether one of his proposed dispositions was too long to be

---

[43] Support for this view can be found in Budziak, "The Effect of Visiting Judges on the Treatment of Legal Policy in the U.S. Courts of Appeals," The "district judge from Hoboken" is mythical, not only because no District of New Jersey judge sits there but also because no judge from D.N.J. sat with the Ninth Circuit.

[44] See Alfred T. Goodwin (hereafter: ATG), memorandum to panel, Dec. 28, 1993, re: Tamarin v. Adam Caterer, 13 F.3d 51 (2d Cir. 1993).

an Order and therefore should be published, and a Second Circuit judge put the disposition in opinion form.[45]

The judge exhibited the same uncertainty in the Fifth Circuit with respect to publication of a disposition: "I am not sure if the . . . proposed disposition is publishable under your practices, so I am submitting it in this form [with alternative captions for a per curiam if not to be published, but signed by him if to be published]. I request my fellow panelists to decide whether it should be published."[46] As to whether another opinion should be signed, he wrote to his colleagues, "If it does shed any light on Trademark dilution, I have no objection to publication, and am willing to sign the opinion to protect the innocent."[47] At another time, he proposed that his disposition be published "because the question in the context of this case appears to be a question of first impression in the circuit," and the opinion was published (as a per curiam).[48]

Somewhat later, Judge Goodwin observed that, for the Fifth and Eleventh Circuits, "there were minor differences in terminology, but no major procedural differences between Ninth Circuit and the other big circuits."[49] He reported that "[b]oth circuits let the writing judge recommend publication after the disposition is drafted, and both usually treat the question collegially but decide, as a panel, whether to publish." Furthermore, "If it is to be decided 'without opinion' both circuits decide, at the post argument conference, that no written disposition is required, and the presiding judge sends the clerk an AWOP [Affirmed Without Opinion] order reciting the local rule of court that authorizes the practice."[50] Both circuits, he said, "use many more AWOPs than we do, but on the longer written dispositions, most of which are NOT published in F.3d, both follow procedures that would seem familiar to our judges."[51] Another difference in procedure became apparent when the judge sat in the

---

45 ATG, memorandum to panel, Dec. 17, 1993, Gierlinger v. New York State Police, 15 F.3d 32 (2d Cir. 1994); see also ATG, memorandum to panel, Dec. 17, 1993, LaChance v. Reno, 13 F.3d 586 (2d Cir. 1994).

46 ATG, memorandum to panel, March 13, 1996, *re*: Lott v. Hargett, 80 F.3d 161 (5th Cir. 1996).

47 ATG, memorandum to panel, November 30, 2000, *re*: Pulse EFT Ass'n v. Sears Roebuck & Co., 247 F.3d 240 (5th Cir. 2001) (table).

48 ATG, memorandum to panel, February 4, 2000, *re*: United States v. Romines, 204 F.3d 1067 (11th Cir. 2000).

49 ATG, e-mail to Stephen L. Wasby, January 8, 2001, 5:03PM EST.

50 These took the form of "Affirmed. See Rule 36-1."

51 He further observed that an AWOP disposition was "a fate that befalls a lot of Fifth and Eleventh Circuit cases that are noted in West 'Tables' as affirmed with no discussion of issues or holdings."

Seventh Circuit in 1994. A law clerk observed then, "The Seventh Circuit does not make the case record, or even excerpts of record, available until after oral argument,"[52] which affected the law clerk's preparation of materials for the judge's sitting. Also related to procedure was the judge's inquiry of a fellow Seventh Circuit panel member as to whether he could join that judge's concurrence "if that would be appropriate and permissible."[53] And in the Eleventh Circuit, the court he visited most frequently, he explained in sending some substitute language for another judge's draft opinion, "When sitting with my Ninth Circuit colleagues and carping at them about an opinion, we are expected to submit suggested language."[54]

Illustrative of the problem that visiting judges, once back in their home circuits, get caught up in matters there and thus are tardy in dealing with the visited circuit's cases, Judge Goodwin was to find himself apologizing for delay in getting back to his colleagues: "Shortly after I undertook the task [of revising an opinion] I became involved in several calendars at home and had difficulty getting back to this interesting case."[55] Later he was again to apologize for delay: "December has been busy for me . . . so I have neglected collegial duties on this case."[56] Despite the first delay, the panel's presiding judge wrote to express gratitude for receiving the revised opinion, saying, "Appreciate your good work for our court!!!"[57] This message was not unlike one Goodwin had earlier received upon sitting in the Fifth Circuit; that message said that the judges "are indeed grateful for your help. On a personal note, John [Duhé] and I very much enjoyed sitting with you."[58] The message was repeated after a later Eleventh Circuit sitting, by Judge Stanley Marcus, "Many thanks for all your help. It was a pleasure sitting with you."[59]

---

[52] Harry Mittleman, memorandum to ATG, October 1, 1994, re: United States v. Dvorak, 41 F.3d 1215 (7th Cir. 1994).

[53] ATG, memorandum to panel, B.H. et al. v. McDonald (Appeal of Murphy), 49 F.3d 294 (7th Cir. 1995).

[54] ATG, memorandum to panel, January 23, 1996, re: Mooney v. CSX Transportation, 79 F.3d 1159 (11th Cir. 1996) (table).

[55] ATG, memorandum to panel, June 28, 2001, re: United States v. Le, 256 F.3d 1229 (11th Cir. 2001).

[56] ATG, memorandum to panel, Dec. 20 2006, Thompson v. Glades County Board of County Commissioners, 493 F.3d 1253 (11th Cir. 2007).

[57] Judge Paul Roney, memorandum to panel, July 9, 2001, re: Le.

[58] "Hank" [Henry Politz, C.J.], memorandum to panel, March 18, 1996, re: Lott v. Hargett, 80 F.3d 161 (5th Cir. 1996).

[59] Stanley Marcus, memorandum to panel, December 4, 2001.

Actions that Judge Goodwin took, and his messages to the colleagues he was visiting, say something about his view of a visiting judge's use of the law of his home circuit. In preparing opinions during one of his two 1995 Eleventh Circuit sittings, Judge Goodwin used Ninth Circuit precedent in one case and in another rejected it. A prisoner had filed a Section 1983 suit to challenge malicious prosecution initiated to cover up a beating. In ruling that prosecutors, like judges, were immune from conspiracy claims, Judge Goodwin wrote:

> All of our sister circuits that have examined the question agree that the same rule that applies to judges applies to prosecutors acting within the scope of their authority as prosecutors. See, e.g., Ashelman v. Pope, 793 F.2d 1072 (9th Cir. 1980) (en banc) (overruling earlier cases narrowly applying immunity and following [an Eleventh Circuit case]).[60]

However, he also showed that, as a visitor, he could adopt a position at variance with his own circuit's rule. An appeal from a conviction for being in the United States after an earlier deportation contained a sentencing issue. In ruling that the statute applicable to an alien convicted of an aggravated felony provided for an enhancement, not a separate offense, Judge Goodwin mentioned, and set aside, one of his own circuit's cases that other circuits had rejected.

> Only one court has treated the subsections as defining separate crimes. See *U.S. v. Campos-Martinez*, 976 F.2d 589 (9th Cir. 1992), *U.S. v. Gonzalez-Medina*, 976 F.2d 570 (9th Cir. 1992). All the other circuits have rejected the Ninth Circuit's line of cases. . . . We join the four other circuits that discovered the legislative evolution of §1326 . . . and concluded that Congress intended §1326 to denounce one substantive crime . . . , with the sentence to be enhanced incrementally for those aliens who commit the offense after they have been deported following convictions for "nonaggravated" or "aggravated" felonies.[61]

Yet later, in another case in which a deportee later in the U.S. had been given an enhanced sentence for a drug trafficking offense, he suggested that the resident circuit judge authoring the opinion remove Ninth Circuit cases from a proposed opinion. "The citation to Ninth Circuit cases . . . could be omitted," he said, pointing out that one was "unpublished and non-precedential" and "cannot be cited within the

---

[60] Elder v. Athens-Clarke Co., Georgia *ex rel.* O'Looney, 54 F.3d 694, 695 (11th Cir. 1995).

[61] United States v. Palacios-Casquette, 55 F.3d 557, 559-560 (11th Cir. 1995).

Ninth Circuit," and as to another, he was "on a panel that is considering distinguishing" a case "because it involved a previous version of the Guidelines that did not include the application note on aiding and abetting, attempt, and conspiracy."[62] The panel vacated and remanded, declaring that a state statute on soliciting to deliver cocaine was not a "drug trafficking" offense.

Judge Goodwin showed concern about a visiting judge's making circuit precedent. This can be seen when he inquired whether the court wanted to use the case on which he was working to make a point— whether he should develop the point that *Brecht* survived the AEDPA "or whether the circuit might prefer a better case for that purpose." As he noted, "As a visitor, I am hesitant to write Fifth Circuit law, but will cheerfully follow suggestions."[63] In general, Judge Goodwin attempted to follow the precedent of the circuit he was visiting. Thus he commented, "I would like to affirm the summary judgment but believe it would be contrary to precedent," and he observed, as to the argument that a district judge "should be trusted to give evidence its proper weight" as to a summary judgment motion, that "such a notion goes against the precedent of this Circuit."[64] In another case, an Eleventh Circuit panel member suggested that Judge Goodwin give greater emphasis to that circuit's precedent in his opinion: "I believe that the interpretation of the interstate commerce requirement contained in this circuit's extortion cases may be of greater relevance in the robbery context than is suggested by your opinion."[65] That suggestion and other exchanges led Judge Goodwin to "suggest that because this work product involves all of us, it is a true per curiam and I should not get the credit for it,"[66] but the resident judges wanted the opinion signed by Judge Goodwin.

At another time, he observed that "[a]s a visitor, I am not sure where this circuit places the burden of showing ambiguity" as to whether a district judge knew of his authority.[67] In another case, he agreed with a

---

[62] ATG, memorandum to panel (Judges Barkett, who wrote the opinion, and Tjoflat), May 12, 2006, *re*: United States v. Aguilar-Ortiz, 450 F.3d 1271 (11th Cir. 2006). The Ninth Circuit case was United States v. Rivera-Sanchez, 247 F.3d 905 (9th Cir. 2001) (en banc).

[63] ATG, memorandum to panel, Dec. 12, 2000, *re*: Ross v. Johnson, 245 F.3d 790 (5th Cir. 2000) (table).

[64] ATG to panel, voting memo, n.d., *re*: *Tamarin*.

[65] Judge Frank Hull, memorandum to panel, May 1, 2001, *re*: United States v. Le, 256 F.3d 1229 (11th Cir. 2001).

[66] ATG, memorandum to panel, July 10, 2001, *re*: *Le*.

[67] ATG, memorandum to panel, n.d., *re*: United States v. Rock, 14 F.3d 591 (2d Cir. 1993) (table).

judge's inserting a paragraph based on a recent decision by that circuit.[68] However, Judge Goodwin did draw on a District of Nevada decision (affirmed by the Ninth Circuit on other grounds) as making sense of facts similar to a Second Circuit case he faced,[69] and in the same case, he also drew on a Ninth Circuit case on which he was working that had somewhat similar facts.

In one of his Eleventh Circuit sittings, Judge Goodwin wrote an opinion drawing heavily on Ninth Circuit law and on the expertise of a Ninth Circuit colleague. Suppression of material had been denied in a child pornography case. Finding no violation of the Wiretap Act because "intercept" didn't cover a hacker's obtaining material that was in storage and thus was not intercepted contemporaneously with being sent, Judge Goodwin had sent his proposed opinion to his Ninth Circuit colleague Sidney Thomas, who had responded that contemporary interception was necessary under the Wiretap Act.[70] As Goodwin explained to his fellow Eleventh Circuit panel members, his delay in getting a proposed opinion to them was partly caused "by my need to check and recheck technical information about the internet with which I had not previously had any experience."[71] The opinion drew heavily on *Konop v. Hawaiian Airlines*,[72] both by "agreeing with the Ninth Circuit" about the complexity of the issue and by saying as to the Ninth Circuit's ruling, "At least one Circuit has held that information stored on a server and conveyed from a private website to users clearly falls within the definition of 'electronic communication'" and has held "that it encompasses only acquisitions contemporaneous with transmission." Judge Goodwin further extensively cited to and quoted from *Konop*. Lest one criticize Judge Goodwin for importing his circuit's law, it should be noted that if the Eleventh Circuit had no prior law on the subject, the author of an opinion, even if a visitor, could reasonably draw on cases from other circuits, as Judge Goodwin did in

---

[68] Richard Cardamone, memorandum to panel, January 11, 1994; ATG to panel, January 12, 1994; see also Jon Newman, memorandum to panel, January 3, 1994, *re*: LaChance v. Reno, 13 F.3d 586 (2d Cir. 1994).

[69] Cleveland v. Beltman North American, 30 F.3d 373 (2d Cir. 1994). See Drucker v. O'Brien's Moving & Storage, 745 F. Supp. 616 (D. Nev. 1990), aff'd on other grounds, 963 F.2d 1174 (9th Cir. 1992). A Second Circuit judge on the panel, however, observed that it was "an opinion I don't think much of." Dennis Jacobs, memorandum to panel, November 9, 1993.

[70] Sidney Thomas, memorandum to ATG, November 14, 2002, *re*: United States v. Steiger, 318 F.3d 1039 (11th Cir. 2002).

[71] ATG, memorandum to panel, n.d., *re*: *Steiger*.

[72] 302 F.3d 868 (9th Cir. 2002).

drawing from both the Ninth Circuit and the Eleventh Circuit's neighbor and prior home, the Fifth Circuit.

Most clearly raising the question of a judge's taking issue with a visited circuit's precedent was an instance during his first sitting in the Eleventh Circuit in 1987, when he faced the issue of whether an injured labor relations assistant for a dry dock company was within the coverage of the Longshore & Harbor Workers Compensation Act.[73] Writing to his fellow panel members, Goodwin began, "I am somewhat diffident (if a federal judge can ever so characterize himself) about meddling in Eleventh Circuit law." He then said that Judge Edmondson's proposed opinion would include all persons in the industry within the Act's coverage, and he was "a little reluctant to hold in effect that the Act was intended as a comprehensive insurance plan for all employees of maritime employers when they set foot on covered premises." However, he went on to say, "Were I laboring within the bounds of my own circuit, I would probably dissent on the ground the majority opinion might become precedent for allowing any white-collar worker, payroll clerk, stenographer or management or other supporting personnel to be covered by the [LHWCA] when injury on a covered work site." However, being in a different circuit, "I concur only because I am inclined to defer to the able judges of this circuit in announcing the circuit's law on questions of first impression within the circuit."[74]

In a libel case during the same sitting, Judge Goodwin did argue for his preferred scope of opinions. He told his fellow panel members that he "favor[ed] shorter, narrowly drawn opinions in all cases" and that "[e]specially in diversity cases in which we are likely to meddle with the law of a state, I favor the narrowest possible writing, and usually go for an unpublished memo disposition because it makes no law at all." He said that while the case "contains what Oregon lawyers call a nice question, one that the Supreme Court may eventually have to decide" as to the dimensions of a "limited public figure," he claimed, "We should say no more than we absolutely must say on this issue." That led him to join one judge's discussion of two issues but he "would prefer not to discuss the other points."[75]

Judge Goodwin also took issue with Eleventh Circuit doctrine during a 1995 sitting, stating it in a special concurrence as to his view of the law.

---

[73] Sanders v. Alabama Dry Dock and Ship Building Co., 841 F.2d 1085 (11th Cir. 1988).

[74] ATG, memorandum to panel, Dec. 28, 1987, re: Sanders.

[75] ATG, memorandum to panel, May 31, 1988, re: Long v. Cooper, 848 F.2d 1202 (11th Cir. 1988). The result was that the latter judge's concurrence became the court's opinion.

The appeal was from summary judgment for the defendant insurer in a suit by the employer's president for the health insurer's fraudulent inducement to purchase a policy not covering pre-existing conditions. The panel's Eleventh Circuit judges had ruled that the insurance broker's status as the president's agent did not compel non-preemption and that actions of the broker and of the insurance company were intertwined with the refusal to pay benefits.[76] Judge Goodwin characterized this case as involving "application of ERISA preemption in removed cases arising out of insurance twisting, common law fraud in the inducement, or other illegal selling practices,"[77] pointed out that application was "not consistent in this circuit, or between circuits," and said he concurred only because an Eleventh Circuit case "appears to bind this court to a rule" which he said "need not be cast in concrete, if it is wrong." He further noted the "obvious tension" between the Eleventh Circuit's rule and the one the Fifth Circuit had announced a year later, and said it "has affected the district courts."[78]

He went on to say that "[a]s a visiting judge from still a third circuit, one is diffident about characterizing the conflict between [the two cases] as a hazard to navigation for the district courts of this circuit," but he followed that with a "But compare" cite to cases from the Southern District of Alabama and the Southern District of Florida.[79] He then said that because of the "demonstrated difficulty faced by the district courts" and because the Fifth Circuit's rule possible was "more consistent than [the Eleventh Circuit's own rule] with federalism, state anti-twisting statutes, and the intent to benefit workers which underlies the ERISA scheme," he thought it "maybe timely and appropriate to suggest an en banc review of the preemption matter," as "it is not impertinent to suggest that clear direction from the Circuit is in order."[80] The court did rehear the case en banc and overturned the panel ruling, finding that the claims lacked sufficient connection with the plan to "relate to" it, so they were not within ERISA preemption, but Judge Goodwin's opinion was not mentioned.[81] That Judge Goodwin was invited again to sit with the Eleventh Circuit shows that its judges did not take umbrage at his taking a position different from theirs. As he wrote later about that case, "I have

---

[76] Morstein v. National Ins. Services, 74 F.3d 1135 (11th Cir. 1996).

[77] Id., at 1139 (11th Cir. 1996) (Goodwin, J., specially concurring).

[78] Id.

[79] Id., at 1140.

[80] Id.

[81] 93 F.3d 715 (11th Cir. 1996) (en banc).

been invited back. . . . Apparently the Circuit has forgiven me for impos-ing the extra work on them."[82]

One of Judge Goodwin's experiences shows how a visiting judge could get in the middle between two resident judges, with resulting discomfort. In a major voting rights case, the district court had denied relief in a challenge to at-large election of county commissioners and the school board. There was disagreement within the panel over an election district which would be 50.23% "minority." Judge Tjoflat's proposed opinion called it an influence district, but, after Judge Goodwin concurred, Judge Rosemary Barkett disagreed. This led Judge Goodwin, in a position of "[n]ever having [had] to apply *Thornburg v. Gingles*, 478 U.S. 30 (1986), to a case until now," to rethink.[83] His discomfort could be seen in his report that he could "but not with enthusiasm" concur in an opinion reversing in part and remanding for more findings.[84] When Goodwin ended up siding with Judge Barkett that the district met *Gingles'* first prong while Judge Tjoflat disagreed, Judge Barkett circulated a new opinion holding that it was clear error to find the remedial plan insuffi-cient to meet the *Gingles* requirement, and Judge Tjoflat dissented.

Another instance illustrating that visiting judges are assigned to major and controversial cases as well as to routine ones, Judge Goodwin was also in the thick of matters as a member of a panel facing a challenge to the denial of a temporary restraining order against metal detector searches of those entering the gate to Ft. Benning, Georgia, in a case resulting from non-violent protests by those who wanted funds cut to a U.S. military school, the Western Hemisphere Institute for Security Cooperation, or School of the Americas. At one point, Judge Goodwin wrote—although perhaps did not send—a memo saying, "As a Fort Benning alumni [sic], perhaps I should recuse, but being a Fourth Amendment afficionado, I am interested in seeing this case through."[85] His memo to Judge Stanley Burch objecting that the case was not moot[86] led to Judge Tjoflat's assuming responsibility for writing the opinion, which held that appellants were entitled to a preliminary injunction, as there had been a Fourth Amendment violation and a burden on free

---

[82] ATG, e-mail to SLW, January 4, 2000.

[83] ATG, memorandum to panel, January 5, 2007, re: *Thompson v. Glades County.*

[84] Id.

[85] ATG, memorandum to panel, n.d., re: Bourgeois v. Peters, 387 F.3d 1303 (11th Cir. 2004).

[86] ATG, memorandum to panel, March 31, 2004, re: *Bourgeois.*

speech and association. Writing later to an old Oregon friend who had congratulated him on the resulting opinion, Goodwin said,

> As a visiting judge, I was somewhat diffident about rocking the boat, but I sent a memo stating that I would have to dissent, setting forth what I thought were good reasons. Judge Tjoflat ... who, like me, is a Nixon appointee, was presiding. He agreed with me and reassigned the case to himself. He and I cooperated in the research and writing, but it is his opinion.[87]

Speculating about whether the court he was visiting would be pleased with his having become this involved, he added, "I don't think I will be invited back to Atlanta, maybe because I am sometimes out of step with the conventional wisdom, and maybe because I turned 80 a couple of years ago and they don't know whether I can make the trip."[88]

---

[87] ATG, letter to Milo Pope (Yervasi Pope, Baker City, Oregon), March 1, 2005.

[88] He also added, "I enjoyed my visiting in other circuits, but did not get around to all of them. I can wear campaign ribbons from the 2nd, 5th, 7th, 8th, and 10th."

4
EXTENT OF USE

Overview

Although all the U.S. courts of appeals are part of a single national judicial system, there is noticeable variation among them. There is, for example, variation in the mix of cases they decide, in part a result of their geographic location. Thus some circuits see many immigration cases—the Second and Ninth Circuits having seen the greatest increase in immigration appeals in recent years—while others see fisheries cases. There are also differences in internal procedures, something on which visiting judges have commented.

And there definitely is variation with respect to the subject at hand—the use of visiting judges and in-circuit district judges. The category "visiting judges" is often thought of as unitary, expanded to include in-circuit district judges, but it should be decomposed, particularly given evidence of differences across circuits in use of appellate judge visitors and visiting district judges, a difference which is important because judges of the courts of appeals and district judges bring different experiences to the courts they visit.

Court of appeals judges, despite procedural variations across circuits, "know the game" and how to think as appellate judges, while out-of-circuit district judges, although perhaps having sat with their own circuits, are primarily trial judges. That said, as visiting district judges are invariably senior judges, they have considerable experience, and some may prefer sitting as appellate judges. For example, Senior District Judge Richard Mills of the Central District of Illinois, a former state appellate judge, reported spending only 15 percent of his time on district court business, with the remainder spent sitting as a court of appeals judge by designation in a number of circuits. Another district judge who became a de facto circuit judge was Judge Talbot Smith, senior judge of the Eastern District of Michigan (Sixth Circuit), who had earlier taught at the University of Missouri (in the Eighth Circuit). After "an ongoing personal feud with one of the judges on the Sixth Circuit," Judge Smith "adopted the Eighth Circuit as his home away from home" and "provided great services to [the] court."[1] Also among the visitors may be retired Supreme Court justices, who by statute may sit in the lower courts.[2] Justice O'Connor has sat in all but the D.C. (and Federal) Circuits, and Justice Souter has been sitting regularly in the First Circuit, of which he had briefly been a member before being elevated to the Supreme Court; his participation, while not equivalent to that of a full-time active judge, has been substantial.

Additional inter-circuit variation can be seen across time and across circuits in the proportion of dispositions in which out-of-circuit visitors and in-circuit district judges take part. Declines in usage of visitors from high levels may take place as vacancies are filled, but other vacancies then occur, perhaps to remain unfilled because of political gridlock, leading to renewed need to continue the use of visitors.

Some U.S. courts of appeals make greater use of out-of-circuit visitors and district judges from within the circuit than do other courts of appeals, and some make considerable use of within-circuit district judges while not having many visitors. For still other circuits, the picture is one in which judges from the circuit serve in other circuits but few come to visit (for such "use and give," see Chapter 5). In short, there is considerable variation among the courts of appeals in their usage of various judges beyond their own circuit judges, although some of that variation may result from the way case sets have been constructed. (For variation in use of a court's own senior judges, see Chapter 8.) The present chapter provides a picture of the circuits' use of visiting judges and in-circuit district judges, including the relative use of the two judge-types.

There is considerable variation across a number of dimensions in the proportion of cases in which various types of judges sit. There are differences in the number of judgeships in each circuit, the First having only 6 and the Ninth Circuit 29, and there are differences in the numbers of senior judges available to hear cases. It is, however, not the *number* of cases in which visitors and in-circuit judges participate that is most important, but the *proportions* of cases in which non-regular judges participate, although in both the Sixth and Ninth Circuits, among the courts of appeals most frequently using "other" judges, both numbers and proportions are large. And there is the variation described below: in use of visitors and in types of visits, in use of in-circuit district judges, and in relative use of visitors and the circuit's own district judges.

---

[1] Donald P. Lay, "Observations of Twenty-Five Years as United States Circuit Judge," 18 Wm. Mitchell Law Review 595, 619, 621 (1992).

[2] See Stephen L. Wasby, "Retired Supreme Court Justices in the Courts of Appeals," 39 Journal of Supreme Court History 146 (2014).

Some use of out-of-circuit judges and in-circuit district judges may be a function of vacancies on a court of appeals as caseload continues to grow even if not all judgeships are filled, but some inter-circuit variation results from definite policy decisions. For example, courts might not use visiting judges or district judges as a matter of policy. The D.C. Circuit, although its policy had earlier been otherwise, during the time examined in this study had a policy of using neither type of judge. No district judges were used because, although some appeals come to the court directly from regulatory bodies, district judges sitting on the court of appeals would have to pass judgment on their district court colleagues. The Seventh Circuit Court of Appeals had also had a policy of not using either visitors or the circuit's own district judges, but the court changed its policy as to district judges during the period studied, so they began to sit with the court of appeals mid-way through the period studied.

While all types of non-regular judges are utilized to deal with the caseload of a visited court to help clear its docket, in-circuit district judges are brought to sit with the court of appeals for an additional reason: to socialize them. They are first brought there shortly after having taken the district bench—often within a year of their appointment—so that they can see how the court of appeals functions and can learn the expectations that appellate judges hold of district judges as the appellate judges "grade their papers." The notion is that, by having sat with the appellate court, district judges will perform better as district judges, at least "better" in the appellate court's view.

The specialized—or at least semi-specialized—Federal Circuit also makes limited use of visiting judges. That the relatively few visitors to the Federal Circuit are district judges is perhaps appropriate because district judges do hear patent cases, all of which come on appeal to the Federal Circuit. No visiting circuit judges are found in this court, probably for the reason that, because of the path that patent appeals follow, judges of the other courts of appeals have no experience with those technical cases. However, Federal Circuit judges do sit in the other circuits. Particularly to be noted is Federal Circuit Judge Kathleen O'Malley, formerly a U.S. district judge in Ohio who had during her tenure there sat with her home circuit, the Sixth, and who, since joining the Federal Circuit, has returned to sit in the Sixth Circuit. Unlike the D.C. Circuit, which superintends the District Court for the District of Columbia, the Federal Circuit lacks its own district courts, unless one wants to consider the Court of International Trade as one. Yet CIT judges do not sit with the Federal Court of Appeals, although they often visit in a number of other circuits.

A Picture Over Time

Before detailed examination of the courts of appeals' use of various types of "other" judges is presented, first in order is a general picture of the various circuits' use of such judges. This will be undertaken circuit-by-circuit, from which it will be clear that some courts of appeals make considerable use of visiting judges and in-circuit district judges, while others make little or no use of them. Further analysis of courts which make greatest use will follow. Presented are the proportions of cases—both those with published opinions and those with non-precedential memoranda, which make a major contribution to docket-clearing—in which all "other" judges participate, with attention to differences between circuits; participation by both visiting judges and in-circuit district judges is examined. In presenting a picture over time, to identify possible changes in circuit usage of these judges, courts which make little use of them are discussed first with respect to their participation in published-opinion cases, followed by examination of courts which make moderate use of them, and then the few courts which use "other" judges heavily. An excursion into participation in "unpublished" dispositions follows, after which the picture moves forward further in time and then refocuses on the heaviest using courts.

Given the way in which the data was collected, the presentation begins with three sets of cases with published opinion, from 2004, 2007, and 2008-2009, and then continues with one case set of non-precedential dispositions, from the first part of 2013. The presentation then turns to sets of published opinions and of non-precedential dispositions paired from roughly but not precisely the same time-frames. Thus, a set of published opinion cases from June-November, 2013, is set alongside the set of unpublished dispositions from May-October, 2013, so that statements about use are not made solely on the basis of, say, published opinions when visiting judges might have participated more (or less) in cases with non-precedential dispositions. (For tables of data, see Appendix A, Table I.A.Parts I and II, for published opinion cases, and Table I.B., for cases with non-precedential dispositions.)

Examination of courts' use of "other" judges will make clear that some of that use is relatively consistent across time, either as to relatively high use or little or no use, with the same courts of appeals tending to be those which make greater use of their own district judges, occasionally including instances in which a district judge sits with the court of appeals and then is elevated to that court. That might happen when cases in which the judge was sitting with the court of appeals were pending decision, with the judge a district judge at the time of oral argument but a circuit judge by the time the panel filed its disposition.[3] However, other courts of appeals exhibit changes over time, as in the instances in which the early case sets show at least moderate use of "other" judges but later case sets reveal much less such use.

Another visible variation is in the types of non-regular judges a court of appeals might use. Some, like the Ninth Circuit, have for some time made greater use of visiting judges than of their own in-circuit district judges, while other circuits, such as the Second and Sixth Circuits, have made far greater use of their own district judges than of visitors. Thus, in addition to differences, at times considerable, across circuits in the proportion of their cases in which non-regular judges participate, within any circuits there may variation in the types of judges visiting.

Little Use. Several circuits have regularly made little use of visiting judges. As already noted, the Federal Circuit's use of out-of-circuit judges would be nil except for the rare participation by a visiting district judge, and no judges from the specialized courts within its subject matter jurisdictions sit on the Federal Circuit. Likewise, as previously noted, the District of Columbia Circuit, although it once used visiting judges, has for some time by policy made no use of them; neither does it use judges from the District Court for the District of Columbia, because they would be sitting in judgment on their colleagues' decisions. Similarly, the Court of Appeals for the Seventh Circuit, again as a matter of policy, does not utilize visiting judges. Until very recently, also as a matter of policy, for an extended period it did not use the services of district judges from within the circuit, but that policy—not the one about out-of-circuit visitors—was changed, and it began to make not insignificant use of them, with 12 district judges participating in 39 cases and 11 district judges participating in 35 in two case sets, numbers that match high usage in a number of other circuits. And one can find occasional F.3d volumes with several such cases, as when district judges participated in 3 of the 12 cases reported in 789 F.3d and in 4 of 19 cases in 821 F.3d, although in 765-763 F.3d cases, only one district judge was present in one case.

In other courts of appeals, there is minimal or negligible use of visiting and/or in-circuit district judges. Thus, some circuits, like the Eighth and Tenth, which do not utilize visitors much, also do not often bring their own district judges to sit with the court. In the first three sets of cases with published opinions, only once did the Tenth Circuit's use of

---

3 One such judge is Jacquelyn Nguyen, formerly of the Central District of California, now of the Ninth Circuit. See also the notation to this effect as to Judge Gregg Costa, formerly of the Southern District of Texas but now of the Fifth Circuit, in Kitchen v. Dallas County, Texas, 759 F.3d 468, 477 n.* (5th Cir. 2014).

"other" judges approach ten percent; with only minimal or nil use of visiting judges, most of the "other" judges sitting with that court were the circuit's own district judges. The Eighth Circuit Court of Appeals, despite relatively infrequent use of the circuit's own district judges, did use them from time to time, as when they sat in 6 of 16 cases reported in 789 F.3d and 3 of 13 cases in 836 F.3d.

The situation in the Fifth Circuit in the same period is only slightly different, with non-regular judges participating in 10% of its cases with published opinion in the first set (358-376 F.3d) and none appearing in cases in 488-500 F.3d, and there are no visiting judges in cases in 550-562 F.3d, although in-circuit district judges participate in 14% of the court's published opinion cases. While district judges sat in 3 of 17 cases in 821 F.3d, there were few others to be found in the later case sets. It should be noted that the number of in-circuit district judges used by a court of appeals does not necessarily map well on the number of cases in which the judges participate. Indeed, at times the number of cases in which they sit does not much exceed the number of judges, as in one case set when the Fourth Circuit used 8 district judges but they only participated in 10 cases; by contrast, in one case set, in the Second Circuit, 7 judges sat in 28 cases. Thus, when each of two appellate courts uses roughly the same number of district judges, the number of cases in which they sit might vary considerably.

Moderate Use. The Third Circuit provides an instance of a court which has made little use of "other" judges in recent cases (from 2013 on), but which earlier did make noticeable use of them. While few in-circuit district judges took part in cases with published opinions in 358-376 F.3d, visiting judges sat in 15% of the cases, with roughly twice as many visiting circuit judges as visiting district judges. Then, in an unusual spike, in cases in 488-500 F.3d, either visiting or in-circuit district judges participated over three-fourths (78.6%) of the 58 cases from that court, with circuit judges making up most of the visitors, before a reduction in which "other" judges sat in less than half (44.4%) of cases in 550-562 F.3d, with visiting circuit judges again outnumbering visiting district judges.

The Second Circuit's use of "other" judges followed somewhat the same pattern as that seen in the Third Circuit, with visiting judges participating initially in 7.3% of cases (358-376 F.3d) and then in slightly over 10% in the next two sets, but in many fewer cases in later sets, where they would show up from time to time, for example 2 cases of 5 reported in 822 F.3d and 3 of 9 in 839 F.3d, but in nowhere near the high numbers of earlier years. Visiting circuit judges considerably outnumbered visiting district judges in the first set of cases, but in the remaining two sets, there were roughly equal numbers of circuit and district judge visitors. The Second Court made greater use of its own district judges, from 18% up to over one-fourth (27%), in these three sets of published-opinion cases. Such district judge usage remained high for some time thereafter, and even after a decline in use of non-regular judges, much later one could still find some consecutive volumes in which the court's own district judges appeared with some frequency, for example, in roughly 35% of the unpublished dispositions appearing in 628-630 Fed. Appx. By contrast, in these early case sets, the Fourth Circuit made some use of district judges, with their sittings ranging from 5% to 21% to 35%, but made less use of visiting judges—7% in two case sets but none in the 488-500 F.3d cases.

Heavy Use. There are other courts of appeals with significant use of non-regular judges, the First, Sixth, Ninth, and Eleventh Circuits, each of which receives greater treatment in this volume. In the First Circuit, in the three earliest sets of cases with published opinions, non-regular judges sat in one-fifth of the cases in the first set but in as many as over-two fifths (41.2%) of cases published in 550-562 F.3d. Conversely, panels composed of three active-duty judges decided as few as one-sixth of cases (15.5%) in the cases in 488-500 F.3d. This is from the time before Justice Souter began to sit with that court, as he was not yet retired from the Supreme Court. When, counter to the myth that he had retreated to a New Hampshire cabin, he did begin to sit with the First Circuit after his retirement,[4] his presence was a reason the First Circuit Court of Appeals could draw less on out-of-circuit visitors and its own district judges.

Circuit judges outnumbered district judges among visiting judges who sat in the First Circuit by something like 3:1 in the first two case sets but by an overwhelming 10:1 in the third set. This is but one example of the fact that circuits which use non-regular judges in more than a negligible number of cases have differing preferences for the types of visiting judges, appellate or district, they use, as well as in their preferences for visitors as against in-circuit district judges. At certain times, the relative use of visiting circuit and district judges can be affected by the unusual situation in which an entire panel of visiting circuit judges decides a case on the recusal of all of a court of appeals' judges.

Writing about the Sixth Circuit, Bergeron reported that the court "tapped the resources of visiting judges [including district judges] at a much higher rate than its sister circuits," and he found that "in five of the years between 1990 and 1999, the Sixth Circuit led all circuits in its percent use of visiting judges," who sat on panels in 12.8% of the court's

---

4 See Wasby, "Retired Supreme Court Justices in the Courts of Appeals."

cases.[5] In the present study, usage of all non-regular judges in the Sixth Circuit stood at three-fifths in the first two sets of published-opinion cases, with non-regular judges sitting in, respectively, 55% and 60% of the cases, but the proportion was barely over one-fifth (22%) in the third set. Within this picture, one finds that out-of-circuit visitors took part in only 9.1% of the cases, but their participation did range as high as one-fifth (358-376 F.3d). In this early period of the present study, the panels in only somewhat over half (56%) of the cases which the court of appeals decided with published opinion were composed solely of circuit judges (both active and senior). However, that figure masked a change from having under two-fifths of the cases decided by such panels (39.5% and 38.8%, for 358-376 F.3d and 488-500 F.3d, respectively) to the much larger proportion of 61.6% (550-562 F.3d), which later was to rise further. Instead of having more circuit judges as visitors than visiting district judges, the reverse was true, at a ratio of 3:1 (district judges: visitors). Indeed, in two of the case sets, there was either only one or no visiting circuit judge. Thus in-circuit district judges make up almost all of the "others" used by the court.

Similar high usage of non-regular judges can be found in the Eleventh Circuit, ranging from under one-half (first set) to just under three-fifths (second set), then decreasing to two-fifths (42%) in the last of the three sets. In the 550-562 F.3d case set, three-fifths of the panels were composed of only Eleventh Circuit judges. In these three sets of cases, there is no particular pattern as to whether visitors are circuit or district judges, with even numbers in one case set, slightly more visiting circuit judges in the second, and mostly visiting district judges in the third.

Thus in cases reported in 488-500 F.3d, visiting circuit judges sat in 25.8% of the cases compared to 20.7% by visiting district judges, while in the cases in 550-562 F.3d, visiting district judges quite outnumbered visiting circuit judges (by 5+:1), after which proportions returned to being relatively close to each other. However, more generally, unlike the Sixth Circuit, which availed itself of far more in-circuit district judges than of visiting judges, the reverse tended to be true in the Eleventh Circuit. And in the latter, there are also cases in which two district judges served on a panel, permissible when a circuit declares a "judicial emergency" because of judicial vacancies.

The Ninth Circuit has regularly used large numbers of both visiting judges and in-circuit district judges, doing so well before the twenty-first century period which is the focus of this study, although variations over

---

[5] Pierre Bergeron, "En Banc Practice in the Sixth Circuit: An Empirical Study, 1990-2000," 68 Tennessee Law Review 771, 793 (2001).

time do appear. In 1970, active-duty circuit judges accounted for four-fifths (80.9%) of the court's judge-sittings, with senior circuit judges adding another 3.1%, so that the court's own judges accounted for almost 85% of the sittings, with the circuit's own district judges (both senior and active-status) in 14.3% of the sittings and visiting judges in only 1.8% of the cases.[6] In 1971 and 1972, active-duty circuit judges' proportion of sittings declined to 77.5% and 70.8%, respectively, but because several judges assumed senior status, substantially increasing the proportion of sittings by senior judges, the proportion of sittings by all circuit judges (active-duty and senior) remained at roughly the same level. With the court's mid-1970s shift to issuing of unpublished dispositions, circuit judges accounted for a decreasing proportion of all sittings—a result of a decline in sittings by active-duty circuit judges—and district judges accounted for an increasing amount.

Participation in the appellate court's work by in-circuit active district judges increased during this period, going from 9.2% of 1972 sittings to 11.6% in 1973 and to 14.0% in 1974, before a slight decline (to 12.4%) in 1975. Senior district judges likewise participated more, from less than 5% in 1972 to more than 7% in 1973 and 1974 and to 9.1% in 1975. A noticeable increase was seen in 1973 in the proportion of panels on which a district judge sat and in the number of cases decided by those panels; whereas in 1972, half the panels contained a district judge, almost three-fifths in 1973 did so. This, along with a stationary (and relatively small) proportion of panels including a visiting judge, meant a further decrease in panels with at least two circuit judges.

In the earlier part of the period covered by the present study, the Ninth Circuit did make less use of non-regular judges than did the Sixth and Eleventh Circuits. Non-regular judges participated in somewhat less than one-fourth (23.6%) of cases with published opinions in the first set, but the proportion rose to over one-third (36%) in cases in 488-500 F.3d. Turning things on their head, the proportion of cases in which the panel was composed of only Ninth Circuit judges, active or senior, reached 75% only once, in the first set, with the noticeably lower 58.3% proportion in the next two sets. This court of appeals used roughly equal numbers of visiting circuit judges and visiting district judges. Relevant to the concern that a panel might have only one active circuit judge is the significant

---

[6] The data presented from the 1970s first appeared in Stephen L. Wasby, "'Extra' Judges in 'The Court Nobody Knows': Some Aspects of Decision-Making in the United States Courts of Appeals," presented to American Political Science Association, Washington, D.C., September 2, 1979, parts of which were published as Wasby, "'Extra' Judges in a Federal Appellate Court: The Ninth Circuit," 15 Law & Society Review 369 (1980-81).

number of such cases—as many as over one-fourth (26.6% for 356-376 F.3d, and 28.6%, for 488-500 F.3d), although later proportions are lower. Illustrative of the variation in usage within a single circuit, the proportion of cases in which Ninth Circuit district judges participated ranged from as much as 17.7% (488-500 F.3d) to a low of 7.0 % (736-748 F.3d); only in the former case set were there identical proportions of visitor participation, and those by in-circuit district judges. Otherwise, the Ninth Circuit made less use of its own district judges than of out-of-circuit visitors, with one recent set (765-783 F.3d) showing the greatest divergence—8.9% participation by in-circuit district judges and three times as much by visitors (27.0%).

The court's calendars, which indicate who sits when and where, provide another way of looking at the presence of non-regular judges in the Ninth Circuit and at the variation in their use. In these calendars, the court's usage was to include in-circuit district judges as "visitors," so the court's "visitors" are our "non-regular" judges. For 2002-2013, the calendars show that the use of such judges moves up and down, with no monotonic decline.[7] In 2002, the proportion of days with a visiting judge was 46.7% and visiting judges accounted for 15.6% of judge-days. This was followed by a two-year decline to 26.8% (8.9% of judge-days) in 2004, before increases—to 36.0% and 40.1%—in 2005 and 2006, before highs of 45.0% (15.0% judge-days) in 2007 and 46.6% (15.2% judge-days) in 2008 were reached. Then came a decline to 30.9% in 2009 followed by two more increases in 2010 and 2011, first to 38.8% and then to the highest level, 47.2% (15.7% judge-days). This was followed by a two-year decline, first to 39.5% (13.2%) and then to the lowest proportion in this series, 29.6% (9.9%) in 2013.

About Unpublished Dispositions. The next picture is of cases examined in which the result was an "unpublished" non-precedential disposition. A brief description is provided of a set of these cases for which there is no match-in-time with a set of published-opinion cases, but first, some discussion of these dispositions is presented.

Non-regular or "other" judges are used, if for no other reason, to assist the courts of appeals with which they sit in clearing their dockets. In turn, the principal way the courts of appeals have adopted to "move" cases is to dispose of them with what were initially called "unpublished" dispositions. Used in less complex cases, these dispositions are generally

---

[7] The calculations were based on counting the number of days on which such judges were to sit. A five-day panel with a visiting judge sitting one day was one-fifth or "20% of the time." Also calculated were judge-days, with three judge-days for one panel or 15 judge-days for a week; a visiting judge sitting one day would be 1/15.

much shorter than published opinions, as they seldom include an extensive statement of the facts—known to the parties—and, because the
outcome is thought to be clearly dictated by existing circuit precedent,
legal analysis is not highly developed; indeed, many unpublished dispositions do little more than cite governing cases. The length of "unpublished"
dispositions does, however, vary across the circuits. Those in the Sixth
Circuit, for example, are no different in length than published opinions
appearing in *Federal Reporter,* and the Fifth Circuit often disposed of
cases with a summary notation of "Affirmed—See Rule 36-1."

An unpublished (non-precedential) disposition resolves the appeal
before the court—that is, it is res judicata for that controversy—but is not
precedent or "law of the circuit." Indeed, as these dispositions were
initially used, the court itself could not cite such dispositions in resolving
another case, nor could lawyers cite those dispositions in their briefs.
However, the Federal Rules of Appellate Procedure were revised to allow
lawyers to cite these cases, but it remains up to the court of appeals to
determine, as a matter of court policy, the weight to be given to those
cited dispositions. Many courts of appeals continue not to give them
precedential weight, so they are perhaps best characterized as "non-
precedential" dispositions.

One aspect of these dispositions that is worth attention is their near
unanimity. The rate of dissent in cases in the U.S. courts of appeals is low,
but it is especially low in these non-precedential rulings. Conversely,
dissent is more likely to be found in published opinions than in "unpublished" memorandums. One reason is that if a ruling is to be non-
precedential, a judge will not wish to take the time to prepare a dissent;
another is that, at least in some courts, a judge intending to dissent in
what was to be a non-precedential disposition may opt to have the
opinion in the case published, which further depresses the dissent rate for
non-precedential rulings.

Memorandum dispositions (or whatever label they carried in other
circuits) were initially properly labeled "unpublished" because, while
printed and released as slip opinions—essentially, small pamphlets, one
per case—they did not appear in the *Federal Reports.* They were available
only in court of appeals libraries, and they were also collected by law firms
with the significant resources. Indeed, one reason behind the non-citation
rule was that some attorneys would have access to them but many others
would not, creating the absence of a level playing field. With the arrival of
electronic legal data retrieval services, however, these "unpublished"
dispositions became available on line, thus expanding the number of
those who could obtain them. In due course, West Publishing Co. began to

issue a case reporter, the *Federal Appendix*, in which the previously-unpublished dispositions appeared. So now the "unpublished" were "published," making "unpublished" somewhat of a misnomer, with "non-precedential" the more appropriate general term.

There are two basic ways in which non-precedential dispositions originate. One is by the decisions of regular three-judge court of appeals panels; the other is from screening panels, to be discussed shortly. In cases assigned to regular (argument or merits) panels, after argument (or submission on the briefs [SOB] if no argument, the judges meet to determine the outcome and to decide which judge will prepare the disposition. At that time, the panel may also decide whether that disposition will be a published opinion (precedential) or a non-precedential memorandum disposition—or summary order, whatever terminology the court might use. At times that publish/not-publish decision is left to the writing judge ("dealer's choice," as some Ninth Circuit conference memoranda put it).[8] Most cases that are not orally argued usually result in non-precedential dispositions.

Few panels issue published opinions in all the cases before them, but some issue only non-precedential dispositions, even in cases in which oral argument has been heard. Screening panels in the Ninth Circuit and elsewhere and in the Second Circuit for immigration cases, and "non-argument calendar" panels in the Eleventh Circuit seldom issue any published opinions. Most panels that are not screening panels issue a combination of published and not-for-publication rulings, and, once the latter became common, a panel's output would most frequently be more non-published than published dispositions.

There are times when after a judge has prepared a non-precedential memorandum, the judge comes to believe that the disposition "makes new law" in the circuit and thus should be published; less frequently, what starts out to be a published opinion is found not to break new ground, so that only a memorandum disposition is necessary. At least in the Ninth Circuit, if a judge dissents to what was to have been a memorandum disposition, the dissenter can opt to have the disposition published. Furthermore, court rules (or General Orders) may contain guidelines as to which cases should be published (or not), but these

---

[8] For more extended treatment of the process, see Stephen L. Wasby, "Unpublished Decisions in the Federal Courts of Appeals: Making the Decision to Publish," 3 Journal of Appellate Practice & Process 325 (2001), and Wasby, "Unpublished Court of Appeals Decisions: A Hard Look at the Process," 14 Southern California Interdisciplinary Law Journal 67 (2004).

criteria are generally not enforceable,[9] although other judges on the court could suggest publication of certain non-precedential dispositions. As well, after a memorandum disposition is filed, the parties or interested on-lookers like trade associations may request publication "because of the importance of the issue" to a certain constituency, and at times, although not often, those requests are granted. In short, the judges on the panel make the determination about publication.

In almost all the courts of appeals, the non-precedential dispositions are "unsigned," that is, the names of the panel judges appear but no author of the disposition is identified; some circuits do designate these "per curiam" but the effect is the same. However, in the Sixth Circuit and, although less frequently, in the First Circuit, the author of a non-precedential ruling does sign the disposition. In part because in most circuits, writing a non-precedential disposition will not show authorship, some have suggested that in-circuit district judges would like to see their name on a case in "Fed. Third" and thus, when they are writing, they would be more likely to lean toward suggesting publication. One result of the non-identification of authorship of these non-precedential dispositions is that only a limited amount can be said about the distribution of authorship among the judges on panels issuing such dispositions, although instances can be identified in which "other" judges constitute a majority of a panel, making their votes dispositive.

Another way in which non-precedential dispositions—indeed, a significant proportion of them—result is through courts of appeals' use of screening panels. These panels, which like other panels consist of three judges (some motions panels have only two, with a third judge available as a tie-breaker), are assigned large numbers of cases that court staff have determined to be of lighter "weight," that is, easily decided under existing circuit precedent or less complex. Then, with the assistance of the court's staff attorneys, the screening panel judges might meet to decide—one could say "dispatch"—upwards of 100 cases in a single day. In the Ninth Circuit, any judge on the screening panel who believes a case to require more attention than the screening panel can give it, because of its complexity or because an important issue lurks in the case, may have the case "kicked," that is, sent to a regular argument panel. It is also possible, that while almost all dispositions from screening panels are non-precedential rulings, the screening panel could determine that a case warranted publication.

---

[9] See Stephen L. Wasby, "Publication (or Not) of Appellate Rulings: An Evaluation of Guidelines," 2 Seton Hall Circuit Review 41 (2005).

An alternative mode of handling screening cases, as in the Second Circuit's adoption of screening panels for its vastly increased volume of immigration appeals and in the Ninth Circuit's earlier use of screening panels, is that a set of three judges is assigned a certain number of cases (a dozen to 20 or so) to be decided without oral argument and with the judges circulating the case files among themselves without meeting.

Courts of appeals which use many non-precedential memoranda and dispose of a high proportion of their cases in this fashion tend to use screening panels. The Fourth and Ninth Circuits are among them, and the Eleventh Circuit has a "Non-Argument Calendar." These devices serve to depress the proportion of such dispositions in which "other" judges take part because screening panels are composed only of the court's regular and senior circuit judges; that is, neither visitors or district judges participate in them. Thus, one can see how the large numbers of non-precedential rulings produced by these panels would minimize the proportion of cases with non-precedential dispositions in which non-regular judges participate.

A lesser percentage of non-regular judges in "unpublished" dispositions than in published opinions cuts against the notion of using visitors primarily to assist with caseload. According to that notion, one would assign visitors and district judges to easier cases, which they could handle effectively—and without disturbing the law of the circuit. Doing that, however, might make it difficult to attract visitors if they knew they would not be given cases with the same range of difficulty as those assigned the court's regular member. Turning over the very easiest cases to the screening panels, with their circuit judge-only composition, allows visitors to have cases with some more meat rather than giving them the dregs, although whether this is a matter of conscious decision (to attract visitors) is not known.

Non-Publication and Unanimity. The composition of panels may affect the extent to which they are unanimous. Although this point was not pursued for the period of the present study except in connection with prompts for en banc rehearing and Supreme Court review (see Chapter 9), its operation in the Ninth Circuit in the early 1970s is illustrative. In 1970 and 1971, more than three-fourths of panels composed only of active-duty circuit judges, which accounted for a large proportion of the court of appeals' output, ever showed disagreement; those "agree panels" accounted for roughly two-thirds of cases decided by panels of only active-duty circuit judges. From 1972 through 1975, over four-fifths of these panels with three active-duty circuit judges never disagreed, and such panels accounted for from close to 90% (in 1972 and 1974) to below

80% (in 1973 and 1975) of all panels of three active-duty circuit judges. The proportion of cases with actual disagreement decided by panels of that composition fluctuated over the period, but it was only 8.9% in 1970 and 7.5% in 1971. With the rate of agreement in such panels high in published cases, it was even higher in the unpublished cases at this beginning of the time when the court began to issue them.

The Ninth Circuit used fewer visiting judges in that period than in the later time at the core of this study, resulting in considerable fluctuation in the data about disagreement in panels containing a visiting judge. (Keep in mind that a panel with a visitor might also contain a Ninth Circuit senior judge or a district judge from within the circuit, not accounted for here.) Disagreement was exhibited in only 10% of cases decided in 1970 by panels with a visiting judge. That proportion dropped to 7.3% in 1971 but then more than doubled, to 15.2%, in 1972. It then declined to 12.3% overall, but was as high as one-sixth in 1973 published-opinion cases, and then rose again in 1974, with a full *36.1%* of published opinion cases from those panels showing disagreement before falling back in 1975.

Panels containing in-circuit active-duty district judges exhibited patterns not unlike those for panels containing only circuit judges. However, panels with district judges reflected more disagreement both in the lower proportion of such panels that agreed in all the cases and in a higher proportion of cases with actual disagreement, which reached 11.1% in 1972 and again exceeded 10% in both 1973 and 1975; disagreement was much higher in published cases, in the 16-18% range for 1973-1975. However, when panels contained a senior in-circuit district judge, there was somewhat less disagreement. Disagreement again was much more likely in cases resulting in published opinions than in "unpublished" memorandum dispositions. For example, in 1974, there was disagreement in 9% of all cases decided by such panels, but in 17.5% for published opinions while only 2.2% in "unpublished" dispositions.

From 1971, when a number of the court's judges took senior status, through 1975, the number of panels with a senior circuit judge naturally increased. (See Chapter 8 for discussion of senior judges.) In this period, the proportion of such panels which agreed in all their cases was roughly 80%, ranging from 78.9% in 1972 to as high as 84.3% in 1975. The proportion of cases decided by these panels in which there was disagreement rose steadily from 1970 to a level of 10% in 1972, where it stabilized before dropping to 6% in 1975. As expected, the published-opinion cases decided by such panels showed a higher proportion of disagreement—11-12% in 1973 and 1975, but 17.3% in 1974—than in unpublished dispositions.

Actual Use. In turning to the courts' use of such dispositions, it should be noted that, while the proportion of cases with non-precedential dispositions exceeds 80% for all courts of appeals combined, there are some appeals courts for which only a very small portion of their dispositions are in this category. (See Table I.B in Appendix A.) Relatively few—compared to the output of such cases in other circuits—can be found in cases from the District of Columbia Circuit, which does not use visitors or in-circuit district judges, and the First, Seventh, and Eighth Circuits and the Court of Appeals for the Federal Circuit, which only occasionally welcomes a visiting district judge (only 3 visiting judges in 116 cases). In the First Circuit, as to which one of its judges has observed that too many of that court's dispositions are long, published opinions when more could be shorter memorandum dispositions, no visitors participated in such cases, true also for the Eighth and Tenth Circuits.

Within the unpublished dispositions appearing in 510-525 *Federal Appendix*, covering much of the first half of 2013, the pattern in which visitors were used was not unlike that seen above in the three earlier sets of published-opinion cases. In this period, the Seventh Circuit had just resumed use of in-circuit district judges, but only three sat in cases in this set. For these cases, the Third Circuit used very few visiting judges and only a few in-circuit district judges, who sat in 3% of the cases. No visiting judges decided these Fourth Circuit unpublished dispositions, and in-circuit district judges appeared in only 1.4% of the cases, perhaps because that court's screening panels, which dispose of many "routine" cases in unpublished dispositions, are composed solely of the court's own circuit judges (active and senior). And in the Fifth Circuit, one finds only two district judges participating in these cases.

What about the courts of appeals seen to have made greater use of non-regular judges in cases in which the court issued published opinions? The patterns earlier noted for them recur for some circuits in this set of cases with unpublished dispositions. In the Second Circuit, for example, visiting judges (more circuit than district) sat in 8.1% of these cases, but in-circuit district judges sat in under one-third of them (30.5%). One also finds few visiting judges in these cases in the Sixth Circuit—they sat in less than 5% of the cases—but considerable use was made of in-circuit district judges, who participated in over two-fifths of these unpublished-disposition cases (43.0%). Indeed, there are even a few cases in which the district judge's position is dispositive because the panel's circuit judges divide, with one either dissenting or concurring separately. By comparison, the Eleventh Circuit, while using both visiting judges and in-circuit district judges, used them less than in the above-noted—and somewhat earlier—published-opinion cases; "other" judges participated in only 10% of these cases, with circuit judges outnumbering district judges 2:1 among the visitors, and with a roughly equal number of visitors and the circuit's district judges taking part.

The Ninth Circuit also used "other" judges to roughly the same extent in these unpublished disposition cases as in the earlier published opinion cases. In this set of cases appearing in 500-525 Fed. Appx., visitors sat in almost one-sixth of the cases (15.3%), with most of those being visiting district judges, while in-circuit district judges participated in 8.0%, thus continuing that circuit's greater use of visitors than of in-circuit district judges.

Moving Forward. A picture can be formed of participation by "other" judges both in cases with published opinions and those decided with unpublished dispositions, using the period of roughly mid-2013 to late in that year—June-November for the former and May-October for the latter. On the whole, courts' usage of "other" judges in both types of dispositions is roughly the same. This would, of course, be expected for the D.C. Circuit, because its non-use of these judges is by court policy, in addition to which that court's very minimal use of non-precedential dispositions would have provided little opportunity for visitors' participation in any event. The situation for the Seventh Circuit is almost identical, with only three district judges taking part in unpublished dispositions and none taking part in the court's published-opinion cases. The Federal Circuit also used no visiting judges in any of its cases during this period.

The courts of appeals which made low use of non-regular judges continued in the same vein as well. For example, there was almost zero participation by "other" judges in either type of Tenth Circuit disposition, and only five district judges took part in unpublished-disposition cases there. No "other" judges participated in the Eighth Circuit's relatively small number of unpublished dispositions, and no visiting judges sat in cases decided with published opinions, although district judges did sit in 8.3% of the latter. Similarly, the Fifth Circuit made no use of visiting judges in either type of case and only very small numbers of district judges, in what was a decline from the earlier noted periods. The Fourth Circuit showed a similar decline from its peak use of non-regular judges— most of them the circuit's own district judges—who had sat in over two-fifths of the court's published-opinion cases in 2008-2009 but then in far less (one-sixth, then 10%). Somewhat contrasting was the Third Circuit, where the use of all non-regular judges was less than 10% in cases with published opinions; the visitors were district judges from other circuits except for one complete panel of circuit judges from other circuits; in cases released with non-precedential rulings, visitors (mostly visiting district judges) sat in only 2.9% of those cases and no in-circuit district judges sat in them.

As the First Circuit has produced very few non-precedential rulings, there were few opportunities for non-regular judges to participate in them. However, in its published opinions at this time, visiting circuit judges and in-circuit district judges sat in roughly 15% of the court's cases; higher usage of visiting circuit judges declined; and the circuit used even fewer of its own district judges than it did of visitors. In its only 10 unpublished rulings, the circuit's own district judges sat in 4 and retired Justice Souter, the only "visitor," sat in 5. In the Second Circuit, visiting judges sat in 7% of cases with published opinions but in only 1% of those with unpublished dispositions. However, as before, the circuit's district judges continued to play a large role, participating in one-fifth of the cases with published opinions and roughly half that (9%) for unpublished dispositions; the difference in rates was likely largely the result of many unpublished dispositions, especially in immigration appeals decided by screening panels of the court's own circuit judges.

Not unlike the Second Circuit pattern is that for the Eleventh Circuit, with greater use of in-circuit district judges than of visitors, but with non-regular judges' participation less in unpublished dispositions than in cases with published opinions. Unlike those circuits where usage of non-regular judges declined from the earlier sets (2004, 2007, 2008-2009), this court's use remained relatively high. In its published opinion cases, visiting judges—circuit judges more than district judges by a 2:1 ratio—sat in one-fourth of those cases, but the circuit's own district judges sat in more than two-fifths, resulting in non-regular judges' participation in more than two-thirds of the court's published opinions. Among the visitors, the proportions of visiting circuit and visiting district judges had earlier been relatively close, with shifts as to which type predominated. Thus, in cases reported in 488-500 F.3d, visiting circuit judges sat in 25.8% of the cases compared to 20.7% by visiting district judges, while in the cases in 550-562 F.3d, visiting district judges quite outnumbered visiting circuit judges (by 5+:1), after which proportions returned to being relatively close to each other. In cases disposed of by non-precedential rulings, by contrast, visitors (again, circuit judges more than district judges, 2:1) and in-circuit district judges each sat in roughly 5% of the cases.

Much greater use of in-circuit district judges than of visitors continued to be evident in the Sixth Circuit, where visitors were a minimal presence in cases with published opinions but sat in 6.2% of the cases with unpublished dispositions, dividing roughly evenly between visiting circuit and visiting district judges. On the other hand, the Ninth Circuit, where there had been variation in whether use of visitors exceeded use of the circuit's own district judges, now was more likely to have visiting judges sit than its own district judges, in both published and unpublished dispositions. In the published opinion cases, non-regular judges were used in roughly two-fifths of cases, with visiting judges participating in 28% and district judges only one-fifth, but in the court's many non-precedential dispositions (over 1,000 in this case set), visitors participated in one-sixth of the cases and district judges, 7.3%. Unlike the situation in some other courts, however, Ninth Circuit visitors were disproportionately district rather than circuit judges, by a 4:1 ratio in published opinion cases and 3.4:1 for non-precedential rulings.

Similar patterns are apparent in the next partly-matched sets of cases, those with published opinions from November, 2013-April, 2014, and non-precedential dispositions from October, 2013-March, 2014. The First Circuit, while using non-regular judges—somewhat more in-circuit district judges than visiting (circuit) judges—in 26.3% of cases with published opinions, issued only 15 non-precedential dispositions, in four of which visitors participated, with no district judges taking part. The Third Circuit continued its low usage of non-regular judges, all but one of whom were visitors to the circuit; they sat in only 5.8% of published-opinion cases and in 4.7% of those with non-precedential dispositions. There was even less usage of non-regular judges in the Eighth Circuit, with no visitors sitting and only three district judges taking part in the published opinion cases; the Tenth Circuit did the same.

The Second Circuit made greater use of non-regular judges, but virtually all of them were the circuit's own district judges. In its published opinion cases, where a few visitors did participate, district judges sat in 10.7% of the cases, while in cases with unpublished dispositions, there was only one visiting judge while in-circuit district judges sat in almost one-eighth of those cases. The Fourth Circuit exhibited a somewhat similar pattern, although fewer district judges took part, sitting in 10% of published-opinion cases but in only 1.2% of unpublished rulings, and only one unpublished disposition had a visiting judge on the panel.

Among the courts of appeals making greater use of non-regular judges, such judges participated in only 11.8% of Eleventh Circuit cases in this set, both those with published opinions and with unpublished dispositions; visitors and district judges sat in roughly equal proportions of cases, with visiting district judges somewhat outnumbering visiting circuit judges. The Sixth Circuit, with a higher proportion of cases in which non-regular judges participated, continued its much heavier use of its own district judges than of visitors. In its published opinion cases, district judges sat in one-third of the cases while visitors participated in only one-eighth; only one visitor was a circuit judge. The picture is the same for non-precedential rulings, with in-circuit district judges sitting in roughly one-third of those cases (31.6%), while visitors sat in only 7.4% of the published opinion cases. The total usage of non-regular judges was 44.7% for published and 38.9% for unpublished dispositions. The largest circuit, the Ninth, also continued its patterns of usage. For both cases with published opinions and those with non-precedential dispositions, visiting judges, most of whom were district judges from other circuits, sat in one-eighth of the cases; their presence was to be much greater than that the circuit's own district judges who sat in 7% of both published and un-published disposition cases. The greater presence of visiting district judges than of visiting circuit judges runs counter to the stated views of some Ninth Circuit judges that if there were to be any visitors, it would be better were they not visiting district judges.

Focus on Heavier Users. As it was clear from the cases through early 2014 that some courts regularly made only minimal use of "other" judges, attention thereafter was focused on the courts that were "heavier users." The examination here is of published opinion cases issued in April into August, 2014 (749-764 F.3d) and, for unpublished dispositions, March into October, 2014 (560-581 Fed. Appx.), and published opinions extending from August, 2014, into April, 2015 (765-783 F.3d) and unpublished dispositions from October, 2014, also into April, 2015 (582-599 Fed. Appx.).

The First Circuit, as earlier noted, issued very few "unpublished" dispositions, but it continued to make noticeable use of "other" judges, with visiting (circuit) judges and in-circuit district judges participating in one-fourth of the first of these two sets of cases; out-of-circuit visitors, however, participated in fewer than 10% of the cases in the first set (9.1%, 720-736 F.3d). In the second set, if one includes retired Justice Souter's participation (5% of the cases), non-regular judges participated in one-fourth of the court's cases. Looking in the other direction, panels composed solely of active-duty circuit judges did not handle more than one-third of the cases in a set (33.7%, 765-783 F.3d). The Second Circuit used few visitors and its own district judges took part in roughly one-eighth of its cases, both those with published opinions and those with non-precedential rulings.

The Sixth Circuit continued heavy use of non-regular judges, who took part in roughly one-third of the court's cases decided with published opinion and even more in cases with unpublished dispositions: 39.5% in the first set and approaching half (45%) in the second. As before, most of these non-regular judges were the circuit's own district judges, by a ratio of roughly 5:1 in published cases and roughly the same proportion in unpublished dispositions (4:1 in one set, 6:1 in the other). The more frequent appearance of non-regular judges in cases with non-precedential dispositions provides evidence of a court's use of such judges to deal with caseload through greater use in less significant cases.

The Ninth Circuit's considerable use of "other" judges, which has attracted attention, continued in these two sets of cases, as those judges sat in over one-third of published-opinion cases in both case sets while appearing less frequently in unpublished dispositions—in one-fourth of those cases in the first set but only 13.6% in the second set—a continued result of the court's practice of using only its own circuit judges for the many cases handled through its screening program, as "screeners" invariably result in non-precedential dispositions. With "screeners" removed from the data (see below), other judges' participation in non-precedential dispositions would likely be closer to the rate of participation in published-opinion cases. Thus in the Ninth Circuit, the greatest "docket-clearing" is undertaken by the court's own judges, not by other judges brought in to assist the court. As was the case earlier, the Ninth Circuit is visited more by other circuits' district judges than by those circuits' appeals court judges.

While the Ninth Circuit's use of "other" judges has attracted attention, heed should also have been given to those judges' role in the Eleventh Circuit. In these two case sets from the 2014-2015 period, such judges sat in an astounding *sixty-plus percent* of the cases with published opinions. Yet they took part in a much smaller proportion of the court's unpublished dispositions (roughly 10%), likely the result of the court of appeals' use of its own circuit judges for its non-argument calendars, which are very likely to result in "unpublished" dispositions. In the cases decided with published opinions, visitors from other circuits sat in one-third of the Eleventh Circuit's cases, with more visiting circuit judges than visiting district judges in one set and slightly more visiting district judges than visiting circuit judges in the other set. The circuit's own district judges continued to sit with the court of appeals frequently, in one-fourth of the first set of cases but almost one-third (30%) in the second set.

Focus on the courts making heaviest use of visiting judges and in-circuit judges continues with two more paired sets of cases, one with published opinions from April-September, 2015 (784-800 F.3d) and "unpublished" dispositions for April-November of the same year (600-

623 Fed. Appx.), and the other a set of published opinion cases from September, 2015-April, 2016 (801-819 F.3d) and of non-precedential dispositions from November, 2015-March, 2016 (623- 640 Fed. Appx.). In these more recent sets of cases, patterns observed in earlier sets of cases generally recurred. The First Circuit continued to decide almost all its cases with published opinions, with non-regular judges' participation remaining above 20%, rising to 28.4% in 801-819 F.3d cases. In addition to making regular use of the services of retired Justice Souter, who sat in almost one-fifth of the more recent cases, this court borrowed appeals court judges—but not district judges—from other circuits, while the court's use of the circuit's own district judges varied from 10% to under one-sixth.

Although visiting judges sat in 10% of the most recent set of Sixth Circuit published-opinion cases, the circuit generally used very few visitors, who took part in well under 5% of its "unpublished" dispositions. However, substantial use of its own district judges continued, as they sat in 30% of the recent published-opinions cases in 801-819 F.3d, although the proportion then dropped to one-eighth. While the proportion of all cases with non-regular judges declined from the earlier nearly one-third to just over one-fifth (21.8%) in the last case set, this use of in-circuit judges remains significant. District judges sat in over one-third of the parallel set of cases with non-precedential dispositions, and, if the few visiting judges are added, the proportion of cases with non-regular judges rose to just under two-fifths (38%).

The picture from the Eleventh Circuit had been one, as in the Sixth Circuit, of considerable use of in-circuit district judges, who sat in one-fifth and one-fourth of the two most recent sets of published-opinion cases, but there were fewer instances than earlier of having two district judges sit in a case. However, unlike the Sixth Circuit, the Eleventh Circuit made significant use of visitors, who were found in roughly two-fifths of the most recent cases decided with published opinions, leading to the extremely high proportion of non-regular judge participation in all these cases of three-fifths in one set and *in excess of two-thirds* in the following one, which surpassed the Ninth Circuit's use of non-regular judges despite the attention given to the latter's use. Although published-opinion cases show high use of non-regular judges, that is not true of cases disposed of by non-precedential rulings, many of which come from the court's non-argument calendars, on which only the court's own circuit judges sit. In the non-precedential-disposition cases, the circuit's district judges sat in fewer than 5% of those cases and the overall proportion of non-regular judges in these cases, while one-eighth in cases in 600-622 Fed. Appx., was under 10% in the following set.

While the Ninth Circuit made less use of non-regular judges in its published opinion cases than did the Eleventh Circuit, in the two most recent published-opinion case sets, non-regular judges sat in over two-fifths (41.8%) of these Ninth Circuit cases in one set and somewhat less, but still over one-third (35.3%), in the other. Just as with the Eleventh Circuit, visiting judges sat in a higher proportion of cases than did in-circuit district judges; the latter participated in about one-eighth of the cases while visitors' participation was either above or below one-fourth. However, counter to the Eleventh Circuit's greater use of visiting circuit judges, the Ninth Circuit continued to avail itself more of visiting district judges than of visiting circuit judges. Just as with the Eleventh Circuit, in the Ninth Circuit, the proportion of cases in which non-regular judges participated in non-precedential dispositions was lower than for cases with published opinions, but, with non-regular judges sitting in roughly one-fourth of the "unpublished" cases, the difference between published and unpublished cases is noticeably smaller than in the Eleventh Circuit. Continuing past practice, there were more district judges than circuit judges among visitors to the Ninth Circuit and greater use of visiting judges than of the Ninth Circuit's own district judges.

Focusing on whether out-of-circuit visitors are primarily judges from the courts of appeals or are out-of-circuit district judges serves to under-score variation in use of types of non-regular judges. In three of the first seven periods, visiting circuit judges' participation exceeded that by visiting district judges. For example, in the cases in 550-562 F.3d, visiting circuit judges accounted for somewhat over one-eighth of case participa-tions (13.2%) compared with somewhat fewer cases with district judges (11.6%). For the more recent periods, however, visiting district judges' case-participations considerably exceeded those by visiting circuit judges. For three consecutive case sets, the latter participated in 5% or less of the cases, while district judge visitors accounted for at least four times as many participations, reaching 21.8% (765-783 F.3d). As already noted, shift in usage runs counter to the view held by some judges that if there are to be visitors, it would be better not to use district judges.

Without "Screeners": A Recount. As earlier noted, a significant pro-portion of non-precedential rulings is issued by the courts of appeals' screening panels, although often case reports do not explicitly indicate that source but Eleventh Circuit cases from the "non-argument calendar" are so designated. It can, however, be determined which panels (Judges A, B, and C) were screening panels by the sheer volume of their decisions—large numbers all handed down in a short time and appearing in two or at most three consecutive volumes of *Federal Appendix*, with the panel containing only the circuit's own circuit judges. When a panel hands down six or seven rulings in a very short span, that might result simply from an argument panel's handling several lighter-weight cases on their calendars, with most of such cases submitted on the briefs (SOB). A panel with a non-regular judge producing a half-dozen dispositions in a short time is obviously not a screening panel, as no non-regular judges sit on them.

There is an exception in the Ninth Circuit to screening panels issuing large number of cases. A panel of three senior judges—in recent years, Senior Judges Procter Hug, Jr., Edward Leavy, and Jerome Farris, with Judge William Canby at times one of the three—has handled screening cases "the old-fashioned way." That is, rather than meet in person (or by video-conference) to hear staff attorney presentations (oral screening panels, or OSP), the judges instead circulate case-files among themselves, either "serially" (to Judge A, then to Judge B, then to Judge C) or "simultaneously" (all three judges receiving the file at once). These panels of three senior judges are intact not only for a couple of days, as is true of the screening panels handling high volumes of cases, but stay in place longer and they dispose of smaller numbers of cases over that longer time.

If cases from screening panels are identified as best as possible—undoubtedly resulting in an undercount of their cases—and their cases are then subtracted from the number of non-precedential dispositions in a case set, the result is to re-set the proportions calculated in the larger case set which included all cases in *Federal Appendix*. With cases from easily-identified Ninth Circuit screening panels removed from the total of all cases decided with non-precedential dispositions, there are shifts in the proportions of cases with visiting judges, in-circuit district judges, and senior judges (see Chapter 8 for primary attention to senior judges). For all the case sets, with "screeners" removed, there is an increase in the proportion of cases with visiting judges and with district judges, while for all but one case set, the proportion of cases with senior judges decreases, and in the case set that is the exception, the difference in proportions represents the smallest percentage-point shift of the sets. Thus among the various case sets, with screeners removed, the proportion of cases in which visiting judges participated increased from 3.7 percent points to a high of 12 points (median: 7.9 points) and for cases in which district judges sit, the increase ranges from a low of 1.4 percentage points to a high of 6.2 (median: 3.7). The smaller shifts in proportion for cases with district judges than for visiting judges results from the Ninth Circuit's use of more visitors than of its own district judges. As to cases in which senior circuit judges sit, the shift in proportions ranges from the above noted increase—of 2.2 points—to the largest decrease, 27.8 points (median: 13.0 points).

5
WHO ARE THE VISITORS?

This chapter presents a picture different from, and complementary to, the one previously provided. The previous chapter provides a picture of the proportion of cases, both those resulting in published opinions and those which end with non-precedential dispositions, in which out-of-circuit visiting judges and in-circuit district judges participate. With that picture of "other" judges' participation in hand, it is important to learn more about who are the visiting judges and in-circuit district judges in courts of appeals cases. Attention is given in this chapter first to courts' "use and give" practices through a delineation of the visiting judges by the circuits which use them and those from which they come, with visiting circuit judges and visiting district judges receiving separate attention. Then the focus turns largely to individual judges, with emphasis on those who visit most frequently; the chapter ends with attention to the set of judges who visit with the greatest frequency, who might be considered a "cadre" of judges in national use. The district judges who sit with their own circuit's court of appeals and the districts from which they come are examined in the next chapter.

Use and Give

Thus far nothing has been said about the courts from which visitors come, as if they were identical peas in a pod, albeit a large nation-wide judicial pod. Yet those courts of appeals which avail themselves of other circuits' judges, that is, which borrow judges from them, do not necessarily draw uniformly from all the other circuits, nor do all circuits serve equally as the source of borrowed judges. While some circuits both use and give, it is clear that, except for an early case set, there were circuits that used but did not give (they were solely borrowers) and vice-versa, letting other courts borrow their judges but not borrowing from those courts. As will be seen in the next chapter, the same is true as to any circuit's use of its own district judges, which may come more from some districts than others. While some circuits (e.g., the Eighth) gave both circuit and district judges to other circuits in roughly equal numbers, some other circuits contributing visitors were more likely to give circuit judges (e.g., the Ninth and Tenth Circuits), while other circuits (e.g., the Second and Seventh Circuits) were more likely to give district judges.

Policy provides a part of the explanation for this variation. Some of that policy originates in the national judiciary, which, through the Judicial Conference of the United States, has developed a set of rules as to the situations in which a court may borrow a judge and when it may "give" one to another circuit. Most relevant are rules that borrowing circuits may not give—at least not active-duty judges, although some active-duty judges nonetheless navigate the processes of the Inter-Circuit Assignment Committee and sit outside their home circuit. The rules create constraints, if not impassable barriers, which serve at least as a partial deterrent to judges from one circuit sitting elsewhere. Yet the picture is not crystal-clear nor fully rule-bound because the court system's giving-and-borrowing rules in effect basically apply only to active-duty judges, who, because of the rules, do not constitute a large proportion of visiting judges, while senior judges constitute the largest number of visitors.

Individual circuits also create policy affecting judges' potential to be visitors when, for example, they adopt a policy not to accept visitors, or, without an explicit policy, make such minimal use of them that they appear to have a *de facto* policy against such use. Most obvious among those courts of appeals which do not accept visitors are the District of Columbia and Seventh Circuits. In both instances, that policy against receiving judges from other circuits does not, however, preclude the judges of those courts from sitting elsewhere, as some of their judges do. For example, in cases with published opinion in 488-500 F.3d, 5 Seventh Circuit judges sat elsewhere in 10 cases, and another 5 judges did so in the cases in 736-748 F.3d, with 4 judges each in 550-562 F.3d and 720-734 F.3d, all of the latter in the Ninth Circuit.

There has been variation as to whether visiting judges come primarily from another court of appeals or are other circuits' district judges. In three of seven periods examined, visiting circuit judges' participation exceeded that by visiting district judges. For example, in 550-562 F.3d, visiting circuit judges accounted for 13.2% of case participations compared with 11.6% for district judges. For the most recent periods, however, visiting district judges' case-participations considerably exceeded those by visiting circuit judges: the latter participated in 5% of the cases or less in the last three case sets, while district judge visitors accounted for at least four times as many sittings, reaching 21.8% (765-783 F.3d), running counter to the previously-noted view held by some judges that if there are to be visitors, it would be better not to use district judges.

Circuit Judges. In this study, the first picture for "trading" of court of appeals judges who participated in cases resolved with published opinions indicates that circuits varied in the number of visiting circuit judges used and the number of cases in which they participated. For example, in the first set of cases (358-376 F.3d), six circuits used 4 or more visiting circuit judges, who participated in 12 cases each in the First, Second, and Third Circuits and in 28 cases each in the Ninth Circuit (11 judges) and Eleventh Circuit (10 judges), and two circuits gave 5 or more such judges to other circuits. In terms of borrowing judges, there was variation among the circuits as to relative using and giving. A half-dozen circuits gave more visitors than they used from other courts. The greatest disparity was in the Eleventh Circuit, which used 10 judges in 28 cases but had only one of its judges sit elsewhere, and the First Circuit, visited by 5 judges sitting in 12 cases while only one First Circuit judge sat elsewhere, in 4 cases. By contrast, the Ninth Circuit used 11 judges (28 cases) while giving eight (18 cases); and two courts of appeals were particularly notable as donors—the Eighth, which provided 5 visiting judges who participated in 28 cases, and the Ninth, as just noted. Each of the five judges who sat in other circuits visited in three different circuits: Judges Eugene Siler of the Sixth Circuit, Richard Cudahy of the Seventh, John Gibson and Frank Magill from the Eighth, and Bobby Baldock of the Tenth, while the Eighth Circuit's Myron Bright and the Federal Circuit's Alan Lourie each participated in 8 cases in two circuits.

For some time thereafter, the First, Third, Ninth, and Eleventh Circuits made the greatest use of visiting circuit judges, so that, for example, for cases published in 488-500 F.3d, each of those circuits used them in from 17 cases (Third Circuit) to as many as 31 cases (Eleventh Circuit, 10 judges). In that case set, four circuits used five or more visitors and only two circuits gave that many; the Fifth and Sixth Circuits did not use visiting circuit judges, while the Eleventh Circuit, which gave no visitors, used 10 visiting judges in 31 cases. The Ninth Circuit gave and used roughly equal numbers of visitors, using 8 (21 cases) while giving 6 judges, who sat in 32 cases. The basic repeated pattern is that a limited number of circuits provided a great number of circuit judges as visitors. Thus in 488-500 F.3d cases, the Eighth Circuit provided 5 judges (12 cases) and the Ninth Circuit provided 6 visitors (21 cases), with Ninth Circuit Judge Arthur Alarcon participating in 13 cases in two other circuits.

In the cases in 550-562 F.3d, the greatest use of visitors was by the First (7 judges, 30 cases) and Ninth (10 judges, 29 cases) Circuits. In this case set, using and giving are scattered, as the First, Fourth, and Eleventh Circuits used but did not give, with the First Circuit using 7 circuit judge visitors who sat in 30 cases, and the Fifth and Tenth Circuits provided visiting circuit judges but did not use any, while the Ninth Circuit both used (13 judges, 26 cases) and gave (4 judges, 16 cases). The Ninth and Tenth Circuits were the primary donors. Three judges, each from a different circuit, came to the Third Circuit for a single case.[1] The first set of "unpublished" cases, covering 510-525 Fed. Appx., shows a similar scatteration, but attracting attention are the Eleventh Circuit, which used 8 circuit judge visitors in 31 cases but provided no other courts with visitors, and the Ninth Circuit, which used 4 visiting circuit judges in 32 cases while using 5 judges in only 9 cases.

For all but the most recent case sets, court of appeals judges visiting the Ninth Circuit came from all the circuits, although the presence of fewer senior circuit judges on other courts of appeals would have affected their ability. Only one judge each came from the District of Columbia, First, and Fourth Circuits, but two judges each came from the Third, Fifth, and Seventh Circuits—in 13, 11, and 16 cases, respectively, with Seventh Circuit Judge Richard Cudahy participating in 10 cases and writing opinions. The Eleventh and Federal Circuits also supplied two visitors each, with the latter's Judge Daniel Friedman sitting in 5 cases and writing opinions in 2.

In the later published opinions in 720-735 F.3d, there was minimal and scattered using and giving, except that the Third Circuit sent a full panel to the Second Circuit; the Ninth Circuit used 7 visitors in 15 cases and gave 4 judges to other circuits but for only 6 cases; and the Eleventh Circuit, which gave no circuit judges to other courts, used 4 from elsewhere in 13 cases. Nor did the picture change when unpublished dispositions from roughly the same time (536-540 Fed. Appx.) are added, as, again, only did the Ninth and Eleventh Circuits make much use of circuit judge visitors—6 judges in each court, in 27 cases in the Ninth Circuit (with Seventh Circuit Judge Kenneth Ripple accounting for 11) and far fewer, only 12, in the Eleventh Circuit.

Cases appearing in 736-748 F.3d again demonstrated no use of visiting circuit judges and minimum donation of such judges in the Second, Fifth, and Eighth Circuits; the Ninth Circuit used 8 visitors but gave only one and the Eleventh Circuit likewise used 7 circuit visitors (13 cases) but only one of its judges sat elsewhere. The First, Ninth, and Eleventh Circuits later continued as greatest users, with visiting circuit judges sitting in 23 First Circuit cases in 736-748 F.3d, a time during which the Tenth Circuit was the only court to give more than two judges (3 judges, 8 cases). The unpublished dispositions from roughly the same period—

---

[1] Common Cause of Pennsylvania v. Pennsylvania, 558 F.3d 249 (3d Cir. 2009) (Judges Pierre Leval of the Second Circuit, Joel Flaum of the Seventh Circuit, and David Ebel of the Tenth Circuit; Judge Ebel wrote for the panel).

those in 541-559 Fed. Appx.—do not change the picture, with the Ninth and Eleventh Circuits the only circuits using more than minimal numbers of visitors.

In the cases in 749-764 F.3d and 560-581 Fed. Appx., almost all circuits neither used nor gave more than a couple of judges. The exceptions, as before, were the Ninth Circuit, in cases with published opinions, using 6 circuit judges in 11 cases and giving 4 (for 13 cases), and the Eleventh Circuit, which used 10 circuit judges in 28 cases while giving none. Changes are few in the picture from parallel non-precedential dispositions, with the Ninth and Eleventh Circuits each using 9 judges, participating, respectively, in 30 and 39 cases.

The Ninth Circuit continued use of visiting judges in cases published in 765-763 F.3d, as it borrowed 9 circuit judges who participated in 16 published-opinion cases, while the Eleventh Circuit used 10 judges in 28 cases. Three other courts of appeals—the Sixth, Eighth, and Tenth— loaned 3 judges each to other circuits, while in cases with non-precedential rulings reported in 582-599 Fed. Appx., the Ninth Circuit used 10 judges sitting in 41 cases, and 5 judges sat in 10 Eleventh Circuit cases. For published-opinion cases, the First Circuit gave only one circuit judge while borrowing 3, and the Tenth Circuit gave 4 judges (10 cases) while borrowing none. The Eleventh Circuit conversely used 8 judges (for 22 cases) but gave none. The Sixth Circuit traded two for two, and the Ninth Circuit borrowed some more than it gave (6 v. 4), with borrowed and donated judges sitting in roughly the same number of cases. The same pattern recurred in cases found in 784-800 F.3d and in 600-623 Fed. Appx., with relatively little trading of appellate judges in most circuits; however, the Ninth and Eleventh Circuits continued to make greater use of those jurists, with the Ninth Circuit using 10 circuit judges in 70 cases with non-precedential dispositions, while the Eleventh Circuit used one more circuit judge (11) but in a smaller number of cases (30). For the roughly parallel sets of 801-919 F.3d and 623-640 Fed. Appx., the patterns remained the same, with generally minimal, and scattered, use and giving of visiting circuit judges, although, in addition, the First Circuit used 5 judges in 17 cases with published opinions. Elevated use continued in the Ninth and Eleventh Circuits—in the Ninth, 6 judges in 11 cases with published opinions and 9 judges in 50 non-precedential dispositions, and in the Eleventh, 10 judges in 22 published-opinion cases and the same number of judges in only 10 unpublished dispositions.

District Judges. The picture for district judges sitting outside their own circuits is much the same as for visiting circuit judges. Excluding those courts whose policy precluded use, some circuits receive visiting judges, some provide them, and some do both. In the earliest case set (358-376 F.3d), all courts of appeals except the Fourth Circuit used visiting district judges, but six circuits did not provide them to sit in other circuits. Visiting district judges participated in 24 cases each in the Sixth and Ninth Circuit and in 32 Eleventh Circuit cases. The Ninth Circuit, later a net user, gave 3 judges in 358-376 F.3d cases and 5 judges (11 cases) in the 550-562 F.3d case set.

In 488-500 F.3d cases, the Tenth Circuit neither used nor gave, while the Ninth Circuit used 13 visiting district judges in 26 cases and gave 5 district judges (interestingly, 3 to the Federal Circuit, an unusual occurrence) for 7 cases, and the Eleventh Circuit used 10 district judge visitors in 20 cases; six Second Circuit district judges sat in 19 cases. In addition to the Ninth and Eleventh Circuits (18 and 24 cases, respectively), visiting district judges participated in 13 Sixth Circuit cases and in 8 each in the Second and Federal Circuits, where visiting judges have been relatively rare but where visiting district judges later participated in 15 cases (550-562 F.3d.). Of Second Circuit visiting district judges, Eastern New York Judge Edward Korman participated in 9 cases in two circuits in that time.

A number of circuits provided several district judges to other courts of appeals at one or more times. For example, the Fourth Circuit provided 4 district judges in cases in 550-562 F.3d, and the Eleventh Circuit gave 5 in 736-748 F.3d, when 8 Second Circuit district judges sat in 15 cases in other circuits, with all but one sitting in the Ninth Circuit although two of those sat elsewhere as well. The Court of International Trade (CIT) regularly contributed a large number of judges—4 in 34 cases in the earliest case set, 5 judges in 14 cases in the next, and in the following set, Judges Richard Goldberg and Jane Restani participated in 15 cases combined.

In the 720-735 F.3d case set, circuits providing visiting district judges but not using them in cases with published opinions were the First, Fourth, Fifth, and Eighth, as well as the Second and Tenth Circuits in the next set. Most circuits saw the presence of visiting judges in the non-precedential rulings decided at roughly the same time. Particularly obvious was the Ninth Circuit, where 26 visiting district judges sat in 86 cases, with 7 Second Circuit district judges, who sat in only 4 cases elsewhere, accounting for 37 of those participations. The Sixth Circuit gave 3 district judges, the same number it borrowed. Exemplary of limited use and giving was the Eleventh Circuit, which used 3 visiting district judges for 5 cases while only one of the circuit's district judges sat elsewhere (in 8 cases). The non-using Seventh Circuit did donate 5 district judges to sit on panels outside the circuit.

There were clear imbalances in some circuits between using and giving district judges. For example, for cases in 720-735 F.3d, the Sixth Circuit had a visiting district judge in only one case while providing 5 judges outside the circuit who sat in 17 cases, and the Second Circuit used 3 district judges from other circuits for 6 cases while providing other circuits 8 district judges for 16 cases. The greatest imbalances were in the Ninth and Eleventh Circuits, where in one case set, the Ninth Circuit borrowed *30* visiting district judges, who participated in 64 cases, but it loaned only 2 judges for 3 cases. This was followed by its use of 26 visiting district judges while loaning only 2, while the Eleventh Circuit first provided only 2 judges while using 7 judges in 12 cases and then used 11 such visitors while providing only 3.

While the Ninth Circuit had made little use of visiting district judges in the cases reported in 720-735 F.3d, it used 36 visiting district judges in 35 cases in 736-749 F.3d, when the Sixth Circuit also used 7 visiting district judges (11 cases) and the Eleventh Circuit, nine (17 cases). The Second Circuit continued its substantial donation of district judges to other circuits for use in cases with "unpublished" dispositions—9 judges sitting in 48 cases. Also donating district judges for non-trivial numbers of cases with such dispositions was the Sixth Circuit. It gave 5 judges, who sat in 26 cases, 10 of which were accounted for by Judge Stephen Murphy (Eastern Michigan), while, in an almost even trade, used 5 judges in 25 cases. The most-frequent user remained the Ninth Circuit, where 27 visiting district judges sat in 156 cases.

The 749-764 F.3d set of published-opinion cases shows that three circuits gave visiting district judges, but none did so in large numbers except the Second Circuit (7 judges, 16 cases). Most circuits sent no visiting district judges elsewhere but used only a few. Use of visiting district judges was considerable in only two circuits—again the Eleventh (7 judges, 16 cases) and the Ninth (21 in 40 cases). The picture as to cases with non-precedential dispositions from the parallel period is much the same, with the Eleventh Circuit using 9 visiting judges in 28 cases (Judge Richard Goldberg of the Court of International Trade sat in 8), and the Ninth Circuit used a greater number of such judges (30) in by far the greatest number of cases in which they participated (141), with 4 Eastern District of New York judges sitting in 34 cases (Judges Frederick Block, 16, and Edward Korman 13). Well behind was the court with the next greatest use, the Sixth Circuit, which used 4 judges in 14 cases. Also notable is that 3 Court of International Trade judges sat in 20 cases throughout the circuits and 3 Eighth Circuit judges participated in 15 cases.

For published-opinion cases in 765-763 F.3d, when only two visiting district judges sat in the Sixth Circuit (4 cases), the Ninth and Eleventh Circuits continued to borrow large numbers of visiting district judges, with 26 judges in 56 cases in the Ninth Circuit and 10 judges in 32 Eleventh Circuit cases. Visiting district judges came to the Ninth Circuit from all circuits and from the Court of International Trade, whose Judge Jane Restani participated in 13 cases, but only one district judge each came from the D.C. and Tenth Circuits.

Most courts do loan district judges but only in small numbers and for not many cases, so, for example, in cases in 765-783 F.3d, the Fifth, Sixth, and Eighth Circuits each gave 4 district judges to other circuits, but for only 10, 7, and 8 cases, respectively, and in the courts visited, the Fifth and Eighth Circuits made little use of non-regular judges. Giving more were the Second and Seventh Circuits, each of which donated a half-dozen district judges—for 13 and 15 cases, respectively. Also, three Court of International Trade judges sat in 14 cases, all in the Eleventh Circuit, which borrowed 6 judges overall for 16 cases while giving 3, who sat in only 4 cases. Continuing the pattern, the Sixth Circuit used 4 judges (only 4 cases with published opinion) and gave only 2 (to the Ninth Circuit, for 6 cases), while six courts of appeals gave but did not use visitors, with the Second Circuit giving the most, as 7 district judges sat in 16 cases in three circuits. The reverse is seen in the Ninth Circuit, where 21 visiting district judges sat in 46 cases, while no Ninth Circuit district judges sat elsewhere. In cases with unpublished dispositions from roughly the same time, the largest numbers of visiting district judges from individual circuits were from the Second—10 judges, sitting in 46 cases—and the Sixth Circuit—6 judges, 42 cases—with the latter using 3 district judges from other circuits in 12 cases. Among Second Circuit visiting district judges, most were from Eastern New York (5 judges, 17 cases) and Southern New York, whose Judges Kevin Duffy and Jed Rakoff sat in 13 cases each. Despite the Seventh Circuit's continuing bar on bringing in visitors, 4 Northern District of Illinois judges went elsewhere to sit in 9 cases, and Judge Lynn Adelman (Eastern Wisconsin) added 8.

In the published-opinion cases appearing in 784-800 F.3d, several courts of appeals used roughly a half-dozen visiting district judges and two used only 3, but the Eleventh Circuit used 7, who sat in 12 cases, and the Ninth Circuit, the heaviest user, used 28, in 60 cases. These heavy users did not, however, contribute district judges to other circuits—none from the Ninth Circuit and only 2 from the Eleventh—but 6 Sixth Circuit district judges sat in 14 cases elsewhere and 5 from the Second Circuit took part in 15 cases. In the companion set of non-precedential rulings in

600-622 Fed. Appx., 4 district judges visited the Sixth Circuit (8 cases), 8 visited the Eleventh Circuit to sit in 30 cases, and fully 35 district judges came to the Ninth Circuit, where they sat in almost 200 cases. Most prominent in contributing visiting district judges were the Second Circuit—8 judges, who sat in 65 cases—and Sixth Circuit, 6 of whose judges sat in 25 cases as visitors.

Little change in patterns of borrowing and giving appears in the most recent sets of cases examined. For published opinion cases appearing in 801-819 F.3d, the Ninth Circuit's use of visiting district judges—28 judges sitting in 53 cases—far exceeds any other circuit's use, with the Eleventh Circuit, although making greater use than other circuits, well behind with its use of 7 district judges in 28 cases. In this period, the Sixth Circuit donated 7 judges who sat in 16 cases, and the Second Circuit donated only 6 judges, all for 10 Ninth Circuit cases. The highest number of visiting judges used in cases decided with non-precedential dispositions was also in the Ninth and Eleventh Circuits: 7 visiting judges sat in the Eleventh Circuit in 14 cases, while 29 judges, from all the circuits, again participated in over 100 cases—indeed, 115. On the "giving" side, two circuits donated 4 judges and another two donated 6 district judges each. The 4 donated Second Circuit district judges sat in 26 cases, all in the Ninth Circuit, and the 6 judges from the Sixth Circuit participated in 24 cases, all but one of which were in the Ninth Circuit.

Individuals' Participation

Visitors Per Circuit. Examination of courts' using and giving of circuit and district judges provided an initial indication of the numbers of visiting judges who came from some circuits. Closer perusal of who those judges are is in order, but before that, somewhat more attention should be given to the number of visiting judges who sat in visited circuits over a period of time. This will provide a picture of the number of "bodies" that visited courts had to assimilate, because it is not only the number of cases in which visiting judges (and in-circuit district judges) sit that is of importance, but also critical is the number of individual non-regular judges who sit with a court over an extended period. (See Table II in Appendix A.)

A court of appeals' own circuit judges have minimal contact with all but a relatively few visiting judges. And although visiting judges may be invited to join the "home town folks" for a meal, in most instances the visitors' contact will be limited to those with whom they are sitting, so that, just as the visited judges have relatively little contact with the visitor, the visitor also sees only a relatively small part of the visited court. While it may not be necessary for *all* members of a receiving court to become familiar with the visitors, the extent of contact is relevant to the point that the more non-regular judges, the more difficult for a court of appeals' own judges to know each other because of the reduction in the number of instances in which they sat with "their own kind" and thus the greater difficulty for any court of appeals judge to deal with what is called "a known court"—a set of judges with a stable composition over some period of time. Even if visiting judges don't bring with them the law of their home circuits, their outlooks are not likely to be the same as that of the judges of the court they are visiting, with the judges of the latter having become more or less accustomed to each other.

Judges who do visit vary considerably in the extent to which they do so. As a result of short stays in any one visited circuit, most visiting circuit judges sitting in any particular circuit take part in only one case or relatively few that result in published opinions, but some visitors do participate in quite a few cases. And while many visiting judges sit in only one other circuit, some may be found in several of the nation's other courts of appeals. Among those who visit only one court, a few are such regulars that the judge is really more a member of the "visited" court than of his own, as noted earlier about Senior Judge Talbot Smith of the Eastern District of Michigan's regular sitting in the Eighth Circuit, but this is not a frequent occurrence.

What about the numbers and sources of these judges? There is no need to examine courts—the District of Columbia or Seventh Circuit Courts of Appeals—which by policy do not accept visiting judges, nor several other courts of appeals, including those for the Fifth and Eighth Circuits, which used no visiting judges during the period examined, The courts of appeals in several other circuits—the Second, Third, Fourth, and Tenth—had so few visitors that they would not have had any difficulty absorbing them on the occasional basis on which they sat. Of course, when a circuit used several visiting circuit judges (or visiting district judges), those judges did not necessarily participate in equal numbers of cases. But attention should be paid to those four circuits which made greater use of visiting judges in the period studied.

As time went by within the period, the First Circuit's use of visiting judges diminished, particularly when retired Supreme Court Justice David H. Souter, who can be considered either a visitor or a de facto senior judge of the court, began to sit regularly with that court of appeals, on which he had sat briefly before being elevated to the Supreme Court. Yet in the early part of the period, the First Circuit made use of a number of visiting circuit judges who sat in numerous cases. They included Judge

John Gibson of the Eighth Circuit, who sat in 7 cases among those appearing in 358-376 F.3d, 5 in 488-500 F.3d, and another 3 in 550-562 F.3d, and the Tenth Circuit's Judge Bobby Baldock, who sat, respectively, in 8, 9, and 10 cases in those three case sets, plus 9 others. In this early period, two Federal Circuit judges sat with the First Circuit: Alan Lourie, in 8 cases in the first case set, and Pauline Newman, in 7 cases in 488-500 F.3d. Later in the period, one saw the same thing: Judge Kenneth Ripple of the Seventh Circuit sat in 9 cases in cases published in 765-783 F.3d, after having sat in 5 in those in 736-748 F.3d, plus 9 others; and Judge Timothy Dyk of the Federal Circuit sat in 6 cases in the 720-735 F.3d case set, 10 cases in 765-784 F.3d, and 10 others.

The Sixth Circuit Court of Appeals, in addition to using a very high number of the circuit's own district judges, also was visited frequently, and judges came to it from seven circuits, with 2 from the Eighth Circuit and 2 more from the Federal Circuit; none of these sat in more than the 6 cases in which Ninth Circuit Judge Arthur Alarcon participated. One Eighth Circuit visitor sat on a panel of three visiting circuit judges (the other two were from the D.C. and Third Circuits) that resulted from the recusal of all Sixth Circuit judges. Visiting district judges came from eight circuits and from roughly a dozen districts (including 3 Florida districts), plus the Court of International Trade. Here the participation of two judges stands out. Judge William Schwarzer of the Northern District of California, at one time the director of the Federal Judicial Center, sat in 15 Sixth Circuit cases over this period, and Judge Richard Mills (of Central Illinois), a former state appellate judge, sat in 10 cases.

The Ninth and Eleventh Circuits further illustrate situations with a very large number of visitors. The Ninth Circuit was visited by *80* judges from 2013 through 2016, 19 of whom were circuit judges and 61 visiting district judges. The visiting appellate judges came from all courts of appeals except the Federal Circuit, with 4 judges from the Tenth Circuit, and the very large number of visiting district judges arrived from all circuits, plus one from the CIT, with the number ranging from one (Third), 2 (Tenth), 3 (First, Fourth), and 4 (Eleventh) through 6 (Fifth, 4 of whom were from Louisiana districts) to 9 (Sixth, 5 being from the Northern District of Ohio) and Seventh, all but one of whom were from Northern Illinois. The greatest contributor of visiting district judges was the Second Circuit, 13 of whose district judges—5 from Eastern New York and 7 from Southern New York, the circuit's biggest districts—sat with the Ninth Circuit Court of Appeals. What makes these numbers even more significant is that to these visitors must be added the 80 in-circuit district judges who sat with the court of appeals, for a total of 160 non-regular judges, nearly *four times* the court's number of active-duty and senior judges combined (43 as of May, 2017).

In the period studied, the Eleventh Circuit had a somewhat smaller but still large number of visitors. There were some 60, almost evenly divided between circuit (27) and district (33) judges, to which, in order to get a sense of the number of non-regular judges with whom the court's own judges had to contend, one must add a somewhat larger number of in-circuit district judges—over 50. Thus, over 100 non-regular judges sat with the court during this time. Given that the Eleventh Circuit had fewer judgeships (11, plus 7 senior judges) than did the Ninth Circuit Court of Appeals, its use of non-regular judges was proportionately greater than that by the Ninth Circuit. Visitors to the Eleventh Circuit, who included retired Justice Sandra Day O'Connor, were from all circuits except the First and Fourth Circuits and the Federal Circuit. Five, who sat in only 10 cases, were from the Fifth Circuit, but their presence should not surprise given that it was the Fifth Circuit from which the Eleventh Circuit had been carved. Only 3 visiting appellate judges participated in more than 10 cases—Sixth Circuit Judge Eugene Siler (14) and Judges Arthur Alarcon (19) and Jerome Farris (18), both of the Ninth Circuit, who accounted for most of the 46 cases in which six Ninth Circuit judges took part.[2] Another half-dozen judges sat in 8 or 9 cases. The District of Columbia and First Circuits provided only one visitor each, with First Circuit Judge Norman Stahl sitting in 8 cases; there were 3 judges from the Second Circuit (11 cases, in 8 of which Judge John Walker sat), while 3 Sixth Circuit judges sat in a total of 25 cases; in addition to Judge Siler, Judge Ronald Gilman sat in 9. Five Eighth Circuit judges visited in 20 cases (Judges Myron Bright in 8, John Gibson in 9).

The visiting district judges came from districts in all circuits, although only one each came from the D.C., First, and Seventh Circuits. Several circuits contributed 4 district judges each (Second, 17 cases; Fifth, 21; and Ninth, 8), with judges tending to come from multiple districts within each of the circuits, except that 4 of the 5 Third circuit judges were from the Eastern District of Pennsylvania. There were also 6 judges from the Court of International Trade, 2 of whom sat in over 20 cases each (Richard Goldberg 22 and Jane Restani 25).

Individual Judges. Which individual judges have been engaged most in sitting in other appellate courts? One can look at this by determining the number of cases in which individual judges sat in a specific circuit in a

---

[2] Judge Farris, whose chambers were in Seattle, maintained a residence in Atlanta, so he was easily available to the Eleventh Circuit, although that court sat in other cities as well.

relatively short period. For example, for cases in 358-376 F.3d, Judge John Gibson of the Eighth Circuit participated in 5 cases in the First Circuit, and Judge Ruggero Aldisert of the Third Circuit participated in an equal number of Ninth Circuit cases. Federal Circuit Judge Daniel Friedman sat in 6 Sixth Circuit cases—and he also sat in 2 in the Ninth Circuit, and Ninth Circuit Judge Jerome Farris participated in 8 cases in the Eleventh Circuit.

Yet, while visiting circuit judges might sit in only a couple of published opinion cases in any one circuit in any time-frame (case set), some judges sat in several circuits, increasing the published-opinion cases in which they took part. In this first set of cases, Judge Eugene Siler of the Sixth Circuit sat in a total of 9 cases in three different circuits (First, Ninth, and Eleventh), and Judge Richard Cudahy of the Seventh Circuit also took part in 9—in the Third, Sixth, and Ninth Circuits. Two Eighth Circuit judges sat in three other circuits—Judge John Gibson in 10 cases in the First, Second, and Ninth Circuits, and Judge Frank Magill in 6 in the Third, Fifth, and Ninth, while Myron Bright sat in 8 cases in two Circuits (Third and Ninth). Tenth Circuit Judge Bobby Baldock also sat in three circuits—the First, Fourth, and Ninth, but for only 6 cases.

For cases in 488-500 F.3d, the Federal Circuit's Judge Pauline Newman participated in 8 cases in the First Circuit, and Ninth Circuit Judge A. Wallace Tashima also sat there in 7 cases, as did Judge Gibson in another 5. Judge Siler sat in another 8 cases in the Ninth Circuit plus an additional 6 in the Third Circuit; with sittings elsewhere, he sat as a visiting circuit in 20 cases in this period and then sat as well in 7 First Circuit cases in the next case set, as did Judge Baldock in 7 cases. And Ninth Circuit Judge Arthur Alarcon participated in 10 Eleventh Circuit cases in addition to 3 elsewhere, to which he added 6 Fourth Circuit cases in the 550-562 F.3d set, a time when the Eighth Circuit's Myron Bright participated in 17 cases in three circuits, including 8 each in the Ninth and Eleventh Circuits. Also continuing with participation in more than a couple of published-opinion cases were Sixth Circuit Judge Siler, with 13 in four circuits, with 7 of those cases in the First Circuit, where his circuit colleague Gilbert Merritt sat in another 5 and Judge Baldock participated in 7. The Eighth Circuit's Judge Gibson participated in 5 cases each in the First and Second Circuits, and Ninth Circuit A. Wallace Tashima participated in another 5 in the Third Circuit. Also contributing large numbers of Ninth Circuit sittings in published-opinion cases were Judges Bright (8) and Thomas Reavley of the Fifth Circuit (6).

Among the cases published in 749-764 F.3d, Judge Bobby Baldock sat in 9 in the First Circuit and in an additional 9 in the 765-783 F.3d case set, as did Seventh Circuit Judge Kenneth Ripple, with the Federal Circuit's Judge Timothy Dyk participating in 10 more. While the large numbers of sittings in First Circuit published cases may be explained in part by that court's issuing almost all its rulings as published opinions rather than as non-precedential dispositions, the numbers of cases in which some judges sat there are still noteworthy, as when Judge Michael Daly Hawkins of the Ninth Circuit participated in 9 cases in the 801-819 F.3d case set, along with Judge Dyk's sitting in another 5. Also of note at this time were Sixth Circuit Judge Eugene Siler's 5 sittings in Eleventh Circuit published-opinion cases.

Like visiting circuit judges, most district judge visitors participated in only one or two cases that resulted in published opinions, but others participated in more such cases in single courts or, at times, in more than one circuit. In the earliest case set, Judge Charles Weiner of Eastern Pennsylvania participated in 7 Ninth Circuit cases, and Central District of Illinois Judge Richard Mills sat there in 10 cases as well as 6 in the Eleventh Circuit. Louis Oberdorfer of the District of Columbia sat in 5 Third Circuit cases and a total of 11 cases in four circuits (also the First, Sixth, and Tenth); and Judge William Stafford of Northern Florida sat in 6 cases in the First Circuit. William Schwarzer of Northern California sat in 6 Sixth Circuit cases (488-500 F.3d) in addition to sitting in another circuit. Unlike the multi-circuit participation of several circuit judges, Judge Schwarzer's may have resulted from his having been Director of the Federal Judicial Center, which made him widely known to the judiciary nationally. Judge Jane Restani of the Court of International Trade, the apparent "energizer bunny" of visiting district judges, is the only other district judge to sit in multiple circuits. Visiting district judges tended not to participate in more than 5 cases with published opinion in any case set, but Judge Frederick Motz (D. Maryland) sat in 6 Ninth Circuit cases among those published in 765-783 F.3d, and, as the usual exception, Judge Restani sat in 9 Eleventh Circuit cases during that time.

Judge Restani's activity calls attention to the high visiting activity of CIT judges, who also included Judge Judith Barzilay in 7 Sixth Circuit cases and, in 8 Eleventh Circuit cases, and Judge Richard Goldberg, who also participated in 5 Eighth Circuit cases (550-562 F.3d). Others were, from the Seventh Circuit, Judge Suzanne Conlon of Northern Illinois, who sat in 5 Ninth Circuit cases, and, from the Eighth Circuit, Judge Lyle Strom (D. Nebraska), who participated in 8 cases in the Eleventh Circuit. Participating in two circuits—the Ninth and the Eleventh—were two Eastern New York judges, Edward Korman and David Trager, who, respectively, sat in a total of 9 cases and 5 cases. Visiting from the Ninth

Circuit, in addition to Judge Schwarzer, was Judge Vaughn Walker (N.D. California), one of the few judges to visit the Federal Circuit, where he participated in 5 cases.

In the first set of "unpublished" disposition cases in this study (510-525 Fed. Appx.), some judges participated in more than a few of these non-precedential dispositions. Among the visiting circuit judges, Third Circuit Judge Jane Roth sat in 8 Sixth Circuit cases, Sixth Circuit Judge Eugene Siler in 7 in the Eleventh Circuit, and the Ninth Circuit's Arthur Alarcon in 6 Eleventh Circuit, while his colleague J. Clifford Wallace took part in 5 Second Circuit cases and another colleague, Jerome Farris, sat in 4 such dispositions in the Eleventh Circuit, as did the Ninth Circuit's Andrew Kleinfeld. In this set of cases, some visiting district judges also had notable participation. Two contributed 15 sittings each to a single court—James Carr of Northern Ohio, sitting in the Ninth Circuit, and in the Second Circuit, Judge Restani, who also sat in such cases in the Second and Eleventh Circuits. Southern District of Texas Judge Lee Rosenthal's 15 case-participations were divided between the Eighth and Ninth Circuits. The Second Circuit's Edward Korman (E.D.N.Y.) sat in 11 Ninth Circuit cases, and the same circuit's Judge Jed Rakoff (S.D.N.Y.) sat in 8 cases in the same court, as did Judge John Tunheim of the Eighth Circuit's District of Minnesota and Judge Martin Garbis of the District of Maryland (Fourth Circuit) in 7 cases.

In the 720-735 F.3d case set, Judge Timothy Dyk of the Federal Circuit participated in another 6 First Circuit cases; that circuit's Judge Kermit Lipez sat in 5 Third Circuit cases; and Seventh Circuit Judge Kenneth Ripple sat in 5 cases each in the First and Ninth Circuits, to which he added 4 Eleventh Circuit cases in the following case set. Of the few visiting district judges with more than minimal participation in such cases, two were from the Sixth Circuit: Jack Zouhary (Northern Ohio) and Gordon Quist (Western Michigan), in, respectively, 7 and 5 Ninth Circuit cases. Among the visiting district judges, Judge Restani, who later appeared in 6 more Eleventh cases, participated in 4 Ninth Circuit cases and 3 Second Circuit cases in the 720-735 F.3d set. Three CIT judges including Judge Restani accounted for all 6 Second Circuit cases in which visiting district judges participated in that period.

In the roughly parallel "unpublished" cases, Judge Ripple stands out for sitting in 11 such cases in the Ninth Circuit. The only other circuit judges with participation in more than a couple of such cases were Sixth Circuit Judge Ronald Gilman (6 cases in Ninth Circuit) and Ninth Circuit Judge Arthur Alarcon's 5 cases in Judge Gilman's court, a functional trade. Tenth Circuit Judge Bobby Baldock had 4 participations in the

Eleventh Circuit. As the Ninth Circuit produces so many more cases with unpublished dispositions than with published opinions, it is not surprising that more visiting district judges, in this period used far more heavily than visiting circuit judges, had non-trivial participation in these non-precedential rulings. Likewise, only 7 judges had as many as 5-8 such sittings in a single circuit, with Northern Ohio's Jack Zouhary's 8 the largest, followed by Eastern New York's Brian Cogan and Edward Korman (7 each), both in the Ninth Circuit, and Southern Texas' Lee Rosenthal (in the Sixth Circuit). In the Ninth Circuit, in addition to Judges Zouhary and Korman, Southern New York's Jed Rakoff and Judge Lawrence Piersol of the District of South Dakota also sat in 6 such cases, and Southern New York's Sidney Stein and Eastern Louisiana's Sarah Vance 5 each. Three of these visiting district judges sat in more than one circuit, with Judge Rakoff adding 4 cases in the Fifth Circuit to his 6 in the Ninth, Judge Donald Walter (Western Louisiana) sat in 3 cases each in the Ninth and Eleventh Circuits; and Northern Florida Judge William Stafford participated in 4 cases each in the Sixth and Ninth Circuits.

In the cases decided with published opinion in 736-748 F.3d, few visiting circuit judges sat in more than a couple of cases. The First Circuit's Kermit Lipez sat in 5 cases in the Third Circuit and, in his own circuit, three visiting circuit judges sat in 4 cases each: Timothy Dyk of the Federal Circuit, who regularly sat there (and only there), Bobby Baldock of the Tenth Circuit, and the Seventh Circuit's Kenneth Ripple, who continued his frequent service as a visitor, which also included sitting in 4 cases in the Eleventh Circuit. The First Circuit also saw retired Justice David Souter, if one considers him a visitor as he was returning to the court of which he had once briefly been a part, participating in 10 cases with published opinions in this time period. Virtually all visiting district judges sat in only one, two, or three published opinion cases. For the equivalent time period, only three judges' participation in non-precedential dispositions is worth noting. Judge Jane Black of the Eleventh Circuit participated in 10 Ninth Circuit cases and Judge Lipez sat in 5 in the Third Circuit, while Judge Kathleen O'Malley of the Federal Circuit, elevated there from her position in the Northern District of Ohio, returned for 5 cases to her home Sixth Circuit, where she had earlier sat by designation while a district judge.

And so the patterns continued. In the published-opinion cases in 749-764 F.3d, visiting circuit judges for the most part contributed limited participation scattered among the circuits except for some concentration in the First, Ninth, and Eleventh Circuits; likewise, few visiting district judges sat in more than 4 such cases. Among the visiting circuit judges,

Judge Kenneth Ripple, continuing as a preeminent visitor, sat in 4 published First Circuit cases and 5 in the Eleventh Circuit, where Judge Arthur Alarcon of the Ninth Circuit also sat in 5 cases as well as in the Sixth Circuit, and Judge Baldock sat in 9 such cases in the First Circuit. In this period, the D.C. Circuit's Judge David Sentelle began to make an appearance as a visitor, sitting in 4 Eleventh Circuit cases.

In the parallel set of "unpublished" cases in 560-581 Fed. Appx., Judge Ripple added 14 Ninth Circuit cases to his published-opinion cases elsewhere. Sixth Circuit Judge Eugene Siler sat in 6 such cases in the Eleventh Circuit, where the Ninth Circuit's Judge Jerome Farris was a greater contributor to that court's dispositions. Judge O'Malley added 6 more participations in the Sixth Circuit, and another new visiting judge, Fortunato Benavides of the Fifth Circuit, took part in 8 Ninth Circuit non-precedential dispositions as well as two Eleventh Circuit cases.

Over a dozen visiting district judges participated in one circuit or another in at least 5 cases with unpublished dispositions. Two Second Circuit Eastern District of New York judges had over a dozen participations in the Ninth Circuit: Frederick Block (16) and Edward Korman (13). In the Second Circuit, neighbor Court of International Trade Judge Richard Eaton was a participant in 6 cases, while his colleague Richard Goldberg went to the Eleventh Circuit for 8 cases. Northern Florida Judge William Stafford sat in the same number in the Sixth Circuit, as did Southern Florida Judge Paul Huck in the Ninth Circuit. The latter circuit, with its heavy use of visiting district judges, saw several district judges participating in more than few cases. In addition to Judges Block and Korman, Judge Richard Friedman from the District Court for the District of Columbia sat in 10, along with Judges Martin Garbis (D. Maryland) (8), Ivan Lemelle (E.D. Louisiana) (7), Jack Zouhary (N.D. Ohio) (7), and Robert Pratt (S.D. Iowa) (8).

Going forward, in 765-783 F.3d, the same circuit judges remained predominant visitors participating in cases with published opinions. The First Circuit saw three: returning Judges Ripple and Baldock, in 9 cases each, and Dyk in 10, while the Fifth Circuit's Judge Benavides sat in 4 cases in the Eleventh Circuit and 3 in the Ninth Circuit. In addition were the Sixth Circuit's Eugene Siler (5 Eleventh Circuit cases) and Ronald Gilman with 4 there and 3 in the Ninth Circuit. The presence of more visiting district judges meant fewer cases per judge, with none participating in more than the 6 Ninth Circuit cases in which Frederick Motz (D. Maryland) sat; Northern District of Illinois Judge Robert Gettelman sat in another 5 there.

In the "unpublished" dispositions of roughly the same time (582-599 Fed. Appx.), some of these judges added more sittings, for example, Judges Benavides in the Ninth Circuit (8) and Judge Gilman 3 there and 6 in the Eleventh Circuit, but there were now other visiting circuit judges in cases with published opinion—Andre Davis of the Fourth Circuit (6 cases in the Ninth Circuit), the Tenth Circuit's David Ebel (8 cases, same circuit), and Barrington Parker of the Second Circuit (4 cases, also same court). Along with quite a number of visiting district judges sitting in only two or three cases with non-precedential rulings, there were some with significant participation in such cases who had not participated in any published-opinion cases. Not surprisingly, most of the frequent participants appeared in the Ninth Circuit, although Judge Robert Dow (N.D. Illinois) sat in 6 Sixth Circuit cases. Many with notable numbers were renewing earlier visits, including Southern New York's Jed Rakoff and Kevin Duffy (13 cases each), Lawrence Piersol of the District of South Dakota (9), Jack Zouhary of Northern Ohio (7) and Gordon Quist of Western Michigan (11) from the Sixth Circuit, and Eastern Wisconsin's Lynn Adelman (8); quite a number of others sat in 4 or 5 cases. Also now appearing among the visiting district judges were, from the First Circuit, Michael Ponsor (D. Massachusetts) (6 cases) and from the Sixth Circuit, Stephen Murphy of Eastern Michigan (9) and Solomon Oliver of Northern Ohio (6). CIT Judges Richard Eaton and Jane Restani together sat in 11 Eleventh Circuit cases.

Both circuit and district visiting judges participating in published-opinion cases in 784-800 F.3d sat in only a few cases each, but some circuit judge visitors took part in large numbers released with non-precedential rulings in 600-622 Fed. Appx. Among them was D.C. Circuit Judge David Sentelle, with 8 Eleventh Circuit cases. Several judges visiting in the Ninth Circuit contributed even greater numbers, most notably Judge Gilman's 13 and Judge Benavides' 15, as well as Second Circuit Judge Robert Sack's 9, and 7 each by three judges—Lipez (First), Davis (Fourth), and Ebel (Tenth). Not surprisingly, only in the Eleventh and (especially) the Ninth Circuits do we find visiting district judges with large numbers of case participations. The Court of International Trade's Richard Goldberg stands out in the Eleventh Circuit with 10 such cases; his colleague Jane Restani sat in an equal number in the Ninth Circuit, where five other judges, all of whom had visited before, participated in 10 or 11 cases—Judge Michael Ponsor (D. Massachusetts), Eastern New York's Frederick Block and Edward Korman, and, from the Southern District of New York, Kevin Duffy (14) and Jed Rakoff (15). Other continuing regulars had slightly fewer cases (6-8)—Paul Friedman of the District of Columbia, Eastern Louisiana's Ivan Lemelle, Lee Rosenthal of the Southern District of Texas, and District of Minnesota Judge John Tunheim, along with more recently-appearing Friedman college Royce Lamberth and Joan Lekflow of Northern Illinois.

Before moving further forward, note that, for the cases decided with published opinion, visiting circuit judges came from all the circuits, but only one judge each came from the District of Columbia, First, and Fourth Circuits. The two judges each from the Third, Fifth, and Seventh Circuits sat in 13, 11, and 16 cases, respectively, with Judge Richard Cudahy (7th Cir.) sitting in 10 cases and writing 3 opinions. The Eleventh and Federal Circuits also supplied two visitors, with the latter's Judge Daniel Friedman sitting in 5 cases and writing opinions in 2. Visiting district judges hailed from all the circuits and from the Court of International Trade (Judge Jane Restani in 13 cases), although there was only one judge each from the D.C. and Tenth Circuits. Use of judges from the Federal Circuit and the Court of International Trade cuts against some judges' concerns about using judges from specialized courts, although others thought it advantageous that they weren't wedded to the circuit precedent of another general-jurisdiction court of appeals.

Apart from Judge Restani, only three other judges sat in 10 or more cases—Kevin Duffy of Southern New York (13 cases), Edward Korman of Eastern New York (10 cases), and Judge Gordon Quist of Western Michigan (13 cases). The Second Circuit contributed the most district judges, 15, in 65 cases, with almost half of those judges (7) from Southern New York, sitting in 30 cases. The Sixth and Seventh Circuits each supplied nine judges: those from the Sixth Circuit sat in 47 cases and judges from the Seventh Circuit, which itself did not use visitors, sat in another 30 cases.

To return to visiting judge participation, "newcomers" sitting in more than a few cases with published opinions in 801-819 F.3d were Judges Michael Melloy of the Eighth Circuit (4 Ninth Circuit cases) and the Ninth Circuit's Michael Daly Hawkins, in 9 First Circuit cases. Among regular visiting judges, two from the Sixth Circuit—Judges Siler (5 cases) and Gilman (4)—sat in the Eleventh Circuit. Of those district judges participating in published-opinion cases, unlike past periods, none who sat in the Ninth Circuit participated in more than 5 cases, which Judges Lee Rosenthal (Southern Texas) and Elizabeth Foote (Western Louisiana) did. However, in the Eleventh Circuit, where regular visitor Richard Goldberg (CIT) participated in 7 cases with published opinion, two Eastern Pennsylvania judges—Eduardo Robreno and Harvey Bartle III—sat in 9 and 4 cases, respectively. Once again, in roughly parallel non-precedential dispositions (623-640 Fed. Appx.), some circuit judges' participation is more prominent than in the published-opinion cases. Examples are Judge Barrington Parker (2d Cir.) in 9 such dispositions and Ronald Gilman, in 8, both in the Ninth Circuit, where Tenth Circuit Judge Carlos Lucero sat in 6. The only visiting district judges prominent in these cases with non-precedential rulings, except for Judge Restani's 6 case-sittings in the Eleventh Circuit, were all in the Ninth Circuit. The Eastern District of Michigan Judge George Caram Steeh sat in 12 cases, Judge Lefkow in 10, and seven others sat in 6-8 cases. All but a couple of them were regulars like Southern New York's Judges Duffy and Rakoff and Judges Motz of Maryland, Adelman of Eastern Wisconsin, and Piersol of South Dakota, to whom should be added William Smith, Chief Judge of the District of Rhode Island and thus unusual as a visitor because an active-status judge, and Sarah Scheindlin of Southern New York, only recently a senior judge.

The Cadre

Examination of the prominence of individual visiting judges, especially in circuits which borrow visitors the most, has revealed regularly recurring names among the many who were visitors at one time or another. Of course, changes in the "top ten" occur over time, both as new names have joined the list, largely as judges assumed senior status, making it easier for them to visit, and aging and mortality removed others.

The judges who sat most frequently in other circuits can be said to be part of a cadre of judges who, as they move from their home circuits to visited courts, make for a more national judiciary by better tying the circuits together. (When a retired Supreme Court justice sits in all—or almost all—the circuits, as retired Justices Tom Clark and Sandra Day O'Connor did, that serves further to tie the courts of appeals together.) The presence of a possible cadre can perhaps be seen most obviously in the large number of district judges who come from the East—and especially from two New York districts in the Second Circuit—to the West's Ninth Circuit; who come from points west to sit in Boston with the First Circuit; or who move south to participate in the Eleventh Circuit's work. There is no formal cadre. This grouping has no specific designation nor do its "members" have an additional title designating them as "Member of the Cadre." However, they are not far from being the "flying squadron" of national judges contemplated by earlier jurists who thought of a regionally-based national judicial system.

Sitting in more than one circuit seems a necessary prerequisite for a judge to be considered in the cadre. Certainly the assistance a judge might give to a single visited circuit is important to that circuit—and to the judge—but the relationship of Judge A to Circuit X, without more, may well be idiosyncratic. By contrast, a judge's willingness to sit in more than one circuit indicates a broader—one could say more national—perspective.

Many circuit and district judges participate in non-trivial numbers of cases as visitors but sit in only one circuit other than their own. For example, Judges Rhesa Hawkins Barksdale and Patrick Higginbotham of the Fifth Circuit have sat only in the neighboring Eleventh Circuit, which, it must be remembered, was part of the "old Fifth." Another example is Judge Timothy Dyk of the Federal Circuit, who has sat only in the First Circuit. Some other Federal Circuit and Court of International Trade judges have visited only one circuit. Notwithstanding the important contribution these judges have made, for one reason or another they have not demonstrated the mobility manifested by judges who have visited in more than one circuit.

Over the several years of this study, there were 25 circuit judges and 28 district judges who served as a visiting judge in more than one circuit. If we do not further sort these judges by the number of cases in which they participated, we have a cadre of 50 judges, although with the extent of their participation varying. Five of the circuit judges served in 4 or 5 different courts of appeals: Judge Eugene Siler of the Sixth Circuit, Richard Cudahy and Kenneth Ripple of the Seventh, and Myron Bright and John Gibson of the Eighth Circuit; 2 other Eighth Circuit judges—Frank Magill and Michael Melloy—also sat in multiple circuits. Among the multi-circuit visitors coming from the Ninth Circuit were Judges Arthur Alarcon, Jerome Farris, A. Wallace Tashima, and J. Clifford Wallace, and the Tenth Circuit supplied 3 more—Judges Bobby Baldock, David Ebel, and Carlos Lucero. The visiting district judges who sat in multiple courts of appeals came from all circuits, with Second Circuit districts contributing the most—5 judges, 3 from Eastern New York (Raymond Dearie, Edward Korman, and David Trager) and 2 from Southern New York (Kevin Duffy and Jed Rakoff). The single source of most such judges was the Court of International Trade, with 4: Judges Judith Barzilay, Richard Eaton, Richard Goldberg, and the seemingly omnipresent and highly-participant Jane Restani.

Doing Double Duty. If we identify the 50 judges just discussed as a national cadre of judges who have shown their willingness to sit through-out the federal judicial system, there is another set of judges, ones who may be said to do "double duty"—district judges who both visited other circuits *and* sat by designation with their own courts of appeals. Some district judges both sat in their own circuit's courts of appeals and in those courts in other circuits. Circuit judges who visit other courts are by definition doing double duty, as they continue to sit in their home circuits in addition to being visiting judges.

In addition to the fact that active-duty district judges would be far less likely to sit out-of-circuit because to do so they must go through the procedures of the Inter-Circuit Assignment Committee, and because "newbie" district judges are brought to the court of appeals to be socialized to its work with no thought they would—or would even be able to—sit outside the circuit, the extent to which district judges sit with their own circuit but do not visit other circuits is striking nonetheless. Conversely, there are some district judges, relatively few, who visit in other circuits and also sit by designation with their own circuits; indeed, some visiting district judges do not sit at all with their own appellate courts. Ultimately a relatively small proportion of district judges sitting by designation perform "double duty," and quite a number of those on the double-duty list have sat in only a few cases in either other courts of appeals or their own circuit.

District judges visiting other circuits may be doing double duty, that is, sitting by designation in their own circuit and visiting elsewhere, although actually this is "triple duty"—handling calendars in their own districts, sitting by designation with the court of appeals, and serving as visiting judges. However, some senior district judges who serve as visitors in other circuits limit their home-duty work and concentrate on visiting, for example, as noted earlier, Judge Richard Mills of Central Illinois, who maintained only 15% of a load in his home court, and the late Talbot Smith. Those judges may find appellate work more appealing (yes, a pun), they have a proclivity for it, and they also may find it less taxing. When district judges visit elsewhere but don't sit with their own circuit, it may result not only from a yen to "see the world" but from lessened need for them in their home district.

The list of district judges who performed "double duty" in the period covered by this research reaches almost 50. However, a dozen of these judges have only small numbers of sittings either as visitors or as by-designation judges in their own circuit. Another 9 did double duty but most of that was as visiting judges, with little participation in the work of their own circuit's courts of appeals.

Besides some judges with considerable service both as visiting judges and as by-designation district judges on courts of appeals, there are also 10 double-duty judges who, as visitors, sat in multiple circuits. There are, from the First Circuit, Judge William Smith of the District of Rhode Island; participating even while serving as his district's chief judge;

Judges Jed Rakoff (S.D.N.Y.) and Edward Korman (E.D.N.Y.) from the Second; two Third Circuit judges from Eastern Pennsylvania—Louis Pollak earlier and, more recently, Michael Baylson; Judges Donald Walter (Western District of Louisiana) and Lee Rosenthal (Southern Texas) from the Fifth Circuit; Judge Joseph Hood of Eastern Kentucky and Western Michigan's Gordon Quist from the Sixth Circuit; Northern District of California's Judge William Schwarzer from the Ninth Circuit; and, from the Eleventh Circuit, Judge Paul Huck of Florida Southern.

Only some 20 district judges overall visited other circuits and sat with their own circuit's court of appeals. In the first set of cases, Judge William Schwarzer of Northern California was the only one, but he also did "double duty" in the next two case sets. Two Second Circuit district judges sat both elsewhere and with their own court of appeals in two time periods—Edward Korman (E.D.N.Y.), in both 488-500 F.3d and 550-562 F.3d cases, and Jed Rakoff (S.D.N.Y.), in the two most recent case sets. Three other Eastern New York judges—David Trager, Frederick Block, and Brian Cogan—at one time or another sat both outside their circuit and with their court of appeals, as did Southern New York Judges Leonard Sand and Sidney Stein. The only First Circuit judge to do so was Rhode Island's William Smith and, from the Third Circuit, only Judge Louis Pollak of Eastern Pennsylvania. The only such judges from the Fourth Circuit were Judges T.S. Ellis II and Liam O'Grady, both of Eastern Virginia. More recently, Judges Ivan Lemelle (E.D. Louisiana) and Lee Rosenthal (S.D. Texas) both sat outside the circuit and with their own Fifth Circuit Court of Appeals. Likewise, from the Eleventh Circuit, Southern Florida Judge Paul Huck sat with his own circuit and outside it in recent cases; so did Northern Florida Judge Roger Vinson.

The Sixth and Ninth Circuits each had somewhat more "double duty" judges. Northern District of Ohio Judge Katherine O'Malley sat with the Sixth Circuit and also visited with the Federal Circuit, to which she was later appointed. (And, in a later case, she sat as a visitor back in her original home Sixth Circuit.) In the 550-562 F.3d case set, Judge Joseph Hood (Eastern Kentucky) sat both within and outside the circuit, as did three Northern District of Ohio judges—Jack Zouhary, James Gwin (720-735 F.3d), and James Carr (736-748 F.3d). In addition to Judge Schwarzer, other Ninth Circuit judges sitting both outside and with their court of appeals were his Northern California colleagues Ronald Whyte (488-500 F.3d) and Vaughn Walker (550-562 F.3d) and Judge Marilyn Huff from Southern California (also 550-562 F.3d).

6
DISTRICT JUDGES

The views of judges whose courts use in-circuit district judges have been presented earlier. Here, to complement the picture of district judges visiting outside their own circuits, an examination of their patterns of sitting with their own circuit's court of appeals is presented. The patterns of visiting judge use should be kept in mind, because there can be a relationship between use of visitors and use of the circuit's own district judges; they are related, not separate, matters, and greater use of one type might lead to less use of another. And a visiting district judge might feel more comfortable in the role of visitor in a court of appeals that was accustomed to using many of its own district judges. In this treatment of district judges, attention is also given to a specific problem that has arisen in one circuit: a court of appeals' use of district judges to sit on cases from the district judge's own district.

The courts of appeals bring the circuit's own district judges to sit with them not only to help with caseload but also to help socialize new district judges to the expectations of their "superiors"—those who "grade their papers." This reason for their use may help explain why many district judges participate in only part of a court's calendar week and sit in only a small number of cases, or why their presence in the composition of panels might lead to the inference that they are "filling spots." However, from time to time, some district judges do participate more frequently, making return appearances at the appellate court. It might be noted that, just as district judges sit with the court of appeals to learn the latter's ways of functioning, some judges of the courts of appeals, especially those who earlier in their careers had not been state or federal trial judges, at times sit in the district court to gain a better understanding of the work of the district judges whose decisions they review. (Some other court of appeals judges, who *were* trial judges, sit in a nearby district court to help out and/or simply because they like trial court work.[1])

This chapter begins with examination of various circuits' use of their own district judges, followed by a look at the particular districts within circuits from which the district judges come. Attention then shifts to

---

[1] In the Ninth Circuit, Judges Alfred T. Goodwin, formerly a state trial judge and a judge of the District of Oregon, and A. Wallace Tashima, earlier on the Central District of California, have sat as district judges from time to time.

individual judges—first, the number of judges with whom a court of appeals' own judges must interact and then, particular district judges who have sat frequently with their courts of appeals. The chapter ends with examination of the Second Circuit's use of district judges in cases from those judges' own district courts.

Use of District Judges

Use by Circuit. The U.S. courts of appeals vary in their use of their circuits' own district judges. This may be a reflection of differing "circuit cultures," with district judges—apart from the necessity of their use—more welcome on some courts of appeals but less welcome in others. Over time—at least over the period of this study—courts of appeals which make greater use of their own district judges tend to be the same.[2] Three circuits—the First, Ninth, and Eleventh—make greater use of visiting judges than of their own in-circuit district judges, while, on the other hand, five circuits—the Second, Fourth, Sixth, Eighth, and Tenth—make far greater use of the circuit's own district judges than of visiting judges. In both the Second and Sixth Circuits, in-circuit district judges participate in far more cases than do out-of-circuit visitors.

It should be remembered that the District of Columbia Circuit makes no use of its own circuit's district judges because, with only one district in the circuit, the judges from that district would be sitting in appellate judgment on their own district court colleagues (in this regard, see below for discussion of the Second Circuit). The Seventh Circuit, for an extended period, also did not, as a matter of policy, have any in-circuit district judges sit with the court of appeals, although that policy has since been abrogated and some now do so sit.

Minimal or negligible use by courts of appeals of in-circuit district judges is found in many circuits. For example, in the earliest case set, in six circuits only six or fewer such judges sat in their courts of appeals in 5 or fewer cases with published opinions. As with their use of visiting judges, the Fifth, Eighth, and Tenth Circuits made relatively little use of their own district judges. In 488-500 F.3d cases, only 2 district judges sat with the Eighth Circuit; the Tenth Circuit made the least use of these judges in 550-562 F.3d cases; and in the 720-735 F.3d case set, the Third and Tenth Circuits used only one judge each, while in 736-748 F.3d cases,

---

[2] As noted earlier as to Judges Nguyen of the Ninth Circuit and Costa of the Fifth Circuit, there is an occasional instance in which a district judge sits by designation with his or her court of appeals and then is elevated to the latter court while cases are in process.

the Third Circuit used only one of its own district judges, and 3 other appeals courts used only 2 district judges apiece.

Some circuits used somewhat more of their own district judges in any given period. Several used 6-9, with both the Fourth and Fifth Circuits making use of 6 of the circuit's own district judges in the first set, while in 488-500 F.3d cases; at this level of usage were the Fourth Circuit again (7 judges, 12 cases), the First Circuit (6 judges, 14 cases), and the Tenth Circuit (7 judges, 9 cases). In the 550-562 F.3d set of cases, far more courts of appeals were at this tier of usage, with the First Circuit again using 6 district judges (for 23 cases), as did the Third Circuit (16 cases). Seven district judges, deciding a much larger number of cases (35), sat with the Eighth Circuit, while the 8 district judges participating in the Fifth Circuit's work sat in only 18 cases. The Fourth and Eleventh Circuits each used 9 district judges in this case set, but they sat in only 11 cases in the Eleventh while doing so in 31 Fourth Circuit cases. (See Table III.Part I in Appendix A.)

These data illustrate that the number of district judges that a court of appeals uses does not necessarily map well on the number of cases in which the judges participate. As one can see in the just-noted Eleventh Circuit numbers, at times the number of cases did not much exceed the number of judges, as when the Fourth Circuit used 8 district judges but for only 10 cases, but, by comparison, the Second Circuit's cases in 720-735 F.3d reveal use of 7 judges for 28 cases. And the just-shown comparison of the Fourth and Eleventh Circuits indicates that when roughly the same number of district judges participate in each of two appellate courts, the number of cases in which they sit might vary considerably.

Several courts of appeals have regularly made greater, sometimes much greater, use of the circuit's own district judges. In the published opinions appearing in 358-376 F.3d, while some circuits were seen to have used only 2, 3, or 4 district judges, the Ninth Circuit drew on 13, who participated in 29 cases, while the Second and Sixth Circuits used almost twice that number; district judges sat with the Second Circuit in 35 cases and 25 sat in 63 Sixth Circuit cases. With the Sixth and Ninth Circuits continuing, along with the Second Circuit, to be heavy users of their circuit's district judges, in 488-500 F.3d cases, 26 in-circuit district judges sat in 39 Ninth Circuit cases while in the Sixth Circuit, 31 sat in 76 cases, and, in 550-562 F.3d cases, the Ninth Circuit used somewhat more judges (20, in 31 cases) than the Sixth (15, in 25 cases). That high use continued in the published opinion cases in 720-735 F.3d, with 21 Ninth Circuit district judges participating in 34 appeals and 25 Sixth Circuit district judges helping to decide 50 cases. The Sixth Circuit's substantial use continued with 19 judges in 34 cases (736-748 F.3d), with comparable figures for the next four case sets—20 or so district judges sitting in over 30 cases per set, e.g., 21 judges in 35 cases in 801-801 F.3d. This is, of course, only district judge participation in cases resulting in published opinions. A look at parallel sets of non-precedential-disposition cases indicates that in Sixth Circuit, the same frequent use of district judges is found, with the number of judges participating in cases in each case set running from 28-32 except for one instance of 39 sitting (526-540 Fed. Appx.), with those judges participating in between 104 and 150 cases. (See Table III.Part II in Appendix A.)

Somewhat later, the Ninth Circuit exhibited a decline to limited district judge participation in published cases. In the 736-748 F.3d case set, only 10 judges sat in 13 cases, but higher use then resumed, with 18 judges in 27 cases, in 744-763 F.3d; 19 judges in 765-783 F.3d cases (22 cases); and 17 judges in 784-800 F.3d cases (only 21), although in cases published in 801-819 F.3d, 23 Ninth Circuit district judges sat in 34 cases. There is no comparable dip in district judge participation in cases with non-precedential dispositions; indeed, the number of district judges sitting was higher than for cases with published rulings, although here, too, there was variation across time, from 22 judges in one case set (54 cases) to as high as 39 judges in another (140 cases).

In the cases in 720-735 F.3d and 736-748 F.3d, the Second and Eleventh Circuits had joined the courts of appeals which made considerable use of the circuit's own district judges, with the Second Circuit using, respectively, 17 judges (28 cases) and 13 judges (but in only 13 cases) and the Eleventh Circuit making use of 14 judges (27 cases) and 23 judges (39 cases). Heavy use persisted in both circuits in their unpublished cases. In the Second Circuit, from 13 to 26 district judges sat in such cases per case set, accounting for from 27 cases to a one-time high of 76. In the Eleventh Circuit, in cases published in 749-764 F.3d, 23 district judges participated in 51 cases and, in those cases in 765-783 F.3d, 22 judges sat in 55 cases, before a modest decline to 17 judges in 29 cases (784-800 F.3d) and 14 judges in 27 cases (800-819 F.3d), yet as many as 24 district judges sat in cases with "unpublished" dispositions in 560-581 Fed. Appx. Overall, there was roughly the same decline seen in cases with published opinions, with the next highest number of district judges at 18 and, in the last "unpublished"-disposition case set, only 10 judges taking part in only 22 cases, down from a high of 66 cases when 24 district judges participated. It should be noted that, in the Eleventh Circuit, one finds a not-insignificant number of cases in which two district judges participated, a result of the court's "judicial emergency" situation. The resulting alignment of one (active) circuit judge and two district judges is not the only time a panel contains two "non-regular" judges, but at least one of those two "non-regulars" is likely a senior circuit judge or a visiting circuit judge.

If one looks not at raw numbers but instead at proportions of cases in which judges participated, at times there is moderate use of in-circuit district judges in cases decided with published opinion, as in 2007 in the Fifth Circuit (14.3%) and Eighth Circuit (14.1%), with the Seventh Circuit district judges sitting in a comparable proportion of cases (15.1%) shortly after that court resumed their use. On the other hand, in the Tenth Circuit the proportion has never exceeded 7.5% and usually has been well below that. The Second and Sixth Circuits made high use of in-circuit district judges throughout, although in the Second Circuit, the proportion, over 20% for a while, dipped to just over 10% starting with cases in 736-748 F.3d. In the Sixth Circuit, the proportion of cases with district judges never fell below one-fifth (21.6%, 784-800 F.3d) and was at or exceeded one-fourth for the remainder of the time, and at one point (736-748 F.3d) it reached one-third (33.0%). Variation did occur, however, with the proportion declining from over one-half (51.7%) in cases in 488-500 F.3d to only one-fourth (24.9%) in the 765-783 F.3d case set.

The Eleventh Circuit made only moderate use (10.3%-16.8%) of district judges in the earliest three case sets, but later the court made quite high usage of district judges. Starting with 720-735 F.3d, the proportion of cases in which they sat always exceeded one-fifth, and it exceeded one-third in a couple of case sets (37.3%, 720-735 F.3d; 34.4%, 784-800 F.3d). The Ninth Circuit's district judge usage is moderate throughout, staying within a range of 7.0% to 17.7%. The First Circuit's use of its own district judges was moderately low—6.7% or less overall, but only 2.9% in 801-819 F.3d and negligible in another set—although it did exceed one-eighth (14.5%) in cases in 749-764 F.3d. Indeed, the First Circuit provides evidence for up-and-down variation that could take place in district judges' participation, as it ranged from 14.8% of the cases in 358-376 F.3d to 10.9% (488-500 F.3d), before moving all the way up to 16.8% (550-562 F.3d) before dropping to 6.6% and 6.4% (720-735 F.3d, 736-748 F.3d) before a new rise to 14.8% (740-764 F.3d) and a drop back to 6.6% (765-783 F.3d).

Generally the same picture appears for cases decided with non-precedential rulings as with published-opinion decisions, at least for the Second, Sixth, and Ninth Circuits. (See Table III.Part II in Appendix A.) In the Second Circuit, the proportion of cases with "unpublished" dispositions in which district judges participated was within the narrow range of

9.0-13.2%, while the range was even narrower in the Ninth Circuit—6.1-8.8%—and a couple of times it was 4-5 percentage points lower than for district judge participation in published-opinion cases. For the Sixth Circuit, the proportion was 31.6%-36.7% for all but one set (526-540 Fed. Appx.), where it was 44.4%, all a bit higher than for cases with published opinion. For the Eleventh Circuit, however, one sees considerably fewer instances of district judges sitting in cases with unpublished dispositions than in published-opinion cases. Where the proportion of published opinion cases in which a district sat never fell below 20%, it never rose above 8.6% (526-540 F.3d) for the non-precedential dispositions, and after that set it fell to being regularly under 5%, These results largely stem from this court's use of the non-argument calendar for many cases, as only active circuit judges sit on them.

Particular Districts. A court of appeals might draw widely from most of the districts in the circuit for judges to sit with it by designation, with such participation scattered among the circuit's districts. On the other hand, one particular district might account for most of the district judges participating in the court of appeals' work. The latter was the regular pattern in the Second Circuit. Thus, in the cases in 358-376 F.3d, 13 of 24 district judges sitting with the court of appeals were from the Southern District of New York, with another five from Eastern New York; those two districts accounted for 11 of 14 district judges (and 20 of 24 cases) in cases published in 488-500 F.3d and for 13 of 18 district judges (20 of 33 cases) in 550-562 F.3d. The Southern District's judges also accounted for 12 of 17 district judges in Second Circuit cases in 720-735 F.3d cases and for 10 of 13 in 736-748 F.3d. Part of the explanation for the predominance of judges from the two districts is their large number of judges, but a major reason may be their proximity to the site of court of appeals argument, which made it easier for them to be borrowed; this may also help explain why most Southern District judges participated in only one case. This pattern continued, as when in later published-opinion cases in 765-783 F.3d, Southern District and Eastern District judges accounted for 12 of 14 by-designation district judges and 15 of 19 cases in which district judges took part.

Proximity, along with a district's large number of judges, may also help explain the occasional predominance of Eastern District of Pennsylvania judges among district judges sitting in the Third Circuit, as the headquarters of both courts was in Philadelphia. In cases published in 488-500 F.3d, 8 of the 14 Third Circuit district judges sitting by designation, accounting for 16 of 25 cases, were from Eastern Pennsylvania. However, judges from a district not geographically proximate may predominate, as occurred in First Circuit cases in 550-562 F.3d, when 5 of the 6 district judges participating, accounting for 16 of 23 cases, were from Puerto Rico, or, in the Fifth Circuit, where the Western District of Texas gave 5 of 8 district judges (12 of 18 cases).

Even when district judges' chambers and the court of appeals are in close proximity, it does not necessarily follow that the district judges will sit often with the appellate court. For example, most District of Massachusetts judges are in the same courthouse as the First Circuit Court of Appeals, but few of those district judges participated in more than one case in a case set, a likely indication that they were "borrowed" to fill out an appellate panel. Indeed, travel requirements made it more likely that judges from Puerto Rico, if they sat, would sit for more days and thus participate in more cases. In fact, District of Puerto Rico Judges Jay Garcia-Gregory (12 cases) and Gustavo Gelpi (7) sat as frequently at one point as did Judges William Smith of Rhode Island and Joseph DiClerico of New Hampshire (10 and 11 cases, respectively).

For many circuits, because the appellate court used so few district judges overall, we cannot speak of one district predominating in its contribution of district judges, as in the Eighth and Tenth Circuits. There are also instances in which, with district judges appearing only infrequently, one district might contribute the largest proportion of district judges, as when, in the Fourth Circuit, there were two consecutive case sets in which the Eastern District of Virginia provided 6 of 8 district judges (7 of 10 cases).

Even when the number of district judges used by a court of appeals was of some magnitude, no district might stand out in its contribution of these judges. In the Eleventh Circuit, which used 9-11 district judges in the cases in each of the earliest case sets, no district stood out in its contribution. Those district judges who did sit on the appeals court at that time came from all the circuit's districts, but the number of judges from each district varied from one (Southern Alabama), two (Middle Georgia), and three (Middle Alabama) to as many as 11 judges from Florida Southern, sitting in 42 cases, and Florida Middle, whose 13 participating district judges accounted for 57 participations.

Starting with the cases in 720-735 F.3d, there was an increase in the number of district judges, ranging from 14-23. Individual districts, particularly those in Florida, stood out, although the contribution of any individual district was not great because the "spread" was much greater than in the Second Circuit. For example, in the 736-748 F.3d case set, the court of appeals borrowed 5 of 23 judges, sitting in 11 of 39 cases, from Middle Florida, with Southern Florida giving another 4 judges. Middle

Florida regularly made a noticeable contribution in later case sets, for example, 5 judges sitting in 13 cases from a total of 23 district judges participating in 51 cases, and 5 judges in 10 cases or 14 judges sitting in 27 cases. Southern Florida judges also appeared often, with 6 (in 13 cases) of 28 judges (51 cases) and, in the following period, 6 judges in 11 cases of a total of 22 judges sitting in 55 cases.

Another aspect of the Eleventh Circuit's use of its district judges is their presence with other non-regular judges on panels, that is, two such judges might be participating in a single case, because of the circuit's "judicial emergency" rule. Indeed, the Eleventh Circuit saw the presence of two non-regular judges on a panel in as many as one eighth (765-783 F.3d) or one-sixth (749-754 F.3d) of the court of appeals' cases, with at least one visiting judge among the two non-regular judges in 27 cases. The most frequent combination of two non-regular judges was two in-circuit district judges, at times from the same district, in 21 instances, and a combination of a visiting district judge and an in-circuit district judge occurred in 16 cases. Other combinations appearing in smaller numbers of cases were that of a visiting circuit judge and an in-circuit district judge, or two visitors (a visiting circuit judge and a visiting district judge).

The Sixth and Ninth Circuits, both of which used considerable numbers of in-circuit district judges, did draw from all districts in the circuit but at times tended to draw heavily from particular ones. The Sixth Circuit's "draw" was more even than took place in the Second Circuit. Of the 25 district judges who sat in the Sixth Circuit Court of Appeals in cases reported in 358-376 F.3d, there were 8 judges from Eastern Michigan, perhaps because it has more judges, but 3 each were also borrowed from Western Michigan and Southern Ohio, 4 from Northern Ohio, and 5 from Eastern Kentucky. In the next case set (488-500 F.3d), of 31 district judges sitting by designation, 5 each came from the Eastern District of Kentucky and the Southern District of Ohio, 6 from Eastern Michigan, and 8 from Ohio Northern.

Somewhat later, in the cases in 720-735 F.3d, the two Ohio districts accounted for half the participating district judges (13 of 25), with another eight from Eastern Michigan, which continued to be a major contributor of district judges to the circuit. For example, in 736-748 F.3d, it provided 9 of 19 district judges but only in 9 of 34 cases, then, consecutively, in 749-764 F.3d., 6 of 19 judges and a healthier 14 of 32 cases; 6 of 25 judges but only 12 of 41 cases; and 8 judges of 17 (but only 9 of 26 cases). However, in a more recent case set (808-819 F.3d), only two Eastern Michigan judges sat, in one case each. One (or both) of Ohio's two districts also donated district judges, providing as many as had Eastern

Michigan at times, but the Ohio judges usually took part in fewer cases than those from Eastern Michigan. As an indication of variation in patterns over time, however, 4 judges from Northern Ohio and 8 from Southern Ohio seriously outnumbered the 2 from Eastern Michigan in cases published in 891-819 F.3d. While many of the district judges who sat with the Sixth Circuit were senior judges, from time to time one also could find district chief judges sitting with the court of appeals, perhaps combining their sittings with a meeting with the circuit's chief judge or with circuit staff.

The Ninth Circuit, which one should remember used far more *visiting* district judges than its own district judges, with a certain proportion of sittings by the latter resulting from newly-appointed district judges going to the court of appeals for socialization to its concerns, presents a mixed picture. The circuit contains many districts and the very large Central District of California, based in Los Angeles. There are instances, as in cases in 358-376 F.3d and later in 736-748 F.3d, in which the district judges sitting with the court of appeals did not come predominantly from any particular district. However, in cases published in 488-500 F.3d, half the district judges (13 of 26), accounting for half the cases in which district judges sat (20 of 39), came from three of California's four districts. More obviously, in the 720-735 F.3d case set, Northern California and Southern California contributed 5 district judges each to the 20 sitting with the court of appeals. There were other instances in which slightly more judges from a single district sat without constituting a major source of district judges, for example, 4 District of Nevada judges out of 18 district judges but only in 5 cases, or 4 Northern District of California judges of 19 but in only 4 cases.

Counter to what might have been expected, California's four districts generally were not, individually or cumulatively, predominant, although in cases in one set (784-800 F.3d), 9 of 17 district judges the court of appeals used, sitting in 11 of 21 cases, were from the California districts, with individual California districts varying in their contributions; and in various periods, non-California districts sent as many judges to the Ninth Circuit as did any of the California districts. Of the latter, Eastern California provided the least and Central California the most to the Ninth Circuit Court of Appeals, a reflection of the relative size of their judge rosters. Most judges participated in only one, two, or three cases; in fact, only roughly a half-dozen judges sat in 5 or more cases.

Across the full set of data on cases with published opinions, judges from *all* the circuit's districts sat on Ninth Circuit panels at one time or another. Not surprisingly, however, the districts differed in the size of their contribution, with the smallest contribution by Montana and Oregon, districts with smaller caseloads. A small district's contribution could, however, be boosted by a single judge's frequent participation, as when Judge David Ezra, one of four District of Hawai'i judges sitting with the Ninth Circuit, took part in 13 cases there. Five District of Alaska judges participated in twice as many cases (26) as did the same number from the District of Arizona, and at one point, the District of Nevada had contributed 10 judges who sat in only 24 cases, two fewer than the judges from Alaska. Likewise, 7 Western Washington judges sat in 22 cases, with only one (Ronald Leighton) participating in more than 5; but 4 Eastern Washington judges sat in only 7 cases. The larger case-participations by judges from distant districts (Alaska and Hawai'i) can be explained in terms of their travel time to oral argument; it would make little sense to bring a judge from Anchorage to the "lower 48" for only a couple of cases, while judges who have to travel smaller distances for argument could sensibly be used in fewer cases.

Thus far, this description has been only of district judge participation in cases resulting in published opinions. Those patterns are repeated in the often-voluminous numbers of non-precedential dispositions the courts have produced. Thus in the Second Circuit, Southern District of New York judges constituted most district judges sitting in these cases, accounting for as many as 17 of 25 judges sitting with the court of appeals, in 76 of 80 cases; 13 of 17 judges, in 36 of 44 cases; 13 of 18 judges, in 27 of 39 cases; and 16 of 24 judges, in 54 of 79 cases, although Southern New York's dominance is somewhat less in the last two case sets—11 of 21 judges, in 26 of 48 cases, and 11 of 26 judges, in only 19 of 52 cases.

In the Sixth Circuit, in any period, as many as four or five districts made major contributions of district judges sitting by designation, but no one district was anywhere as dominant as was Southern New York in the Second Circuit. None contributed one-third of the district judges, with the closest being Eastern Michigan's 9 judges (of 28) in cases in 541-559 Fed. Appx. and 9 of 30 judges in cases in 560-581 Fed. Appx., and the Northern District of Ohio's 8 judges, sitting in 34 cases, in 582-599 Fed. Appx. However, the judges from some districts participated in more than one-third of the circuit's non-precedential rulings, as when 5 Eastern District of Kentucky judges sat in 65 of 192 cases in the 510-525 Fed. Appx. set; Eastern Michigan judges sat in 53 of 150 such cases (560-581 Fed. Appx.); 8 Northern District of Ohio judges took part in 34 of 106 cases reported in 582-599 Fed. Appx.; or 9 Eastern District of Michigan judges helped decide 44 cases of 142 in 600-622 Fed. Appx. Throughout, many Eastern Michigan and Northern Ohio judges were among those sitting by designation, and Southern Ohio judges also appeared in all but two sets; Eastern Kentucky judges participated less but are notable as well. In the Eleventh Circuit, while the Middle District of Florida made a large contribution of district judges in "unpublished" cases, as it had in ones with published opinions, providing as many as 7 of 14 judges (19 of 50 cases), at other times its contribution is less, for example: only 4 of 12 judges (and only 7 of 18 cases) in one set, or 5 of 24 judges (and only 11 of 66 cases) in another, and there are case sets when no district's contribution is noteworthy.

No single Ninth Circuit district contributed a particularly large proportion of cases resulting in non-precedential rulings, but district judges from almost all the circuit's districts sat in them. The exception is Idaho, which had limited judicial resources so that a judge could not be spared to sit with the court of appeals. Three California districts combined (Northern, Central, and Southern) contributed no more than 14 judges of 40, sitting in 44 of 152 cases reported in 600-622 Fed. Appx. District of Alaska judges' participation in these cases is interesting, however. For example, in the 526-540 Fed. Appx. case set, 5 judges from there sat in 17 of 62 cases, more than the 15 cases in which the same number of Central District of California judges participated, and then 3 Alaska judges participated in 18 cases of 85, and, still later, 4 sat in 35 cases of 125. As suggested earlier, this over-representation may result from travel considerations.

Another Cut. Another question to ask is, "Roughly what proportions of the judges in each district sit with the court of appeals?" What is most important here, to provide another view of variation in judge-use, is the proportion of judges in each particular district who sit with the appellate court. And there definitely is wide variation, from districts none of whose judges sit with the court of appeals, to those roughly half of whose judges (active-duty and senior combined) participate in appellate work, and to some districts where all the judges have sat by designation. It is not surprising that some of a district's judges would not sit with the court of appeals in any given period, even if for several years, as some may have done so years before and have been through their "socialization sitting" and a number are now senior judges handling a reduced caseload.

Here, the question is not the number of *cases* in which the district judges sat but the low bar of simply whether they sat with the court of appeals at least once during the period of this study. This standard will, if anything, result in an undercount, as judges may have participated in the appeals court's work before the 2012-2016 period or judges appointed only in 2014-2015 might have sat with the court of appeals in cases handed down late in 2016 or thereafter and thus are not included in this data. A further counting problem is that some senior judges remain on a district court roster despite minimal service or that which has for all practical purposes ceased; their presence reduces the proportion of district judges who have sat with their appellate colleagues. A similar counting problem is created by some senior district judges who visit other circuits but do not sit by designation in their own circuits.

As was done earlier, in this discussion, circuits are grouped by the frequency of their use of district judges by designation—limited, moderate, and heavy use. The circuits whose courts of appeals made least use of in-circuit district judges—excluding the D.C. Circuit with its policy of no such use—were the Third, Fifth, Eighth, and Tenth Circuits. In the Third Circuit, low proportions of district judges in all the circuit's districts sat with the courts of appeals, with the highest being a ratio of 1:2 (judge sitting : judges not sitting) for Eastern Pennsylvania judges; that ratio was 1:4 for Middle Pennsylvania, and no Western Pennsylvania judges sat with the court of appeals. Half of the judges from two Fifth Circuit districts sat in their court of appeals: Eastern Louisiana, whose headquarters is where the Fifth Circuit sits, in New Orleans, and Western Texas, the furthest away from New Orleans. Except for those two districts, there was low or no participation from other districts' judges, with none at all from the Mississippi districts, even from Southern Mississippi's 10 judges; only one of 12 Northern Texas judges and one of 7 from Eastern Texas; and a ratio of 1:8 for Southern Texas (3 judges sitting, 24 not).

Four of the Eighth Circuit's nine districts provided no judges to the court of appeals. In only one district, North Dakota, small in terms of caseload, did all the judges sit by designation, and in only three districts did ratios reach 1:3, but in two of those, 6 of 9 of those not sitting were senior judges. The districts nearest where the court of appeals heard argument, St. Louis and St. Paul, had the highest proportions: those were Eastern Missouri (5 of 13 judges) and the District of Minnesota (4 of 9). There is some indication that courts of appeals, especially those which don't generally utilize many district judges, might be more likely to draw on "locals" to fill spots when required late in panel composition process. The District of Colorado, containing the Tenth Circuit's Denver headquarters, had the largest number of judges sitting with the court of appeals although that number is not high (5 sitting, 8 not). The only court with an even 1:1 ratio of those sat to those who did not was the District of Wyoming (2 and 2), also a district of lesser caseload. Only one District of Utah judge participated in the court of appeals work while 10 others did not, and all three Oklahoma districts had negative ratios, as did Kansas (1:2) and New Mexico (2:7).

The courts of appeals in two circuits, the Fourth and Seventh, made moderate use of their own district judges. In the Fourth Circuit, the proportions ran from 1:5 in two North Carolina districts (Eastern and Middle) to 4 of 7 Western North Carolina judges sitting with the court of appeals, to roughly even sit/non-sit proportions: 1:1 proportions for the Eastern District of Virginia, with the largest number of judges and where circuit headquarters was located, and the District of South Carolina; the proportion for the District of Maryland was 1:2+. Even some judges from districts not near circuit headquarters participated, such as one of 3 judges from the Northern District of West Virginia and 2 of 6 from Southern West Virginia. That the Seventh Circuit had only recently resumed having its district judges sit with the court of appeals may explain why only one district (Eastern Wisconsin) had an even split—3 judges sitting with the appellate court, 3 not, but one of that district's judges visited frequently out-of-circuit—and one, Northern Illinois, the circuit's predominant district, had an almost even split (16 sittings, 17 not, with 4 of the latter judges regularly visiting other circuits). Of the other districts, no Western Wisconsin judges participated in the Seventh Circuit's work, while in other districts, fewer judges sat than did not.

What was the picture in those circuits which made relatively higher use of district judges? In the First Circuit, a high proportion of judges from all districts but one sat with the appeals court. All District of New Hampshire and District of Rhode Island judges, for whom participation required some travel to Boston, participated, even though the small numbers of judges in those districts (5 and 3) would usually push *against* having them all sit by designation because of their need to attend to their districts' dockets. In the District of Massachusetts, most of whose judges had chambers in the same courthouse as the court of appeals, the proportion of judges sitting was 2:1. The only district whose judges sat minimally with the court of appeals was the District of Puerto Rico, perhaps in part a result of extended travel, but an observer has suggested that the First Circuit's judges lack respect for them.

The Second Circuit Court of Appeals, although its use of the circuit's own district judges declined at the very end of the period studied and beyond, made considerable use of them, with a high proportion of judges from all districts sitting with the court of appeals, true even for those districts where travel was required to Foley Square in New York City, such as the Northern and Western Districts of New York, with most of their "non-sitting" judges either senior judges or quite recent appointees, or the

District of Vermont, all 4 of whose judges sat. The District of Connecticut had a 1:1 ratio, but one of the "non-sitters" was appointed only in 2014 and another was a senior judge.[3] As to Eastern and Southern New York, the two districts with very large judge rosters, the proportion of judges who sat with the court of appeals was 4:1 for the Southern District, most of whose judges are at the same location as the court of appeals, while the Eastern District, occupying far-off Brooklyn and Long Island, had roughly equal numbers (16-14), with 3 of the non-sitting judges appointed only in 2014-2015 and the others being senior judges.

In the Sixth Circuit, only two districts showed negative proportions of judges sitting—the small Middle District of Tennessee, possibly not having enough judges to spare resources the court of appeals could borrow, and the Western District of Kentucky, also with few judges (only 1 of 5 sitting). Of the other seven districts, only one was close to an even split (3 sat, 2 did not), while the others had high positive ratios or had only a single senior judge not sitting with the court of appeals at this time (Eastern Kentucky and Eastern Tennessee, both 8:1, and Southern Ohio, 13:1). The ratio for Northern Ohio was in excess of 3:1 (13 and 4), and the largest district, Eastern Michigan, contributed 19 judges while 7 did not participate in this period.

In the Eleventh Circuit, there was considerable variation in the extent to which the court of appeals borrowed judges from various districts. In two, more judges sat with the court of appeals than did not: Southern Georgia (4-1) and Northern Florida (6-3), and in three others, the ratio of those who sat to those who did not was at or close to 1:1—two smaller districts, Middle and Northern Alabama (2-2 and 5-5, respectively) and one of the two largest, Middle Florida (15-16). The four remaining districts had "negative balances": Southern Alabama (1-2), Middle Georgia (2-4), and Northern Georgia (6-9, or a 2:3 ratio); in the other large district, Southern Florida, the split was 12-15.

The Ninth Circuit Court of Appeals, it must be remembered, for much of the time studied used more visiting district judges than in-circuit district judges, but nonetheless it engaged in a "heavy draw" on the latter. It is interesting that in this circuit, the nation's geographically largest, stretching from Fairbanks and Honolulu to Billings, Phoenix, and San Diego, distance from circuit headquarters at San Francisco or other principal places of holding argument (Portland, Seattle, and Pasadena[4]) does not explain the districts from which the district judges were drawn to

---

[3] Charles Haight, originally a judge in the Southern District of New York but shown on the roster of the District of Connecticut.

[4] There are also less-frequent calendars at Anchorage and Honolulu.

sit with the court of appeals. All 6 District of Alaska judges did so, as did 5 of 8 District of Hawaii judges, with the 3 who did not being senior judges. Neither District of Idaho judge, one a senior judge, participated in the court of appeals' work, but 4 of Montana's 6 did so. Of the other non-California districts (excluding Guam and the Northern Marianas, whose judges lack Art. III status and thus cannot sit with the court of appeals[5]), only Oregon had a negative proportion of judges who sat in the appeals court (1:4). The ratio for District of Nevada judges was a positive high 4:1; for Arizona, it was only 1:1 but 4 of the 9 non-sitters were senior judges. The four California districts also varied in the proportion of their judges who sat with the court of appeals, ranging from Eastern California's negative 1:2 to Southern California's positive 2:1, with both Central California (the largest district) and Northern California between them—Northern California a positive 13-11 (with two non-sitters appointed only in 2014 so less likely to have been called upon to sit yet) and Central California at roughly 1:2 (13 judges sitting with the court of appeals, 23 not).

Individual Judges

Numbers of Judges. As with visiting judges, it is not only the number or proportion of cases in which in-circuit judges participate that is important. Also crucial is the number of *individual judges* who sit over an extended period, as the larger the number of "stranger" bodies present, the more different points of view which a court of appeals must learn and to which its judges must accommodate, as district judges, even though they will have been applying that circuit precedent, are not likely to have the same views as those of judges of the court of appeals. A possible result some have suggested is that it will be more difficult to maintain the stability of the circuit's law.

When the sheer numbers of in-circuit district judges who sit with each court of appeals is calculated, one sees the same variation among circuits previously portrayed, but the raw numbers are nonetheless important in their own right. For the period covering cases with published opinions from 720 F.3d forward and those with "unpublished" dispositions from 510 Fed. Appx. forward, in four circuits the numbers of district judges were so minimal, sitting in fewer than 10 cases in each of those circuits—that absorbing their participation was not likely to be difficult for the court. They are the Third (5 judges), Fifth (9, one of whom became a member of the appeals court), Eighth (8), and Tenth (6) Circuits. Hosting

---

5 See Nguyen v. United States, 539 U.S. 69 (2003).

not many more was the First Circuit, with which 15 district judges sat in this period, but that seemingly small number is two-and-a-half times the six court of appeals active-duty judges. The number of in-circuit district judges used by two more courts of appeals was in the low-to-mid 20's: the Fourth Circuit, at 22, a number not much larger than the court's own 17 active-duty and senior judges together, and the Seventh Circuit, at 25, which had only recently resumed allowing such judges to participate in appellate cases.

Then there are four courts of appeals which made such considerable use of district judges—*more than 50* in each—that the numbers of individual district judges exceeded, at times by a considerable amount, the court of appeals' active and senior judges combined. These were those for the Second Circuit, in which 61 district judges sat in this period; the Sixth, 59; the Eleventh, 50; and the Ninth Circuit, the "grand-daddy" of them all, in which 80 different district judges sat—even though that court made use of fewer such judges than of visitors.

Particular Judges. At times, many by-designation district judges participate in only one or at most two cases in a case set, but some take part in as many as a half-dozen—or more. One judge (or perhaps two) out of a larger number may account for participation in many of the appeals cases in which district judges take part. For example, Judge John Nangle of the Eastern District of Missouri sat in 9 of the 10 Eighth Circuit cases published in 488-500 F.3d in which a district judge participated. In the Eleventh Circuit, among participation by 4 Northern District of Florida judges in 15 cases published in 765-783 F.3d, Judge Robert Hinkle sat in 8, and, among another 4 Middle District of Florida judges sitting in 13 cases, Judge Harvey Schlesinger accounted for 9. In cases in 736-748 F.3d, Eastern Michigan's Judge Lawrence Zatkoff sat in 7 of the 19 appellate cases in which his district's judges took part. Judge Jay Garcia-Gregory of Puerto Rico sat with the First Circuit in 10 of 16 cases in which that district's judges participated in 550-562 F.3d.

However, even among those taking part in more than one case, no one judge may be predominant. For example, Eastern New York Judge Edward Korman's 6 cases in the Second Circuit in 550-562 F.3d were less than one-fifth of the 33 in which district judges took part. District of New Hampshire Judge Joseph DiClerico sat in 7 First Circuit cases in 550-562 F.3d, but they were less than one-third of the 23 cases with a district judge. And the 5 Fourth Circuit cases in 736-748 F.3d in which Judge Joseph Anderson (District of South Carolina) took part were less than half the 11 cases with district judges.

Yet, within any cohort of judges from a particular district, the higher participation of one or two may well stand out. Thus Judge Karl Forester of Eastern Kentucky accounted for half of the Sixth Circuit's cases with a district judge in the 488-500 F.3d case set, and his colleague William Bertelsman accounted for 6 of the 8 cases in which Eastern Kentucky judges sat with the circuit in 736-748 F.3d. And in the 16 cases in which Fifth Circuit district judges took part in 720-735 F.3d, two judges accounted for 10—Philip Martinez (Western Texas) (6) and Ivan Lemelle (Eastern Louisiana) (4). In "unpublished" dispositions in 526-540 Fed. Appx., when 12 district judges took part in 34 cases, among the Southern District of New York judges sitting, Judge Jed Rakoff sat in 9 and Judge John Keenan in 7.

The same phenomenon is evident in a number of instances in cases decided by non-precedential rulings. In dispositions reported in 510-525 Fed. Appx., Judge Joseph Hood was in 33 of the 65 cases decided by 5 Eastern District of Kentucky judges. His colleague Gregory Van Tatenhove accounted for another 21 cases, so together they accounted for 54 of 65 cases in that set. Judge Hood also participated in 10 cases of 28 (again by 5 judges from that district) in 623-640 Fed. Appx. Judge W. Harold Albritton of Middle Alabama participated in 11 cases appearing in 541-559 Fed. Appx.; Judge Brian Cogan, in 8 of 19 cases by 5 Eastern New York judges (510-525 Fed. Appx.); and Judge Edward Rice (E.D. Washington), in 11 cases found in 582-594 Fed. Appx.

The Ninth Circuit also provides a number of instances. For example, Judge Barbara Rothstein sat in 8 of 12 cases in which Western Washington judges participated in 560-581 Fed. Appx. and in 9 of 14 cases in which 4 judges from that district participated in 582-699 Fed. Appx. cases. Judge David Ezra sat in 12 of 19 cases in which 4 District of Hawai'i judges participated (582-599 Fed. Appx.). Judges of the District of Alaska judges provide further examples:

- Judge John Singleton, 11 of 19 cases by 3 judges (541-559 Fed. Appx.)
- Judge Ralph Beistline, 8 of 17 cases by 5 judges (536-540 Fed. Appx.)
- Judge John Sedwick, 14 of 35 cases by 4 judges (582-599 Fed. Appx.)

Despite this single-judge dominance, participation is likely to be more widespread. For example, once the Seventh Circuit began to make regular use of its district judges: among those sitting in multiple cases published in 720-735 F.3d were Judges John Lee (Northern Illinois) and Sarah

Barker Evans (Southern Indiana) in 5 cases each, and Judges Jane Darrow (Central Illinois), Joseph Stadtmueller (Eastern Wisconsin), and James Zagel (Northern Illinois), each sitting in 6 cases. In cases published in 749-764 F.3d, among the 6 Northern Illinois judges in 30 cases, Judge Amy St. Eve sat in 8 and Judges Frederick Kapala and Virginia Kendall in 6 each. Similar instances can be found in other circuits. In the Second Circuit, in the set of unpublished dispositions in 520-525 Fed. Appx., among the 17 district judges sitting in 76 cases, Judge Rakoff sat in 13 and Judges John Koeltl and Jesse Furman sat in 9 each. In the somewhat later cases in 560-581 Fed. Appx., among 16 district judges sitting in 54 cases, Judges Lewis Kaplan and Valerie Caprioni took part in 9 each and Judge Paul Engelmayer in 6.

The Sixth Circuit also provides indications of the "spread" in participation among the judges from a specific district sitting with the court of appeals. In unpublished dispositions appearing in 526-540 Fed. Appx., 11 judges from the Eastern District of Michigan participated in 37 cases, among them Judges David Lawson and Avern Cohn in 7 each and Judges Lawrence Zatkoff and Paul Borman 5 each. In cases in 560-581 Fed. Appx., judges from the district sat in 53 Sixth Circuit cases, with two sitting in 8 each (Robert Cleland, George Karam Steeh), while 4 more participated in 6 cases each (Judges Cohn, Robert Drain, Stephen Murphy, and Arthur Tarnow). This pattern continued in Sixth Circuit cases appearing in 600-622 Fed. Appx., when another 9 Eastern Michigan judges participated in 44 cases, with Judge Thomas Ludington in 10, followed by Judges Murphy (9) and Cohn (8), and in those in 623-640 Fed. Appx., 11 judges participated in 28 cases, with Judges Cleland and Denise Hood sitting in 6 each and Judge Ludington in 5 cases. The participation of Southern District of Ohio judges is similar. In cases in 526- 540 Fed. Appx., when 7 judges from that district sat in 30 cases, two (Sandra Beckwith and James Graham) were in 6 cases, while 3 more were in 5 cases each (Judges Algernon Marbley, Edmund Sargus, and Michael Watson), while in the 560-581 Fed. Appx. case set, of the 7 judges sitting in 48 cases, Judge Sargus participated in 10, Graham in 9, and Watson in 8, and none of the participating judges sat in less than 4 cases.

Cumulative Numbers. If sets of cases are combined, the cumulative participation by some district judges in court of appeals cases stands out from that by others. Thus, when the three earlier sets of published-opinion cases are combined, for example, of 8 First Circuit district judges sitting their court of appeals, Judge Joseph DiClerico (D. New Hampshire) sat in 11 cases but no one else sat in more than 6, while, in the Third Circuit, Judge Louis Pollak of Eastern Pennsylvania participated in 12 but none of the other 16 judges sat in more than 6 cases. The distinction was even more stark in the Second Circuit, where, of 28 district judges, Judge Edward Korman of Eastern New York sat in 13 appellate cases while no other judge sat in more than 7, and, overall, all but 3 judges sat in no more than 3 cases each. In the Ninth Circuit, apart from Judge Schwarzer's 12 participations, no other of the 34 district judges sat in more than 4 cases.

When 2013-2015 cases with published opinions and non-precedential dispositions are combined, although there are courts of appeals with no district judge who particularly stands out in the number of court of appeals sittings, some other judges do. In the Second Circuit, among judges from Southern New York, Judge Jed Rakoff's 51 participations far exceed the 24 cases of the next-most-frequent participant, Judge Lewis Kaplan, and the 21 cases of Judge John Keenan. The numbers then drop to 13 sittings (Judge Paul Engelmayer) and 12 (Judge Alison Nathan), while Eastern New York's Edward Korman also sat in 12—in addition to 13 cases with published opinion from the earlier period.

In addition to one judge participating far more than did the judge's colleagues, there are instances where several follow the "top hitter" closely. In the Eleventh Circuit, the 36 sittings of Judge Harvey Schlesinger (Middle Florida) are followed by Judges Robert Hinkle (Northern Florida), with 29; Paul Huck (Southern Florida) at 23; and two judges who each sat in 22 cases—L. Scott Coogler (Northern Alabama) and Dudley Bowen (Southern Georgia). In the Ninth Circuit, among the 80 district judges with greatest appellate court participation, two judges, each from a low-volume district, have the highest number of Ninth Circuit sittings. Judges David Ezra of Hawai'i (39) and John Singleton of Alaska (30) have the most frequent participation, with Eastern District of Washington Judge Edward Rice next at 27 and 6 others at or over 20 sittings: District of Alaska's Ralph Beistline and Sharon Gleason (each 23); Arizona's Raner Collins (20); Leslie Kobayashi (like Judge Ezra, from Hawai'i) and Judges Robert Lasnik (22) and Barbara Rothstein of Western Washington. In the Sixth Circuit, which, while smaller than the Ninth Circuit, makes proportionally greatest use of district judges among the circuits, not only is there the leading district judge participant in U.S. court of appeals sittings—Joseph Hood of the Eastern District of Kentucky, with 79, and two other district judges, also from the same district, participating in 52 cases each—William Bertelsman and Gregory Van Tatenhove—but there are also 6 judges with 30-39 sittings and 14 more in the 20's.

The Second Circuit Problem[6]

Examination of the districts from which in-circuit district judges are drawn to sit with the courts of appeals gives rise to the issue of those judges sitting in appeals from their own districts. The almost instinctual answer to the question, "Should judges temporarily sitting in an appellate capacity review the work of colleagues from their 'home' courts?," is likely to be "No," even if it took place earlier in our judicial history. Before there were federal intermediate appellate courts, Supreme Court justices rode circuit and they once sat in review of the rulings they had made while on circuit. More to the current point, observers in the court community feel that the presence of district judges on appeals from their own districts is most definitely to be avoided. As one observer stated it, "There is nothing worse than creating awkwardness in the district by letting one district judge overturn another on appeal"[7]—that is, having a district judge participate in reversal of the district court may lead to friction within the district. An additional concern leading to avoidance of the practice is that the district judge sitting as an appellate judge will be "soft" on—that is, defer to—the judge's own district court colleague and will hesitate to engage even in deserved criticism of the ruling under review.

In most circuits, it is agreed that it is inappropriate for district judges serving as temporary appellate judges to review the work of their current district court colleagues. "Most," but not all, for there is an important exception, a court of appeals in which district judges sitting there by designation do, with some frequency, sit in appeals from their own districts. That is the Second Circuit Court of Appeals, whose practice is examined in this section.

The Problem. Except perhaps for capital cases, there seem to be no limitations on the types of cases in which district judges sitting by designation might participate. Yet, apart from the subject matters of the cases on which they sit, there is the question of whether they should participate in cases originating from their own districts. There is no statutory prohibition on district judges sitting in such appeals, but there is a strong norm to the same effect, and it certainly is not considered "best practice." A court administrator has observed that even if a court has no codified operating procedure on the matter, the practice remains a conflict. He adds that if a judge has to recuse from a case if one of the

---

[6] This section is based on, and revised from, Stephen L. Wasby, "The Second Circuit— District Judges' Reviewing Colleagues' Cases," 26 Law & Courts Newsletter 10-12 (#2, 2016).

[7] Christina Boyd, e-mail to Stephen L. Wasby, January 7, 2015.

judge's recent law clerks is appearing for a party, recusal should also be required when the trial judge in the case was a district court colleague. Indeed, that relationship, being a present one, is stronger than the former relationship with a law clerk or with the judge's own former law firm.

For courts of appeals which make no or little use of in-circuit district judges, whether district judges might participate in appeals from their own districts is a non-issue. That is also true when a circuit contains no single large or dominant district, one with a heavy caseload and many district judges. In the latter circumstance, however, using district judges to help the court of appeals process its caseload can create a logistical problem in avoiding assigning judges from such a dominant district to the review of that district's cases.

Avoidance. There is evidence, to be seen shortly, that courts of appeals make efforts to avoid the problem.[8] Although the matter is not pursued here, it should also be noted that courts of appeals with whom district judges sit use low-visibility practices to protect them from the friction that might result from their reversing fellow district judges, even from districts other than their own. One method is not to have them write for the panel in reversing a district judge from *another* district; another is to have the panel issue its disposition per curiam, so that the district judge sitting with the appeals court doesn't take flak for being "out there" in such situations.

This latter process was at work in a 1992 Ninth Circuit case, in which a district judge appeared to have punished a defendant for not pleading guilty by handing down a harsher sentence after the subsequent trial. The Ninth Circuit panel included a district judge sitting by designation, and the panel, while trying to soften the blow a bit by saying in its opinion, "We do not believe that the experienced trial judge actually punished the defendant for standing trial," faced the situation that "the record leaves unrebutted the inference drawn by the defendant" of such punishment. That led the panel to rule that the record must show that no improper weight was given to the failure to plead guilty.[9]

On remand, the district judge would not reconsider his action to make that determination. The panel's two circuit judges, Alfred Goodwin and Shirley Hufstedler, then suggested to the district judge sitting with them, Otto Skopil (D. Oregon), that he recuse so a third circuit judge could be drawn to decide the case. As Judge Goodwin wrote to Judge Skopil, referring to an earlier Skopil ruling reversing the same district judge,

---

[8] And see Jeffrey Brudney and Corey Ditslear, "Designated Diffidence: District Court Judges on the Court of Appeals," 35 Law & Society Review 564, 572 n.10 (2001).

[9] United States v. Stockwell, 472 F.2d 1186, 1187-88 (9th Cir. 1992).

"Charlie Carr will never forgive you for the dirty business you did in January, but at least you won't have to incur his further rage."[10] As Judge Hufstedler wrote to her Ninth Circuit colleague Ben Duniway, who had been drawn to replace Judge Skopil, "Because we have to set down Judge Carr, we thought it desirable that the panel be 3 circuit judges."[11] Then-Chief Judge Richard Chambers went even further, suggesting that the panel's order be worded to allow a judge not in the Central District of California (Judge Carr's district), perhaps an "outside" judge there on assignment, to be chosen to hear the remand, as the regular method would have put the matter before Judge Carr's colleagues.[12] When Judge Carr remained recalcitrant, Chief Judge Chambers had to work to persuade him to get off the case.

Despite the picture this story presents, one does find district judges willing to join in action that in effect disciplines a colleague by reassigning the case to another judge, as when a by-designation district judge joined a circuit judge to form a two-judge majority to do that, over a dissent, albeit in an "unpublished"—and thus lower-visibility—disposition.[13]

Some courts have explicit policies to avoid the difficult situation of district judges sitting on appeals from their district colleagues. Thus the Court of Appeals for the District of Columbia, by policy, makes no use of the judges of the District Court for the District of Columbia, as any such use would put those judges in the position of reviewing their colleagues' cases—unless one restricted them to sitting on appeals to the D.C. Circuit that come directly from administrative agencies. Likewise, the Seventh Circuit Court of Appeals, as a matter of policy, not only declined to accept out-of-circuit visitors but also refused the services of its own district judges to hear appeals. However, as noted earlier, that court recently resumed the use of in-circuit district judges, but in doing so, it has been careful not to have judges of the Northern District of Illinois judges, although most of them are conveniently located in the same courthouse with the court of appeals, sit on appeals from that district.

Other courts of appeals appear to lack an explicit policy on the matter, but they maintain a norm to the same effect. At times, this norm is implemented by informal means. As reported earlier, a district judge from Montana noted that when he sat on the Ninth Circuit's Portland/ Seattle

---

10 Alfred T. Goodwin, memorandum to Otto Skopil, July 16, 1973, *re: Stockwell.*

11 Shirley Hufstedler, memorandum to Ben Duniway, August 8, 1973, *re: Stockwell.*

12 Chief Judge Richard Chambers, memorandum to panel, n.d., *re: Stockwell.*

13 United States v. Espinoza, 653 Fed. Appx. 873 (9th Cir. 2016) (Pregerson, J. and Bastian, J. [E.D. Wash.] / "Callahan").

calendar (two days in Portland, three in Seattle), he couldn't sit on any Montana cases, so he and a fellow district judge from Idaho, who also sat with the Ninth Circuit, had an "arrangement," in which the Idaho judge "would sit on the panel with the Montana cases and I'd sit on the panel with the Idaho cases."[14]

More recently, the Ninth Circuit has gone further toward hardening the norm into policy.[15] In-circuit district judges sitting with the court of appeals are assigned to cases in such a way as to avoid the situation. The court of appeals hears cases in several locations, with cases for a particular location drawn from nearby districts. District judges sitting by designation for argument are not assigned to hear cases near their own chambers, so the problem does not occur. Northern District of California judges thus will most likely not sit in appeals argued at San Francisco, where appeals from their own Northern District are heard, but they will sit with the court of appeals court at Pasadena, where cases from some other districts but not the Northern District are calendared, or they will be assigned to calendars at Portland or Seattle.

Despite all this preparation and formal and informal arrangements, occasional instances have occurred in which a district judge sitting by designation would find cases on the calendar from the judge's own district. Yet as one judge observed, "When clerical error has produced that, I have informed them and they have changed judges."[16] Even with these corrective methods, a case could be missed. One judge told of a case in which an order had been written by a district court colleague but the case had been filed under the name of a different judge who had begun work on the case, and this was not discovered until later, so Judge Gus Solomon, the colleague of the by-designation judge "was not happy" about being reversed.[17] And there are instances in other circuits where, despite care by the Clerk of Court, a district judge has sat in judgment on a

---

14 Interview with Judge William Jameson (D. Mont.), Pasadena, Cal., April 11, 1986.

15 That the court "observ[es] that court policy is for district judges not to participate in disposition of appeals from their own district" is noted by Brudney and Ditslear, "Designated Diffidence," at 572 n.10.

16 Interview with Judge Albert Wollenberg (N.D. Cal.), San Francisco, Cal., February 13, 1977.

17 Interview with Judge William East (D. Or.) And, for an earlier instance which apparently had not been caught, see Rabang v. Boyd, 234 F.2d 909 (9th Cir. 1956), a case from the Western District of Washington (Lindberg, J.), in which Judge George Boldt of that same district was a member of the Ninth Circuit panel.

colleague's decision; they have been found in the Eleventh Circuit[18] and in the First Circuit.[19]

The Second Circuit. Despite most circuits' avoidance, the problem exists in the Second Circuit and does so with considerable frequency, indicating that it could not have been inadvertent. Many cases are decided by panels including a judge from the district from which the appeal has been taken, particularly true for judges of the Southern and Eastern Districts of New York.

An example is *In re Herald* (2014),[20] in which a panel of Circuit Judges Parker and Carney and Southern District Judge Rakoff, in a per curiam opinion, affirmed a ruling by Judge Berman of the Southern District. Another example, with a further twist, is *United States v. Pena*,[21] in which a panel of Circuit Judges Jacobs and Pooler and Southern District of New York Judge Roman, in a per curiam opinion, vacated a ruling by Southern District Judge Loretta Preska, an instance in which a new district judge participated in overturning a ruling by a much senior district court colleague (later the district's Chief Judge). And there was even a case in which a panel with a Southern District judge ruled in a single case on actions of several of the latter's colleagues, when a panel of Circuit Judges Katzmann and Hall and District Judge Rakoff decided a case in which, in the district court, Judge Sprizzo had the original assignment; there was a temporary reassignment to Judge Duffy, who denied a motion to dismiss the indictment; the case then went back to Judge Sprizzo for a bench trial, and, after Sprizzo's death, Judge Alvin Hellerstein carried out the sentencing. The Second Circuit panel on which Judge Rakoff sat vacated and remanded.[22]

If instances such as these were isolated, one might not bother to call attention to the situation, and indeed one might even say there was no

---

[18] See United States v. Smith, 957 F.2d 835 (11th Cir. 1992), in which District Judge Clyde Atkins of the Southern District of Florida sat on an appeal from Judge Paine of the same district, and Motorcity of Jacksonville v. Southeast Bank, 39 F.3d 292 (11th Cir. 1994), also from the Southern District of Florida (Highsmith, J.), where Judge William Hoeveler (S.D. Fla.) was a member of the panel.

[19] See two cases from the District of Puerto Rico, in which Judge Gustavo Gelpi of that district sat on the appeals court panel: United States v. Guzman-Montanez, 756 F.3d 1 (1st Cir. 2014); Conjugal Partnership Acevedo-Principe v. United States, 768 F.3d 51 (1st Cir. 2014). Another member of the panel was the one member of the First Circuit from Puerto Rico, Judge Juan Torruella, and it has been suggested, in a private communication, that there is a likelihood that situation did not occur by chance.

[20] Initially 540 Fed. Appx. 19 (2d Cir. 2014), on petition for rehearing, 753 F.3d 110 (2d Cir. 2014),

[21] 751 F.3d 101 (2d Cir. 2014).

[22] United States v. Cerna, 603 F.3d 32 (2d Cir. 2010).

"problem." However, the instances are *not* isolated and the frequency is great. That frequency is more important because many, many instances came in cases resulting in published opinions, that is, the rulings that made circuit precedent. Over two dozen instances, most involving Southern District of New York judges, were discovered during initial work on courts of appeals' use of in-circuit district judges. That prompted further exploration, a Lexis search covering all of the *Federal Reporter Third Series* from 1 F.3d in 1993 and extending to mid-2015. That search revealed *515* such instances involving Southern District judges. A separate search, covering the same period, revealed *80* instances in which a judge from the Eastern District of New York sat in a panel considering an appeal from that district. In many more instances, cases resulted in non-precedential dispositions.

The search turned up a very few cases that don't raise the basic concern but which, because of the small numbers, do not affect the basic picture. In one case, the ruling in the Southern District of New York was by a judge from another district (William Young, of the District of Massachusetts), so the Southern New York judge on the Second Circuit panel was not sitting in judgment on the ruling of a district court colleague. And in an appeal from the Southern District's bankruptcy court, the Southern New York judge on the Second Circuit panel was not sitting directly in judgment on a district court colleague, but bankruptcy judges are selected by the Circuit Council, which contains district judges as well as judges from the court of appeals.

There are also instances in which a panel as constructed included a Southern District of New York judge, for example, Denny Chin, who, by the time the opinion was filed, had been elevated to the Second Circuit Court of Appeals.[23] Even though one cannot easily say in this situation that the "*district judge* voted to affirm [reverse] the judge's own colleagues," yet when the panel was constructed, such judges were placed on panels that were then tasked with hearing cases from their own districts. For the same reason, also of concern are cases in which a Southern District of New York judge was placed on a panel but recused before decision in the case, leaving it to be decided by the two circuit judges who remained and constituted a quorum.[24] As the basis of the recusals is

---

[23] See, e.g., Penguin Group v. American Buddha, 640 F.3d 487 (2d Cir. 2011), and NY SMS Ltd. Partnership v. Town of Clarkston, 612 F.3d 97 (2d Cir. 2010).

[24] See, e.g., Capital Management Select Fund v. Bennett, 680 F.3d 214 (2d Cir. 2012) (Judge Rakoff), and United States v. Kozeny, 667 F.3d 122 (2d Cir. 2011) (Judge Bianco).

unknown, we cannot know if the district judge might have recused to avoid ruling on a decision by a district court colleague.

Reasons? It is unclear what would warrant such a high frequency of deviation from practices that are standard elsewhere. An occasional instance could result from a failure by the Clerk of Court staff to catch this type of match of judge and source of appeal, but the large number of instances argues against such explanation. Yet it is not apparent that what is evident is a matter of policy. The mechanism by which the panels and cases are matched for these particular cases is not known. Specifically asked if there were instructions to the Clerk's office to avoid the situation, the circuit's chief judge replied, "No, there isn't."[25] He did say that it was "not a practice to assign" judges to cases from their own districts, but it happened because cases are assigned to panels randomly. That explanation, however, seems unsatisfying.

Among various possible reasons for the high frequency of these occurrences, the most likely is geography, especially district judges' proximity to the seat of the court of appeals, and geography may be almost uniquely important in the Second Circuit. As another judge of that court of appeals reported,[26] the Second Circuit has "so many great SDNY [Southern District of New York] judges that we use them a lot." That is also true of the Second Circuit's use of judges from the Court of International Trade, "located across Foley Square from us." The chief judge acknowledged that district judges were most likely to come from the Southern and Eastern Districts of New York, not from the Northern and Western Districts of New York, because, when all the district judges are asked each year whether they want to sit with the court of appeals and for how many days, N.D.N.Y. and W.D.N.Y. judges find it convenient to sit for more than a couple of days, and as expenses must be watched, travel costs are added to the mix, which reinforces use of nearby rather than upstate district judges. Yet the use of "next door" judges, particularly when a district such as Southern New York—and its New York City neighbor, the Eastern District—generates many cases, increases the risk that district judges might sit on appeals from their own district, although that could occur even if a district judge's chambers were not adjacent to the court of appeals.

The recognition of geography as a major contributing factor does not, however, alter the existence of the problem and its prevalence. The chief

---

[25] Telephone conversation between Chief Judge Robert Katzmann (2d Cir.) and the author, September 22, 2015. Following references to the chief judge's comments are drawn from that conversation.

[26] Personal communication with a Second Circuit judge.

judge did report that, after the matter, including the above-noted data, was brought to his attention, he discussed it with court of appeals colleagues and some district judges who had sat with his court. He conceded that there might be "awkwardness" in passing judgment on one's colleagues, but he reported that judges told him that the situation "hasn't affected" them. The district judges told him it isn't personal and that colleagues understand that it is part of the process, and he said that newer district judges feel that the judges are all colleagues and that these cases come with the territory; even with some awkwardness, so that "at the end of the day," there aren't problems. However, it is interesting that, going beyond external appearances and internal awkwardness, the chief judge himself raised the possibility that if judges liked or disliked each other, it would be part of the problem. Yet he also said that the situation was no different from court of appeals judges having long-standing professional and personal relations with district judges.

Such responses, not received promptly, are unsatisfying. For one thing, comments by the district judges who have sat in cases from their own districts were responses to questions asked by *their circuit's chief judge* about their reactions to a practice that had been on-going, and one could surmise that their answers might well have been different if the question were put to them by someone not part of the court and definitely not at least a nominal "superior." Most important, the responses seem protective of "we've always done it this way," and, both surprising and more troubling, they seem to reflect a lack of awareness of other circuits' practices.

A Closer Look at Cases. If district judges sitting by designation participated only in cases on routine matters resulting in unanimous decisions affirming other district judges from the formers' home districts, the situation might not be especially problematic, perhaps apart from showing district judges to be too deferential to their own district court colleagues. Yet the subject matter of some of these cases is significant, such as post-9/11 litigation[27] and challenges to New York City's campaign finance rules.[28] This raises the question whether district judges should be

---

[27] For example, In re Terrorist Attacks on September 11, 2001 (Asat Trust Reg., et al.), 719 F.3d 659 (2d Cir. 2012) (Judges Cabranes, Raggi, and Rakoff (S.D.N.Y.)) (on jurisdictional discovery), plus two related cases. For a later instance, involving a suit over PLO terrorist attacks, in which the by-designation district judge wrote for the panel, see Waldman v. PLO, 835 F.3d 317 (2d Cir. 2016) ("Koeltl" [S.D.N.Y.] + Leval + Droney).

[28] Ognibene v. Parkes, 671 F.3d 174 (2d Cir. 2012) ("Crotty" + Calabresi + Livingston (i/p); "Calabresi"; "Livingston" (i/p + judgment)).

participating even in cases with unanimous affirmances, just as other circuits do not place them on capital appeals.

To obtain a clear picture of what happens when Southern District of New York judges sit on Second Circuit panels deciding cases from that district, some 200 cases from a roughly ten-year period, October, 2004-May, 2015, were examined. The panels in these cases more often affirmed in full (109 cases) than reversed or vacated in whole or in part (83 cases); 4 appeals were dismissed, the equivalent of at least a temporary affirmance, and 4 cases were certified to the New York Court of Appeals, the state's highest court.

In keeping with the low rates of disagreement associated with the U.S. courts of appeals, all cases except for a quite small number of published rulings were unanimous. (Unanimous affirmances were also the most common outcome in cases decided with non-precedential rulings.) There were only 19 opinions in which any judges on the panel did not fully join the majority opinion, plus 5 in which a judge wrote separately after joining the majority opinion in full. In cases in which the panels affirmed fully, the panels were unanimous in 99, to which should be added the decisions dismissing appeals and certifying cases. In only 3 of the cases affirming did the panel's district judge dissent, and only once did a district judge write a concurring opinion when the panel affirmed, but that judge also joined the majority opinion. In only 2 rulings affirming did a district judge join a circuit judge to form a majority against a dissenting circuit judge, and in 5 other such cases a circuit judge wrote a separate opinion concurring only in the judgment.

Unanimous affirmances are, however, not the only outcomes from these panels. For one thing, in a large proportion of the 200 cases (43.2%), the district court was not affirmed, which indicates that the presence on panels of district judges from the district whose ruling was being reviewed hardly precluded overturning the colleagues of the district judges sitting on the panels. There were periods when this was even more evident. In the 9 cases in 358-376 F.3d in which district judges sat in judgment in cases from their own districts, 5 resulted in reversals in whole or in part, and in 2 of the reversals, the district judge authored the panel's disposition.

In district judges' occasional dissents instead of joining the panel's two circuit judges, one sees evidence that the district judge has not deferred to judges of the appellate court, but it may say more, depending on the direction of the majority's judgment in the case. Where the court of appeals majority affirms the district court, dissent by the panel's district judge means that judge would reverse a district court colleague.[29] Conversely, and more importantly in terms of district judges' supposed deference to their colleagues, when a circuit judge panel majority has voted to reverse or vacate the district court's judgment, a dissent by the sitting district judge serves to uphold the work of that judge's district court colleague.[30]

Likewise, participation in unanimous reversals of the district court puts the district judge in the position of reversing a district colleague.[31] Reversals in part pose the same issue,[32] as do rulings affirming in part and vacating and remanding in part.[33] The same is true of cases in which the panel of two circuit judges and the district judge vacate and remand the district court ruling.[34] When the panel reversed or vacated in whole or in part, only twice did district judges dissent, which would have been a vote for affirming the judge's colleague. Among cases overturning the district court, the district judge joined a circuit judge in 6 to form a majority while the second circuit judge dissented, and in 3 of these 6 cases, the district judge wrote the opinion. There was only one reversal in which a district judge joined a circuit judge while the other circuit judge concurred only in the judgment.

Determinative Votes and Opinions. Issues concerning district judges' participation in the work of the court of appeals is most starkly confronted when those judges provide the determinative vote on a panel. A district judge has the "casting" (determinative) vote when the two circuit judges

---

[29] For example, Anditi v. Lighthouse International, 676 F.3d 294 (2d Cir. 2012) ("Chin" + Straub / "Preska" (S.D.N.Y,)); Enron Creditor Recovery Corp. v. Alta, 651 F.3d 329 (2d Cir. 2011) ("Walker" + Cabranes / "Koeltl" (S.D.N.Y.)).

[30] For example, Chesapeake Energy Corp. v. Bank of New York Mellon Trust, 773 F.3d 110 (2d Cir. 2014) (Fialla, J., S.D.N.Y., dissenting from reversal); UBS Financial Services v. West Virginia University Hospitals, 660 F.3d 643 (2d Cir. 2011) (Preska, J., S.D.N.Y., dissenting from a ruling vacating and remanding in part).

[31] See, for example, IRS v. World Com, 723 F.3d 346 (2d Cir. 2012) ("Katzmann"-Kearse-Rakoff (S.D.N.Y.)); Priestly v. Headminder, 647 F.3d 497 (2d Cir. 2011) (per curiam) (McLaughlin-Hall-Berman (S.D.N.Y.)); Highland Capital Management v. Schneider, 607 F.3d 322 (2d Cir. 2010) ("Leval"-Raggi-Cote (S.D.N.Y.)).

[32] For example, ACLU v. Dept. of Justice, 681 F.3d 61 (2d Cir. 2012) (Wesley-Carney-Cedarbaum (S.D.N.Y.)).

[33] For example, Novella v. Westchester County, 661 F.3d 129 (2d Cir. 2011) ("Sack"-Walker-Koeltl (S.D.N.Y.)) (statute of limitations problem).

[34] For example, Johnson v. Nextel Communications, 660 F.3d 131 (2d Cir. 2011) ("Winter"-Hall-Cedarbaum (S.D.N.Y.)); Stevenson v. Bank of New York County, 609 F.3d 56 (2d Cir. 2010) (Walker-Raggi-Rakoff (S.D.N.Y.)) (vacating and remanding to order remand to state court).

on the panel divide, with one dissenting.[35] In the 200 cases examined, there were 14 such cases—7 each in which the panel affirmed and in which it reversed lower court or agency. The district judge's vote on the opinion is also determinative when one of the circuit judges concurs only in the judgment[36] and in situations in which one of the panel's circuit judges did not participate in the decision, either because of recusal, even after the panel has been constituted, or departure, as when Judge Sotomayor was elevated to the Supreme Court. In those latter situations, the result is decision by a two-judge panel, permissible under quorum rules; in those situations, obviously a sitting district judge holds one of the two votes.[37]

Overall, Southern District of New York judges wrote opinions in one-fifth of all of the cases in which the Second Circuit panel on which they sat reviewed Southern District rulings, and, excluding per curiam dispositions where identifying the author is not possible, in 22.7% of all signed opinions, in which there were 17 affirmances and 7 decisions overruling the district court. The Southern District judges wrote opinions in 14 of the 103 signed opinions affirming their district court colleagues, but it is particularly significant that district judges were more likely to write for panels *not* fully upholding the district judge's colleagues. In 74 cases, the district judges wrote 19 opinions reversing in whole or in part (25.7%), while they did so in only 13.6% of the unanimous affirmances.

If one of the panel's two circuit judges writes the opinion, it is possible that the by-designation district judge went along out of deference to that judicial "superior." However, a district judge writing the panel's opinion reversing has brought disagreement with a district court colleague into the open.[38] Such instances show that, by neither taking the

---

[35] See, e.g., NRDC v. U.S. FDA, 760 F.3d 151 (2d Cir. 2014) ("Lynch" + Forrest (S.D.N.Y.) / "Katzmann" (dissenting)); Kwan v. Andalex Corp., 737 F.3d 834 (2d Cir. 2013) ("Koeltl" (S.D.N.Y.) + Lohier (+ Parker i/p); "Parker" (dissenting i/p)); HOP Energy v. Local 553 Pension Fund, 678 F.3d 157 (2d Cir. 2012) ("Wesley" + Sullivan (S.D.N.Y.) / "Jacobs" (dissenting)).

[36] For example, Townsend v. Benjamin Enterprises, 679 F.3d 41 (2d Cir. 2012) ("Koeltl" (S.D.N.Y.) + Livingston (+ Lohier i/p); "Lohier" (i/p + judgment)).

[37] See, e.g., Bryant v. Media Rights Production, 603 F.3d 135 (2d Cir. 2010) (decision by "Wood" (S.D.N.Y.) and Livingston). See also NY SMS Ltd. Partnership v. Town of Clarkston, 612 F.3d 97 (2d Cir. 2010) (decision by "McLaughlin" and Chin [district judge when panel composed]).

[38] See, for example, three cases in which S.D.N.Y. Judge Rakoff wrote for the panel reversing the judgment from his own district: Bayerische Landesbank v. Aladdin Capital Management, 692 F.3d 42 (2d Cir. 2012); SEC v. Gabelli, 653 F.3d 49 (2d Cir. 2011), rev'd, Gabelli v. SEC, 568 U.S. 442 (2013); and Applied Energetics v. Newark Capital Market, 645 F.3d 822 (2d Cir. 2011), and, for instances in which a district judge wrote for the panel in a partial reversal: MBIA v. Federal Insurance Co., 652 F.3d 152

assignment for themselves nor resorting to an unsigned per curiam disposition, the panel's circuit judges are also not attempting to "protect" the district judge. And, even if not writing for the panel, the district judge may join in language critical of the district court, as when a panel vacated and remanded "[b]ecause we find that mandatory abstention was required in these cases under the test we laid out in our prior opinion."[39]

Postscript. After the period studied, there was a decrease in the Second Circuit's use of its own district judges to assist in deciding cases. Thus there were fewer opportunities for such judges to sit in appeals from their own districts. If the duration of the problem described here had been brief, the decline in district judge use might indicate little more than cyclical variation. However, given the duration and extent of the problem, something else is likely to have been at work in the decline, although the court has made no statement on the subject. Did the court, once faced with the record facts, realize that there *was* a problem?

While it may have seemed that the problem had passed, that was most certainly not the case. In Second Circuit non-precedential rulings from the latter part of 2016 appearing in 661 Fed. Appx., an indication of district judges' lessened participation is that in only 4 of the 44 cases did a district judge sit on a Second Circuit panel. However, in *three of the four* cases, the district judges sitting with the court of appeals were from the district from which the appeal had been taken.[40] Shortly thereafter, in 6 more non-precedential rulings, panels containing a Southern District of New York judge reviewed 4 cases from that district, and panels with an Eastern District judge reviewed 2 cases from that district.[41] Here a simple

---

(2d Cir. 2011) (Preska, J.); and L-7 Designs v. Old Navy, 647 F.3d 419 (2d Cir. 2011) (Scheindlin, J.).

[39] Parmalat Capital Finances v. Bank of America, 671 F.3d 261, 264 (2d Cir. 2012) (Cabranes-Wesley-Koeltl (S.D.N.Y.)). The earlier opinion, Judge Wesley writing for the same panel, is at 639 F.3d 572 (2d Cir. 2011).

[40] National Railroad Passenger Corp v. Aspen Specialty Insurance Co., 661 Fed. Appx. 12 (2d Cir. 2016), panel of G. Lynch-Carney-Hellerstein (S.D.N.Y.), appeal from S.D.N.Y. (Rakoff, J.); United States v. Lasher, 661 Fed. Appx. 25 (2d Cir. 2016), panel same, appeal from S.D.N.Y. (Buchwald, J.); and Empire State Carpenters Welfare v. Conway Construction of Ithaca, 661 Fed. Appx. 97 (2d Cir. 2016), panel of Leval-Lohier-Korman (E.D.N.Y.), appeal from E.D.N.Y. (Hurley, J.).

[41] Sikhs for Justice v. Kerry, 663 Fed. Appx. 34 (2d Cir. 2016), panel of Chin-Carney-Berman (S.D.N.Y.) reviewing decision by Swain (S.D.N.Y.); In re Helman Brothers Holdings, 663 Fed. Appx. 65 (2d Cir. 2016), panel of Chin-Carney-Forrest reviewing ruling by Ramos (S.D.N.Y.); Mohammad Ladjevardian v. Republic of Argentina, 663 Fed. Appx. 77 (2d Cir. 2016), panel of Chin-Carney-Forrest (S.D.N.Y.), reviewing decision by Griesa (S.D.N.Y.); Salveson v. J.P. Morgan Chase & Co., 663 Fed. Appx. 71 (2d Cir. 2016), panel of Chin-Carney-Cogan (E.D.N.Y.), reviewing ruling by Gleeson and Brodie (E.D.N.Y.); Thomas v. TXX Services, 663 Fed. Appx. 86 (2d Cir. 2016), panel of Chin-Carney-Cogan (E.D.N.Y.) reviewing ruling by Feuerstein (E.D.N.Y.). See

switch of district judges joining the same two Second Circuit judges would have avoided some of the difficulty.[42] Other problem cases from Eastern and Southern New York were to follow.[43] Nor was the problem restricted to non-precedential rulings. In two published Second Circuit opinions in 2017, district judges were found to have sat on panels reviewing cases from their own districts,[44] with one of those cases major antitrust litigation. The appearance of the problem in published-opinion cases could be said to be more serious because of the possible effects on circuit precedent of such district judge review of colleagues. With relatively little overall use of district judges, to have them sit in cases from their own districts can only exhibit a "we don't care" attitude on the court's part, something unworthy of any court of appeals but especially a leading one.

* * *

When, to contend with growing caseloads, U.S. courts of appeals bring district judges from within the circuit to sit with them, they create the possibility that those judges will hear cases from the very districts to which they were appointed. This is considered counter to "best practice," because of the risk that the relationship between a district judge and a district court colleague whose decisions the first judge is evaluating will create a conflict of interest or produce friction with colleagues.

---

also Genger v Genger, 663 Fed. Appx. 44 (2d Cir. 2016), panel of Jacobs-Livingston-Rakoff (S.D.N.Y.), reviewing decision by Forrest (S.D.N.Y.).

[42] With Second Circuit Judges Chin and Carney common to several cases, switching Southern District Judges Berman and Forrest for Eastern District Judge Cogan would have avoided having judges sit in cases from their own districts.

[43] From the Eastern District: Stern v. City of New York, 665 Fed. Appx. 27 (2d Cir. 2016), panel of Livingston-Lohier-Amon (E.D.N.Y.), reviewing decision by Garaufis (E.D.N.Y.); and Choudhury v. Hemze Express Food Corp., 666 Fed. Appx. 59 (2d Cir. 2016), panel of Leval-Lohier-Korman (E.D.N.Y.), reviewing decision by Magistrate Judge Mann (E.D.N.Y.). From the Southern District: Heller v. Bedford Central School District, 665 Fed. Appx. 49 (2d Cir. 2016), panel of Jacobs-Livingston-Rakoff (S.D.N.Y.), reviewing Forrest (S.D.N.Y.); In re Lehr Construction Corp./Flaxer v. Gifford, 666 Fed. Appx. 66 (2d Cir. 2016), panel of Katzmann-Winter-Stein (S.D.N.Y.), reviewing G. Woods (S.D.N.Y.); DeSarrolladona Farallon S. De R.L. de C.V. v. Cargill Financial Services International, 66 Fed. Appx. 17 (2d Cir. 2016), panel of Livingston-Lohier-Rakoff (S.D.N.Y.), reviewing decision by Scheindlin (S.D.N.Y.); In re DNTN Chartered Accountant Securities Litigation, 666 Fed. Appx.78 (2d Cir. 2016), panel of Katzmann-Winter-Stein (S.D.N.Y.), reviewing decision by Gardephe (S.D.N.Y.).

If *Federal Appendix* is to be believed, there is even a case from the Southern District, decided by Judge Jed Rakoff, reviewed by a Second Circuit panel on which Judge Rakoff himself sat, although the use of "by designation" seems to suggest a publishing error. See Dougan v. New York City Department of Education, 665 Fed. Appx. 55 (2d Cir. 2016).

[44] In re Actos End-Payor Antitrust Litigation, 848 F.3d 89 (2d Cir. 2017), panel of "Rakoff" (S.D.N.Y.)-Jacobs-Lynch.

This possibility does not materialize in most circuits, either because the courts of appeals make minimal use of such judges or act to avoid the situation. On the Second Circuit Court of Appeals, however, district judges, especially from the Southern and Eastern Districts of New York, not infrequently sit on cases from their own districts, even in the more important cases resolved by opinions creating circuit precedent. How this state of affairs came about is unclear, although it is partly a result of the proximity of these two large districts to the circuit's headquarters where appellate argument is heard. Whatever the origins, despite the negative reaction of observers elsewhere it seems to continue unabated and without question despite the potential awkwardness of, for example, a newly-appointed district judge sitting in judgment on a ruling by a quite senior judge from the former's own court. The data from a large set of cases suggest that district judges reviewing cases from their own districts do not hesitate to participate in reversing their colleagues in whole or in part almost half the time and even write opinions directly overturning those colleagues, and while the Second Circuit's practice remains a "problem" in the eyes of many involved in court administration, it is, despite these observers' concerns, apparently not so viewed by the judges involved.

7

WHO MAKES THE LAW OF THE CIRCUIT?

Questions at the core of normative concerns about use of non-regular judges are finally addressed in this chapter. Those questions are related to "Who makes the circuit's precedent?" Is it the court's own judges, active or senior, or the circuit's district judges and out-of-circuit visitors? If the latter types of judges are used in only a small proportion of cases, it might seem obvious that their effect would not be great, perhaps reducing concerns about their participation, but even a single significant ruling by a visitor can affect the direction of circuit law.

A recent instance of such a ruling occurred in the Ninth Circuit. In an insider trading case, the Second Circuit had ruled that something more than a close relationship between tipper and tippee was necessary to create insider trading liability.[1] Among those highly critical of that ruling was Judge Jed Rakoff of the Southern District of New York. Then Judge Rakoff came to the Ninth Circuit as a visiting judge and, as it happened, was on a panel that raised the same question. He wrote for the panel, holding that a close tipper-tippee relationship was sufficient.[2] In creating an inter-circuit split, the Ninth Circuit, through Judge Rakoff, had set things up for the Supreme Court to take the issue. The justices did grant review to the Ninth Circuit's ruling and affirmed it,[3] thus allowing Judge Rakoff as a visiting judge to overturn his own circuit's position.

That is, however, not the only instance in which a visiting judge may have played a role in a Supreme Court ruling. In another example, two Ninth Circuit judges on a panel adopted the position that Fannie Mae could remove a case brought in state courts to federal court, which would then have jurisdiction.[4] However, the third panel member, Judge Sidney Stein, visiting from the Southern District of New York (also Judge Rakoff's district) dissented, indicating that there was no such federal court jurisdiction. The Supreme Court, while somewhat criticizing Judge Stein's interpretation of a rule, sided with him.[5] While Judge Rakoff's

---

[1] United States v. Newman, 773 F.3d 438 (2d Cir. 2014).

[2] United States v. Salman, 792 F.3d 1087 (9th Cir. 2015).

[3] Salman v. United States, 137 S. Ct. 420 (2016).

[4] Lightfoot v. Cendant Mortgage Corp., 769 F.3d 681 (9th Cir. 2014).

[5] Lightfoot v. Cendant Mortgage Corp., 137 S. Ct. 553 (2017).

ruling had created an inter-circuit split, in this situation such a split already existed, with the Ninth Circuit decision placing three circuits on each side of the issue. Nonetheless, while Judge Stein did not create a circuit split, his dissent certainly would have raised a signal to the Supreme Court to accept a case—this case—involving such an inter-circuit conflict.

There was an earlier similar instance in which a separate opinion by a judge visiting the Ninth Circuit had implications for a Supreme Court ruling. In a case on the application of Regulation Z under the Truth in Lending Act, a Ninth Circuit panel majority held the regulation applicable, but Seventh Circuit Judge Richard Cudahy dissented.[6] At roughly the same time, a Seventh Circuit panel, of which Judge Cudahy was not a member, disagreed with the Ninth Circuit's reasoning. The Ninth Circuit ruling had created a circuit split with yet another circuit, leading the Supreme Court to take and unanimously reverse the Ninth Circuit case, thus in effect upholding Judge Cudahy's dissent, from which Justice Sotomayor quoted.[7]

As the Judge Stein and Judge Cudahy examples indicate, there are cases in which visitors have written separate concurring opinions or have dissented, also important to show that they don't simply "go along," even though such concurring and dissenting opinions are of less significance for the law of the visited circuit than when the visitor writes for the court. And, although visiting judges' opinions pose the issue most starkly, they are not all that may matter, because their votes may be determinative in a divided three-judge panel. In a recent instance which received attention, a visiting judge was a member of a panel in a case on Amazon's search results. In the panel's first ruling, the visiting judge joined a Ninth Circuit judge to form a majority which went against Amazon. Then, granting Amazon's petition for rehearing, the panel changed course and ruled in Amazon's favor. The visiting judge, Gordon Quist of the Western District of Michigan, did not write opinions either time, but he did change his vote, which was the key one, between the initial ruling and the ultimate one, so the alignment moved from "Bea" + Quist / "Silverman," to "Silverman" + Quist / "Bea."[8]

The importance of the presence of a visiting judge can be seen in another important case, on the question of warrantless use of heat-monitoring devices to detect the presence of a marijuana "grow" in a

---

[6] McCoy v. Chase Bank USA, 559 F.3d 963 (9th Cir. 2009).

[7] Chase Bank USA v. McCoy, 562 U.S. 195 (2011).

[8] Multi Time Machine v. Amazon.com, 792 F.3d 1070 (9th Cir. 2015), on rehearing, 809 F.3d 930 (9th Cir. 2015).

dwelling. A visiting judge had authored the opinion for a divided panel but was replaced for a superseding opinion in the case. (This is perhaps an indication that visitors cannot easily return to the visited court for further developments in a case.) The result of the switch of judges was that the outcome changed. The judge who had joined the initial opinion by the visitor now dissented, but his view was upheld when the case went to the Supreme Court, which ruled the search unconstitutional. In the original opinion, Judge John Noonan joined Judge Robert Mehrige (E.D. Virginia), who wrote for the majority, with Judge Michael Daly Hawkins dissenting. The superseding opinion was written by Judge Hawkins, joined by Judge Melvin Brunetti, who had replaced Judge Mehrige, and Judge Noonan dissented.[9]

In looking at the participation of non-regular judges on court of appeals panels in relation to "Who makes the circuit's precedent?," the concern is that these other judges, even if they sit with the court with some regularity, are not, nor have they been, regular members of the court. This is part of the normative argument opposing courts' use of these "other" judges, based on the premise that, even if caseload requires such use, only a court of appeals' own judges should be writing the law of the circuit, and these "other" judges should not participate. Using them is said to risk having the law of the circuit, which a court of appeals establishes through the court's published opinions, made at least in part by these judges. The notion is that somehow decisions in which "other" judges take part count for less than those by "regular" appellate judges.[10]

This normative position makes suspect a panel not containing three of a circuit's own appellate judges. Yet, given that in some circuits, "other" judges participate with some frequency, it is not uncommon there for a panel to contain only one active-duty judge, making determinative the votes of the court's own senior judges and of "other" judges. To be avoided are situations like those in which a panel includes an out-of-circuit visitor (especially if writing the opinion) joined by a senior circuit judge, with the

---

9 United States v. Kyllo, 140 F.3d 1249 (9th Cir. 1999), superseded by 190 F.3d 1041 (9th Cir. 1999), rev'd, 533 U.S. 27 (2001), order on remand, 258 F.3d 1004 (9th Cir. 2001).

10 The Shepard's Citation system can be used to determine whether cases decided by visiting judges were later cited more or less positively than those decided by a court of appeals' own judges. Budziak has recently reported that rulings in which out-of-circuit judges participate result in more negative treatments in later cases, both in the circuit in which the cases were decided and in other circuits, than is true of panels of all in-circuit appellate judges. This finding does not repeat for cases in which in-circuit district judges participate. See Budziak, "The Effect of Visiting Judges on the Development of Legal Policy in the U.S. Courts of Appeals."

one active-duty judge in dissent, or when two active circuit judges disagree and a visiting judge or district judge provides the deciding vote.

The specific instances which began this chapter involved out-of-circuit visitors. When there is a divided panel and a visiting judge casts the deciding vote, it most directly raises the question of whether another circuit—or certainly a judge of another circuit—is making the law of the visited circuit, so concern is highest. The effect of out-of-circuit visitors on the visited circuit's jurisprudence is thought to be particularly troubling, especially when the visitor casts the decisive vote in a divided panel. Other circuits' judges—whether from the court of appeals or district courts—are thought naturally to be familiar with the law of the circuit in which they reside but to be unfamiliar with the law of the visited circuit. It is feared that the visitors will bring the law of their circuit in their flight bag and will import it, or attempt to inflict it, on the colleagues they are visiting in preference to the law of the visited circuit, thus violating the strong expectation that they apply the visited circuit's precedent and perhaps prompting changes in the visited circuit's doctrine. However, this fear is soundly rejected by many judges on receiving courts, as when a judge specifically asked about visitors importing their law said, "Not a problem. And their law clerks do all the research anyhow." This is a recognition of the ease of finding up-to-date circuit precedent electronically, although in pre-WESTLAW days, identifying other circuits' current cases was more difficult.

While visiting judges pose the greatest concern, having in-circuit district judges cast dispositive votes or write opinions that make circuit precedent is also thought problematic. While they can be said to be "a judge of the circuit," even if not of the court of appeals, and to have become familiar with the circuit's doctrine by having applied it in their district court rulings, the argument is that they have been confirmed *as district judges*, not as court of appeals judges, much less those with appellate authority over other district court judges, and thus they should remain on the district court.

There are somewhat related, if less serious, concerns about use of the court's own senior judges, whose participation is discussed in the next chapter. The concern is that having a court of appeals' own senior judges sit on panels makes those panels unrepresentative of the entire court, but their presence is thought less troubling because they had been active judges on the court and moved seamlessly to senior status. Nonetheless, concerns about their presence may make somewhat suspect a ruling in which they have participated.

"Who writes the law of the circuit?" is also related to the nomination and confirmation of U.S. courts of appeals judges, especially with the recent increasingly drawn-out and contentious nature of the process.[11] Despite the attention given to the process of nomination and particularly confirmation, almost nothing is written about the effect of the confirmed nominations on the new judges' courts. Perhaps it is assumed that new judges will have an immediate effect, but such effects are not likely to be immediate, and considerable time may pass before their presence is felt. Only when a new appointee participates in cases resulting in the courts' published opinions, can that judge affect the law of the circuit. Many months may elapse before the release of an opinion in a case to which a new judge has been assigned, and in some courts, new judges, rather than being immediately assigned a full caseload, may be eased into their work, for example, at first sitting as a non-voting fourth judge and having only a partial calendar for a couple of months,[12] all of which makes their effect less immediate.

Further limiting a new judge's possible effects on the law of the circuit is courts of appeals' substantial use of non-precedential ("unpublished") dispositions. Substantial use by circuits of judges borrowed from other circuits and from the circuit's own districts also can reduce the effect of new active-duty circuit judges. A larger reason, however, is that many of each court's senior judges undertake nearly a full caseload and thus are assigned to as many cases as the court's active judges, including the most recent appointees. Thus, as will be seen later about the appointment of four new judges to the D.C. Circuit, that court's senior judges continued to account for a high proportion of judge sittings.

Who Decides: Data and Dater [13]

Attention will now be paid to authoring of opinions by visiting judges and district judges and to whether those judges' votes are determinative in the cases in which they sit; both constitute direct evidence of "other" judges (which can include senior circuit judges: see Chapter 8) making circuit precedent. This may provide only a partial answer to the questions

---

[11] See the excellent accounts in, for example, Elliot Slotnick, Sara Schiavoni, and Sheldon Goldman, "Writing the Book of Judges: Part I: Obama's Judicial Appoints Record After Six Years," 3 Journal of Law and Courts 331 (2015), and "Part II: "Confirmation Politics in the 113th Congress," 4 Journal of Law and Courts 187 (2016).

[12] See Stephen L. Wasby, "Into the Soup? The Acclimation of Ninth Circuit Appellate Judges," 73 Judicature 10 (June-July 1989).

[13] As the author lives in New England, a New England pronunciation (think JFK) has to be included.

posed because, while "other" judges' participation is a necessary condition for their effect on the law of the circuit, it is not always a sufficient one, which requires their playing a role in developing the substantive content of court of appeals legal doctrine through suggested revisions to proposed opinions.

To be examined here are several U.S. courts of appeals which make considerable use of "other" judges; set aside are those courts which, as a matter of policy or practice, make very little use of "other" judges. The primary focus is on the nation's largest federal appellate court, the U.S. Court of Appeals for the Ninth Circuit, with attention also devoted to the First, Sixth, and Eleventh Circuits. Thus, the smallest U.S. court of appeals and two mid-sized courts are included, providing some variation in the types of non-regular judges used.

Making a Difference. Participation is one thing, but have visitors and district judges made a difference when they sat? This question is related to having the law of the circuit made by the circuit's own appellate judges. It is evident that, at times, non-regular judges engage in disputation with their panel colleagues before a disposition is released, indicating that they are not simply ciphers "filling in" for a regular active circuit judge.[14] An example of a visitor's involvement in decision-making came in an exchange among panel members when the visiting judge on the panel questioned a proposed disposition: "I believe the second sentence of the last paragraph lacks the necessary precision to be a correct statement of Ninth Circuit law." He added that while, "[a]s an invited guest, I am sensitive to conforming to Ninth Circuit customary practice," he was "very uncomfortable reversing another Article III judge without a single citation to controlling precedent or any authoritative case law."[15] Likewise, in a pre-argument communication, a visitor suggested that a case *not* be submitted on the briefs because "the parties are asking the Panel to interpret certain statements made by the district judge during the sentencing hearing. Each side is claiming a different legal significance to those statements. I believe a discussion with counsel would help clarify

---

[14] See the treatment of a visiting judge by a reporter who wrote that the author of an opinion was "joined by two other George W. Bush appointees: 9th Circuit Judge Sandra Ikuta and 8th Circuit Judge Michael J. Melloy, who was *filling in*." Maura Dolan, "Nativity ban is upheld: Federal appeals panel says Santa Monica law does not violate free speech rights," Los Angeles Times, May 4, 2015, p. B3 (emphasis supplied). A senior district judge who sat frequently with the Ninth Circuit said he was there "only to supply a mule to a shorthanded team." Interview with Judge William G. East (D. Oregon), Los Angeles, February 28, 1977.

[15] Mark Bennett (N.D. Iowa), memorandum to panel, July 24, 2010, *re*: D'Angelo v. Winter, 403 Fed. Appx. 181 (9th Cir. 2010).

the differing interpretations";[16] he later suggested changes in the author's proposed memorandum disposition, "in light of the concessions made at oral argument."[17]

Identifying the effects of non-regular judges on a court's opinion is difficult, as it requires access to post-argument conference exchanges among the judges or to changes a visitor suggests to a proposed opinion, but their determinative votes can be identified, although one must keep in mind that the "casting" vote of a visiting judge or by-designation district judge may or may not make a real difference in circuit precedent on a particular point, something that requires further exploration but is outside the scope of the present inquiry. A further complication is that one knows only the final vote recorded on the filed disposition, not whether the judge may have waffled in his or her vote during resolution of the case.

Non-regular judges' determinative votes occur when a panel splits 2-1 and the visiting or district judge is in the majority, and when the panel's result is unanimous but the visitor or a district judge supports the court's opinion while an appeals court judge concurs only in the judgment. Neither situation occurs often because rate of dissent in U.S. courts of appeals cases is low, and separate concurrences in the judgment are rare. Non-regular judges' votes are also determinative when two such judges, for example, a visiting judge and a within-circuit district judge, sit on the same case,[18] or, in a circuit with a judicial emergency, two district judges sit with one circuit judge, as has occurred with some frequency in the Eleventh Circuit.[19] A non-regular judge's vote is also determinative in

---

[16] Jack Zouhary (N.D. Ohio), memorandum to panel, September 19, 2012, re: United States v. Flores-Cortes, 499 Fed. Appx. 683 (9th Cir. 2012).

[17] Zouhary, memorandum to panel, November 15, 2012, re: *Flores-Cortes*.

[18] See Fantini v. Salem State College, 557 F.3d 22 (1st Cir. 2009) ("Dominguez" (D.P.R.)-Dyk (Fed.Cir.)-Boudin)); F.T.C. v. IAB Marketing Associates, 746 F.3d 1228 (11th Cir. 2014), and Osorio v. State Farm Bank,746 F.3d 1242 (11th Cir. 2014), both with Judges Ronald Gilman of the Sixth Circuit and Judge Inge Prytz Johnson of Northern Alabama sitting with the Eleventh Circuit's Judge R. Lanier Anderson; and Caldwell v. Warden, 748 F.3d 1090 (11th Cir. 2014), in which the court's Judge Frank Hull was joined by Judge Richard Goldberg (Court of International Trade) and C. Lynwood Smith of Middle Alabama.

It is relevant to note that two circuits create panels to facilitate having new circuit judges preside over the panel. Marin Levy, "Panel Assignment in the Federal Courts of Appeals," 102 Cornell L. Rev. 65, 87 (2017). A problem in such arrangements is that the presiding judge on a panel must be its most senior active judge. However, if the presiding judge is to be a new active circuit judge, the other panel members must be drawn from the circuit's senior judges, from district judges, or from visiting judges. Id. at 69.

[19] PSINet v. Chapman, 362 F.3d 227 (4th Cir. 2004) ("Spencer" (E.D. Va.)-Davis (D.

cases decided by only two judges, who constitute a quorum after a third panel member's recusal (or death), and one of the two is a non-regular judge.[20] Non-regular judges would also have the determinative votes in instances when, after recusals, the Chief Justice sends judges from other circuits to decide the case, and these visitors are obviously writing the circuit's law. As noted earlier, a full three-judge panel from the Third Circuit heard a Second Circuit case and judges from three circuits decided a Third Circuit case.[21]

In cases in the present study, in only a small number of instances are non-regular judges' votes determinative, even as a proportion of all cases in which such judges participate, and it is nearly infinitesimal as a proportion of all court of appeals cases. For example, in the Fourth Circuit, district judges cast the determinative vote in 11.3% of the cases in which they participated, but this amounted to only 1.8% of the court's published opinions. Likewise, while visiting judges cast determinative votes in 5.8% of Third Circuit cases in which they participated, non-regular judges cast such votes in only 0.9% of all cases. Instances of non-regular judges casting a determinative vote are almost nil in several other circuits, for example, taking place in only one of 93 Eighth Circuit cases with non-regular judges, which is one of 1,142 total cases. Likewise, in the Tenth Circuit, there was one such vote in 32 cases with district judges—one of 632 total cases. The two Fifth Circuit cases in which district judges cast determinative votes out of 55 cases in which they participated (3.3%) accounted for only 0.3% of the circuit's total published output.

Even in circuits with considerably more visiting judge or district judge determinative votes, in no circuit can it be said that these determinative votes were cast in a substantial proportion of cases. In the Sixth Circuit, such votes occur in 4.3% of the cases in which visiting judges participate and in 7.7% of those in which district judges participate, yet the overall proportion is only 3.4%. Not even in the Ninth Circuit, where critics have particularly questioned participation by non-regular judges, does the

---

Md.) / "Niemeyer"); Packard v. Commissioner of Internal Revenue, 746 F.3d 1219 (11th Cir.) ("Wilson"-Bucklew (M.D. Fla.)-Lazzara (M.D. Fla.)).

[20] See American General Life Ins. Co. v. Schoenthal Family, 555 F.3d 1331 (11th Cir. 2009) ("Pryor" + Strom (D. Neb.)), and two Second Circuit cases: Trust for the Certificate Holders of the Merrill Lynch Mortgage Investors v. Love Funding Corp., 556 F.3d 100 (2d Cir. 2009) ("Raggi" + Keenan (S.D.N.Y.) (Judge Calabresi recused)), and Nakahata v. New York-Presbyterian Healthcare System, 723 F.3d 193 (2d Cir. 2013), where Chief Judge Donald Pogue of the Court of International Trade sat with Second Circuit Judge Raymond Lohier (Judge Debra Livingston recused).

[21] Dongguk University v. Yale University, 734 F.3d 113 (2d Cir. 2013) (Judges Fuentes, Smith, and Fisher); Common Cause of Pennsylvania v. Pennsylvania, 558 F.3d 249 (3d Cir. 2009) (Judges Ebel (10th Cir.), Flaum (7th Cir.), and Leval (2d Cir.)).

proportion of all court of appeals published opinion cases in which a non-regular judge casts a determinative vote exceed 5%. Only 2.1% of all cases examined reveal such votes, with the highest proportion, 4.4%, in a recent case set (765-783 F.3d) and the lowest a fraction of one percent (0.3%).[22] Looking only at cases in which non-regular judges participated, the proportion in which they cast determinative votes—8.4%—does not exceed 10%, with the lowest proportion in the first case set (3.4%) and the highest (12.4%) in the most recent set.

Among cases in which non-regular judges cast determinative votes, there are some instances in which a resident judge and a visitor, or a resident judge and district judge, formed a majority. First Circuit Judge Juan Torruella and Northern California Judge William Schwarzer twice constituted a majority, once against a dissent, the other time against a separate concurring opinion.[23] In the Fourth Circuit, Eastern Virginia Judge T. S. Ellis III and circuit Judge Paul Niemeyer formed majorities in two cases against Fourth Circuit Judge Karen Williams, with Judge Ellis writing for the panel in one case, Judge Niemeyer doing so in the other.[24] Judge Ellis also joined Judge Roger Gregory to create such a majority in another case and Judge Clyde Hamilton in still another.[25] In the Third Circuit, Judge Ruggero Aldisert was joined in one case by visiting Judge Jane Restani from the Court of International Trade and in another by Judge Leonard Stark of the District of Delaware to create majorities over dissents by another Third Circuit judge.[26] Eleventh Circuit Judge Frank Hull was joined by Southern District of Georgia Judge Dudley Bowen, Jr., to form a majority over Judge Beverly Martin's opinions concurring in part and dissenting in part.[27]

---

[22] The proportion in the initial case set, 358-376 F.3d, was only 0.8%.

[23] United States v. Hilton, 363 F.3d 58 (1st Cir. 2004), Judge Jeffrey Howard concurring in the judgment, and United States v. Textron Inc. & Subsidiaries, 553 F.3d 87 (1st Cir. 2009), in which Judge Michael Boudin concurred in part and dissented in part. *Textron* was reheard en banc, 577 F.3d 21 (1st Cir. 2009), so the visiting judge did not play a part in the ultimate result, but that judge's presence on the divided panel may have contributed to the court's rehearing the case en banc (on that point, see Chapter 9).

[24] Nianz v. Gonzales, 492 F.3d 505 (4th Cir. 2007), and BellSouth Telecommunications v. Sanford, 494 F.3d 439 (4th Cir. 2007).

[25] United States v. Dews, 551 F.3d 204 (4th Cir. 2008), Judge G. Steven Agee dissenting, and United States v. Roseboro, 551 F.3d 226 (4th Cir. 2009), Judge Niemeyer dissenting.

[26] Sun Wen Chen v. Attorney General, 491 F.3d 100 (3d Cir. 2007), where Judge Theodore McKee concurred in part and dissented in part, and Drake v. Filko, 724 F.3d 426 (3d Cir. 2013), in which Judge Thomas Hardiman dissented.

[27] Bryant v. Warden, 738 F.3d 1253 (11th Cir. 2013), and Mackey v. Warden, 739 F.3d 657 (11th Cir. 2014).

The Sixth Circuit, with its considerable use of district judges, had three of these instances. In one, Judge James Gwin of the Northern District of Ohio wrote for himself and Judge Gilbert Merritt of the Sixth Circuit, with that court's Judge Anne Batchelder dissenting; Judge R. Allen Edgar (E.D. Tennessee) joined Sixth Circuit Judge David McKeague over dissents by Judge Deborah Cook; and Judge Arthur Tarnow of Eastern Michigan joined Judge Karen Nelson Moore to form majorities in two cases over dissents by another resident Sixth Circuit judge.[28] By contrast, the Ninth Circuit, in which there were also many instances in which a visiting judge or by-designation district judge cast the determinative vote, all instances appear to be "one-off."

Authoring Opinions. Whether visiting judges or in-circuit district judges write the published opinions that constitute circuit precedent is at least as important as their determinative votes. Serving as an author does not directly follow from a judge's sitting on a panel because the circuit judges might assign fewer cases to the "other" judges, especially to district judges who must attend to their own dockets once they return to their chambers. In the normal course, each judge on a three-judge panel is assigned preparation of dispositions in one-third of a panel's cases. Most of those dispositions are non-precedential, and they are helpful in clearing the docket, but it is published opinions that are crucial as circuit precedent.

Overall, judges visiting the Ninth Circuit wrote for the panel in one-fifth (19.1%) of the published-opinion cases in which they participated; that rate is depressed to the extent that the court uses per curiam rulings, which, although "through the court" are in fact usually prepared by one judge but one whose identity is not made public. That "less than par" authorship in the Ninth Circuit might be even less but for the court's use of shared bench memoranda, one-third of which each panel member's chambers prepares for circulation to the other panel members. As the judge whose chambers prepare a bench memo usually receives the assignment to write the disposition, a non-regular judge would already have the materials, in bench memo form, from which an opinion could more easily be prepared.

The Ninth Circuit proportion is less than the one-third (34.3%) found in the Sixth Circuit but roughly the same as the 18.8% found in the

---

[28] Haus v. Bechtel Jacobs Co., 491 F.3d 557 (6th Cir. 2007) and Matovski v. Gonzales, 492 F.3d 722 (6th Cir. 2007); United States v. Garcia, 496 F.3d 517 (6th Cir. 2007), and United States v. Pritchett, 496 F.3d 537 (6th Cir. 2007); and United States v. Bailey, 553 F.3d 940 (6th Cir. 2009), Judge Richard Griffin dissenting, and United States v. Shafer, 557 F.3d 440 (6th Cir. 2009), Judge Helene White dissenting.

Eleventh Circuit. Overall, variation across the case sets is within the relatively narrow range of 20-30 percent. Except for the Sixth Circuit, these proportions, less than one-third, are higher than the low proportion some judges suggested in interviews. In the Ninth Circuit, district judges accounted for a slightly higher proportion of panels' published opinions than did the visiting judges—27.7% v. 23.3%—and variation was greater for them than for visiting judges, as district judges wrote in almost the expected one-third of such cases in one set (32.3%, 720-735 F.3d) and almost that much in another (31.0%, 358-376 F.3d), but they wrote as few as 13.3% of their cases in another set (550-562 F.3d). Among circuits making substantial use of their district judges in published opinion dispositions, the Ninth Circuit proportion of 27.7% falls in the middle, well below the First Circuit's 41.2%, slightly below the 30.9% for the Seventh Circuit, which had only recently resumed use of in-circuit district judges; and greater than in the Sixth and Eleventh Circuits (23.8% and 22.2%, respectively).

Separate Opinions. Even if dissents and separate concurring opinions may not much affect circuit precedent, or at least are less central to it than opinions for a panel majority, the fact that visiting judges and district judges write them is important. Just as in undertaking something close to writing their share of opinions for the panel, "other" judges do not always take a back seat at the panel but are at times willing to state their views in writing when those differ from those of the visited circuit's judges. At times they simply object to the outcome in a case or perhaps they use a somewhat different rationale to reach the same result as did their colleagues. And at times, and more importantly, even while agreeing that existing circuit precedent compels the result, they may wish to point the law in a different direction. Visitors' disagreement with panel colleagues does not appear only in separate opinions, but can—indeed, may be more likely to—appear in intra-panel communication leading up to a final opinion, as noted earlier.

No more than 20 dissents were filed by non-regular judges in the Ninth Circuit cases in this study; they were written by 13 visiting judges (7 circuit, 5 district[29]) and 4 Ninth Circuit district judges. The visitors' dissents might reveal nothing unusual, as when Eighth Circuit Judge Myron Bright dissented in a habeas appeal on the basis of evaluating the evidence differently,[30] but visitors did produce quite extensive dissents and make telling points. In a Truth in Lending Act case about a retroactive

---

[29] One visiting district judge, Lynn Adelman (E.D. Wisconsin), wrote two dissenting opinions.

[30] Murdoch v. Castro, 489 F.3d 1083 (9th Cir. 2007).

interest rate increase, Seventh Circuit Judge Richard Cudahy, a not-infrequent Ninth Circuit visitor, said, "Before addressing the myriad arguments made by the majority, it would be helpful to put matters in context" by pointing out that claims the plaintiff and usually some of the same attorneys made had led to opposite results in other forums, including a Ninth Circuit case.[31] In a challenge to Environmental Protection Agency decisions, Judge Lynn Adelman (E.D. Wisconsin) agreed with the majority opinion's granting the review petition and remanding to the EPA but, in dissenting from another part, argued that finding that one agency determination was not supported by substantial evidence meant that the EPA had not shown another determination was so supported. The judge, criticizing majority overreach, wrote to "disagree with the majority's decision to comment on the other issues" petitioner had raised.[32] And another dissent by a visiting district judge that is worthy of note came in the Federal Tort Claims Act case by Jaycee Dugard after her kidnapping by a parolee. The panel majority affirmed the ruling of the trial court that no case would lie, but Chief District Judge William Smith of Rhode Island dissented, "differ[ing] with the majority's conclusions that the law does not allow her" a day in federal court, even though in taking that position, he was voting to reverse the Ninth Circuit judge, Carlos Bea, who had been the trial judge in this case.[33]

Dissents by a circuit's own district judges on the whole have not been much different from those by visiting judges, ranging from evaluating the facts differently from the majority to differing about the law. For example, when a panel majority held that the trial judge lacked subject-matter jurisdiction to hear the government's motion to set aside the District of Montana district judges' standing order to the U.S. Attorney to gather information under the PROTECT Act; the district judge sitting by designation disagreed over jurisdiction and would have upheld the order.[34] And in a partial dissent over whether there should be arbitration under

---

[31] McCoy v. Chase National Bank, 559 F.3d 963, 973 (9th Cir. 2009) (Cudahy, J., of the Seventh Circuit, dissenting). Judge Cudahy had been a member of a state public utilities commission.

[32] Natural Resources Defense Council v. EPA, 735 F.3d 873, 888 (9th Cir. 2013) (Adelman, J., of the Eastern District of Wisconsin, sitting by designation, dissenting).

[33] Dugard v. United States, 833 F.3d 915, 922 (9th Cir. 2016) (Smith, J., of the District of Rhode Island, dissenting).

[34] United States v. Ray, 375 F.3d 981 (9th Cir. 2004) (Brewster, J., of the Southern District of California, sitting by designation, concurring in part, dissenting in part). The alignment here was somewhat complex: "Graber" (+ Brewster, joining in part); "Clifton" (concurring in part, dissenting in part); "Brewster" (concurring in part, dissenting in part).

FINRA (Financial Industry Regulatory Authority Act), another district judge sitting with the court of appeals, while not departing from the majority's view on several matters, drew on other circuits' cases to disagree that a separate clause relieved Goldman, Sachs of its duty to arbitrate.[35] Separate opinions also included criticism of circuit judges' use of the court's own precedents. And the author of a separate opinion could be highly critical, as when, in a separate concurrence that used language not unlike that found in a dissent, a district judge sitting with the court would have used an "entirely different approach" from the majority as to how an administrative law judge should have reached a decision and said the problem was not the ALJ's failure to make a finding but the making of "inconsistent and erroneous findings."[36] And one could even find a panel's district judge dissenting to criticize the district judge whose ruling was under review.[37]

Other Circuits. What about the extent to which non-regular judges wrote opinions for, or provided determinative votes in, other circuits?

First Circuit. In the First Circuit, other judges' votes were dispositive in very few cases, although in the 550-562 F.3d case set, one visiting circuit judge, one visiting district judge, and an in-circuit district judge each joined one of the First Circuit's judges once to form majorities, to which should be added two cases in which a district judge joined with Justice Souter.

As earlier explained, the greatest effect of these "other" judges on the law of the circuit might come when they write published panel opinions. In these First Circuit cases, there are instances where visitors or district judges do write their share of opinions or more, but often they write less, often far less, than their "equal share." (With only published opinions examined here, it is possible that a judge writing fewer published opinions might write more non-precedential dispositions; however, there are very few of the latter in this circuit.) None of the four visiting circuit judges with the highest participation in these cases authored opinions in anywhere near one-third of the cases on which they sat. Judge Kenneth

---

[35] Goldman, Sachs & Co. v. City of Reno, 747 F.3d 733 (9th Cir. 2014) (Battaglia, J., of the Southern District of California, sitting by designation, concurring in part and dissenting in part). Judge Battaglia joined the majority on the point that Goldman, Sachs did not agree to arbitration on arbitrability itself; on the majority's definition of "customer"; and on whether required arbitration could be displaced.

[36] Bray v. Commissioner of Social Security Administration, 554 F.3d 1219, 1229-30 (9th Cir. 2009) (Wu, J., of the Central District of California, sitting by designation, concurring in the judgment).

[37] United States v. Ochoa, 809 F.3d 453, 459 (9th Cir. 2015) (Navarro, J., of the District of Nevada, dissenting).

Ripple (7th Cir.) wrote most frequently, in 6 of 23 cases, and Timothy Dyk (Fed. Cir.) wrote 5 opinions in 26 cases. Writing less frequently was the Eighth Circuit's John Gibson—only 2 opinions in 15 cases, and Tenth Circuit Judge Bobby Baldock wrote *no* opinions in the 36 cases in which he sat with this court.

There was also wide variation in the proportion of cases which the circuit's district judges who sat more frequently wrote for the court. Thus among three District of New Hampshire judges, Judge McAuliffe wrote for the panel in only one of 5 cases, but Judge McCafferty wrote in 2 of his 3 cases, and Judge DiClerico, sitting in 11 cases, wrote in 6, more than half. Among District of Rhode Island judges, Judge Mary Lisi wrote in only one of 10 cases, but Judge William Smith wrote in 4 of 10 and Judge McConnell wrote in 2 of his 4 cases. Two of three District of Puerto Rico judges wrote more than their "share" of opinions: Judge José Fusté wrote in 2 of 3 cases and Judge Jay Garcia-Gregory in 5 of 12, while Judge Gustavo Gelpi wrote in only 2 of 7, only slightly below "fair share."

Sixth Circuit. Despite the substantial participation by non-regular judges in cases in the Sixth Circuit Court of Appeals, seldom was that participation determinative, being so in only 4% across all the sets of cases and seldom above 5% in any case set. A principal reason is that, unlike the situation in the First, Ninth, and Eleventh Circuits, there were no cases in which more than one non-regular judge sat, that is, there was *either* a visitor *or* a by-designation district judge on a case but never *both*.

The share of published rulings authored by non-regular judges overall was smaller than their expected one-third "fair share." The relatively few visiting circuit judges' proportion of opinions was slightly higher than par (36.3%), but some judges contributed opinions disproportionately: Judge Daniel Friedman of the Federal Circuit wrote for the court in 3 of 5 cases and Judge Richard Cudahy of the Seventh Circuit in 2 of 4, but Judge Arthur Alarcon of the Ninth Circuit wrote no opinions in the 6 published opinion cases in which he sat. The larger number of district judges visiting from other circuits wrote in only 27.1% of the cases with published rulings in which they participated, with great variation among them, as six wrote no opinions while Judge Schwarzer wrote for the court in 4 of his 15 cases.

The proportion of cases in which in-circuit district judges wrote opinions was even lower—only 21.9% percent overall—and again the pattern varied widely. Some judges participating frequently wrote in almost one-third of their cases, for example, regularly-visiting Judge Joseph Hood of the District of Eastern Kentucky wrote for the court in 4 of 13 cases; Judge Robert Holmes Bell of Western Michigan wrote in 4 of his 10 cases; and Eastern Michigan's Judge Zatkoff did so in 4 of his 11 cases. On the other hand, Judge Arthur Tarnow, who also sat in 11 cases, wrote for the court in only one. Only one of the two district judges who sat most frequently with the Sixth Circuit wrote frequently: Judge Gwin, in 6 of his 17 cases, slightly higher than his "fair share," while Judge Algernon Marbley (Southern Ohio) wrote in only 4 of his 18 cases. At times, some judges who sat in fewer cases did write disproportionately, for example, Judge Ann Aldrich (N.D. Ohio) wrote in 3 of 5 cases; Judge Robert Cleland wrote in 4 of his 6 cases, and Judge Gerald Rosen (E.D. Michigan) wrote in all 4 of the published opinion cases in which he sat. These latter instances could result from district judges, preferring to have their dispositions published, opting to designate them for publication, although there is no direct evidence to support such a claim. However, in the Sixth Circuit, unlike the practice in other circuits,[38] the not-for-precedential dispositions in *Federal Appendix* have usually been signed by the author, so one finds in-circuit district judges as authors of these "unpublished" rulings; and to the extent those judges' authorship is shown, it might indicate that they don't seek to have opinions in "Fed. Third" solely to see their names in print.

Indeed, of all the circuits, the Sixth Circuit's non-precedential dispositions are most like its published opinions; there is little to distinguish the two, because, in addition to the non-precedential dispositions being signed, their length is equivalent to that for signed opinions. With the author of these dispositions shown, the proportion of cases in which visitors and in-circuit district judges write for the court can be determined, albeit in a rough approximation, rough because there are many cases in which district judges participate that result in per curiam rulings. (The proportion of cases with visiting judges that result in per curiams is lower than the equivalent proportion for cases with district judges, for whom the proportion per curiam doesn't fall below 15% and twice reaches close to one-third.) We cannot know whether the high proportion of per curiams from panels with district judges results from circuit judges' efforts to protect the district judges from criticism by the judges whose decisions are being reviewed, but the non-trivial proportion of per curiams cautions against giving too much weight to these figures.

Across the 7 sets of "unpublished" cases, there is no consistent pattern as to whether visiting judges or district judges write in a higher proportion of cases in which they participate. In only 3 case sets do visiting judges author these dispositions at a proportion near their "fair

---

[38] The other courts of appeals which make significant use of "other" judges and in which "unpublished" dispositions indicate the author of the disposition are the First and Sixth Circuits and, for some cases, the Eleventh Circuit.

share" of one-third, for example, 35.7% for cases in 526-540 Fed. Appx. and 38.9% in 560-581 Fed. Appx.; and at times the proportions are very low, for example, only one of 12 cases in 623-640 Fed. Appx., but small numbers require caution. As long as one remembers the per curiam matter, more credence can be given to district judges' proportion of authorship because their participation is far more frequent. While in none of the 7 sets do district judges write for the panel in the one-third "fair share," they come close to that in most sets, exceeding 30% in 5 sets; the highest proportion is 32.4% (560-581 Fed. Appx.) and the lowest, one-fourth (24.2%, 510-525 Fed. Appx.). It would thus appear that in these non-precedential dispositions, the district judges are carrying nearly their appropriate share of the writing for the panel.

Eleventh Circuit. As in the other circuits examined, in the Eleventh Circuit, participation by visiting judges and in-circuit district judges was determinative in only a small proportion of cases. The raw numbers are very small for the first six case sets, with the overall proportion 8.0%, but the proportion rises considerably once the court of appeals began to use more panels with two "other" judges and only one Eleventh Circuit appellate judge. The non-regular judges cast determinative votes in no more than 2.7% of cases through the 720-735 F.3d case set, but for cases in 749-764 F.3d, these judges played a dispositive role in over one-fifth of the cases (21.4%), although the proportion declined to over one-eighth (13.5%) for cases in 765-783 F.3d.

Shifting from participation to authorship shows clearly that all types of "other" judges wrote for their panels in proportions smaller than one-third. This is true although cases with non-regular judges are more likely to result in published-opinion rulings because panels hearing cases on the court's Non-Argument Calendar were composed solely of the Eleventh Circuit's own appellate judges.

Visiting judges wrote in only one-fourth (24.3%) of their cases overall; district judge visitors wrote at a slightly higher rate than circuit judge visitors (28.2% to 26.6%); in-circuit district judges wrote in only one-sixth of their cases, even when an increasing number of panels included more than one non-regular judge. When panels were composed of a visiting circuit judge, a district judge, and an active circuit judge, the visiting circuit judges wrote in 4 of 7 instances (57%) while the circuit judge wrote in the other 3; when there were two visiting district judges, one of them wrote in all 3 such cases, while in the one case with a visiting circuit and visiting district judge, the latter wrote. With a visiting district judge and an in-circuit district judge on a panel, the visitor wrote in 7 of 16 cases and the in-circuit district judges in 2, thus reaching over half but not reaching two-thirds, while when two in-circuit district judges sat on a panel, they wrote in only 6 of 21 cases, less than even one-third of the time.

As is true with other courts of appeals examined, the proportion of cases in which individual visiting judges and district judges wrote opinions varied considerably, from authoring no opinions to doing so in more than par. While the more cases in which a judge sat, the more likely it was that the judge would author at least one opinion, Judge Lyle Strom (D. Nebraska) wrote no opinions in 11 cases and Judge Myron Bright (8th Cir.) wrote none in 8 cases. However, there are instances in which a judge wrote in the only case in which the judge sat or, as with Judge Paul Friedman (D.D.C.), wrote in 2 of the 3 cases in which he participated.

Visiting circuit judges who participated the most in Eleventh Circuit cases wrote at very different rates: The Sixth Circuit's Eugene Siler wrote in 9 of his 14 cases, while Judge Jerome Farris of the Ninth Circuit did so in only 2 of 18 and his Ninth Circuit colleague Judge Alarcon in 5 of 19; Judges Norman Stahl (First Circuit) and John Walker (Second Circuit) each wrote in 2 cases of 8. Interestingly, the circuit judges visiting from the Sixth Circuit, taken together, wrote in *half* of their cases (13 of 26), while those from the Ninth Circuit wrote in only 7 of 40. Likewise, among visiting district judges, Judge Richard Goldberg of the Court of International Trade wrote in only 4 of 22 cases, but his colleague Jane Restani came closer to the expected one-third by writing in 7 of 25. The CIT judges combined wrote in 15 of their 62 sittings, below the expected proportion but in fitting with the general finding that visiting district judges write less than regular members of the court. Among visiting district judges with much (but less) participation who did write, Judge Michael Baylson (E.D. Pennsylvania) wrote in 4 of his 5 cases and Judge Lee Rosenthal (S.D. Texas) did so in 5 of 9 sittings.

Visitors and Immigration[39]

Thus far, in the discussion of "other" judges' participation in Ninth Circuit cases and whether they cast determinative votes, not examined were the subject matters the judges addressed. Yet if "other" judges vote differently from resident court of appeals judges on a particular subject or issue, it might affect the visited court's case outcomes. Examination across a number of subject matters is beyond the scope of the present

---

[39] This section is drawn from Stephen L. Wasby, "Immigration Appeals: A Not-so-Brief Tale of Two Courts," paper presented to the American Political Science Association, Washington, D.C., August 30, 2014.

study, but a specific area of law illustrates that "other" judges do not necessarily vote as do the judges of the court on which they are sitting by designation. The subject is immigration, particularly important for the Ninth Circuit Court of Appeals as one of two courts (the other is the Second Circuit) which in recent years have seen the greatest increase in the number of immigration appeals. In a separate study, the votes of visiting judges and in-circuit district judges were compared with those of the court of appeals' active-duty and senior judges. In what follows, data from that study for both published opinions and unpublished memorandum dispositions are presented, as the latter not only represent the largest share of the court of appeals' output but many immigration appeals have been handled by screening panels, which almost invariably produce memorandum dispositions.

Published Opinions. In the 200 *Federal Reporter* volumes covering 2007-2012 (488-686 F.3d), the Ninth Circuit issued just short of 350 published opinions in immigration appeals. Forty-eight Ninth Circuit Court of Appeals judges participated in these cases, many in 25 or more cases each but 7 judges in 5 or fewer cases. Ninth Circuit district judges and judges from outside the circuit accounted for 13.8% of the votes cast.

Using the simple measure of granting or denying the alien's petition to vacate or reverse the Board of Immigration Appeals' decision, there is no particular pattern of support given by all "other" judges to the petitioners in these immigration appeals resulting in precedential opinions. Their level of support is 39.7% overall, with relatively little variation over time. The nine visiting circuit judges who participated in roughly two dozen cases with published opinions supported petitioners at a very high rate (65.2%), but only two took part in more than two cases: Robert Cowen (3d Cir.), with 3 grants and 2 denials of petitions, and Eugene Siler (6th Cir.), who in 8 cases voted to grant the petition in 3 cases and to grant it in part in another. The 25 out-of-circuit district judges participating in these cases supported petitioners 29.4% of the time, and that support increased in later years. Ten of these judges sat in only one case and 13 in two or more cases. Only two visiting district judges, both from the Eastern District of New York, took part in as many as 5 cases, with Judge Edward Korman casting no votes favoring the petitioner and Judge Frederick Block voting to grant one petition and another in part; Judge Louis Oberdorfer from the District of Columbia cast 4 votes against granting petitions.

Some 34 Ninth Circuit district judges provided petitioners more support (39.9%) than did visiting district judges but less than their own Ninth Circuit appellate judicial colleagues. All district judges (Ninth

Circuit and visitors) provided less support (33.5%) than did circuit judges. Fifteen in-circuit district judges sat in only one immigration appeal each, but two others participated in at least four cases. Judges from the four California districts accounted for almost two-thirds of the Ninth Circuit district judge sittings, and their overall support (41.8%) was close to that by all district judges. However, the judges from Northern California and Southern California gave petitioners higher support (66.7% and 55.5%, respectively), while Central District of California judges supported only one-sixth of the petitions.

"Unpublished" Dispositions. The Ninth Circuit decided most immigration appeals by means of non-precedential dispositions, an indication that these cases were thought relatively routine. What is most important for present purposes is that, unlike the situation with cases resulting in published opinions, when non-precedential memorandum dispositions result, support for aliens by "other" judges was consistently higher than for the court of appeals' own judges.

In the 230 cases from 2002 available in 31-49 Federal Appendix, more than 40 active and senior Ninth Circuit Court of Appeals judges participated, as did a half-dozen visiting circuit judges, 4 out-of-circuit district judges, and 21 Ninth Circuit district judges. Overall, the circuit judges supported petitioners in 20.8% of these cases, while judges sitting with the court by designation supported petitioners at a slightly higher rate (24.4%), resulting in support by all judges at slightly over one-fifth (21.2%). A few of these "other" judges—Donald Lay (Eighth Circuit), Jane Restani (Court of International Trade), and James Fitzgerald (District of Alaska)—took part in a half-dozen or more cases.

"Other" judges participated in almost 80 of the roughly 750 immigration appeals from 2005-2006 reported in 135-164 Fed. Appx. The three visiting circuit judges provided lower support for petitioners than did the Ninth Circuit's own judges, largely the result of Fifth Circuit Judge Thomas Reavley's 6 negative votes and 5 by Federal Circuit Judge Jay Plager, while Eighth Circuit Judge Donald Lay supported the petitioner in 2 of 4 cases. Among the 5 out-of-circuit district judges, Judge Kevin Duffy (S.D.N.Y.) supported only one petitioner in 8 cases, but overall these judges voted to grant the petition one-fourth of the time. Ninth Circuit district judges provided support higher than Ninth Circuit Court of Appeals judges but still voted against petitioners in 25.8% of 31 cases.

In the 950 or so immigration appeals disposed of in 180-211 Fed. Appx., the Ninth Circuit's own judges voted to grant the petitions roughly one-eighth of the time (13.6%), while higher support was provided by judges from outside the Ninth Circuit—41.3% for visiting circuit judges and 19.1% for both in-circuit and visiting district judges. With the number of immigration appeals increasing, evident in the almost 1,500 such cases decided in 2006-2007 that appeared in 212-244 Fed. Appx., the caseload increase was accompanied by a decrease in support for petitioners by Ninth Circuit appellate judges to 10.9%, with support by all judges at 11.3%. Only 92 of the 4,409 votes cast in these appeals were by judges who were not regular members of the Ninth Circuit Court of Appeals. Of the 5 visiting circuit judges, each of whom supported petitioner in whole or in part more than half the time, Judge Robert Cowen (3d Cir.) sat in 4 cases and Sixth Circuit Judge Eugene Siler in 6; none of the 9 visiting district judges participated in more than 4 of these cases. The overall support for petitioners by each type of "other" judge was, however, well above that by Ninth Circuit judges. Both out-of-circuit appellate and district judges had support scores of over one-third—circuit judges, 34%; district judges, 39.5%—and the 21 Ninth Circuit district judges who participated voted for petitioner in almost one-fourth of the cases (24.5%), roughly two-and-a-half times the rate for Ninth Circuit appellate judges.

Ninth Circuit appellate judges' support for petitioners rebounded to 13.8% in the 570 immigration appeals reported in 245-272 Fed. Appx. from 2007-2008. "Other" judges continued to have higher support (32.6%), bringing overall support to 16%. Eighteen Ninth Circuit district judges supported petitioners 38.9% of the time, with visiting circuit judges doing so in half their 20 votes, while out-of-circuit district judges provided support one-fourth of the time. Variation among individual judges could be seen in the fact that Judge Richard Mills (C.D. Illinois) cast 7 votes to deny petitions while Judge Frederick Block (E.D.N.Y.) voted for petitioner in whole or in part in 6 of 7 cases.

More than 1,550 immigration appeals appeared in 2008-2009 in 273-279 and 286-324 Fed. Appx. Those cases showed continued decreasing support for petitioners, as the judges cast only 10.6% of their votes to support a petition in whole or in part. The Ninth Circuit's own judges were more stingy, with a support level of only 10.0%, than were the "other" judges, who supported petitioners over one-third of time (34.1%). Ten visiting circuit judges participating in these cases voted to grant petitions one-fifth of the time (21.2%), while visiting district judges supported immigrants more than twice as much (45.2%). The Ninth Circuit's own district judges were only slightly behind at 37.8%, a rate which exceeded circuit judges' support by over three-and-one-half times.

There were 1,250 immigration appeals in 331-367 Fed. Appx. from 2009-2010. Ninth Circuit judges, who individually heard from two to almost 300 cases, very slightly increased their support of petitioners to

10.8%, with all judges supporting petitioners in 11.3% of the cases because "other" judges again showed much higher support (29.9%). Visiting district judges gave the greatest support—one-third—with Ninth Circuit district judges somewhat lower at 28.1% and visiting circuit judges less but still casting one-fourth of their votes for petitioners (26.2%). The more than 1,000 immigration appeals from 2010 in 368-397 Fed. Appx. also reveal a temporary increase in overall support of petitioners by Ninth Circuit appeals court judges from 10.8% to 12.4%, with "other" judges again supporting petitioners more than the appeals court's own judges. In 17 cases, visiting circuit judges cast 35.8% of their votes for petitioners, while visiting district judges did so with 27.7% of theirs, a level more than twice that of Ninth Circuit judges, while in-circuit district judges showed not only lower support than other "other" judges, but gave less support than the circuit's appellate judges (11.4% to 12.4%).

More than 1,000 Ninth Circuit immigration appeals from 2010-2011 appear in 398-431 Fed. Appx. Judges' overall support for petitioners in these cases was 12%, with the court's own judges giving support to 11.4% of the petitions, and, as had been the case, "other" judges providing higher support; their 28.5% again was more than double that of the circuit's own judges. Visiting circuit judges, although participating in only 12 cases, provided support in just under half (45.8%), visiting district judges gave 30 percent support, and Ninth Circuit district judges supported over one-fifth of the petitions (21.3%).

The last set of cases examined, 432-481 Fed. Appx., contained 1,070 immigration appeals. Here Ninth Circuit appeals court judges supported petitions at a 14.2% rate, somewhat higher than immediately before. Again, the many "other" judges participating in these appeals supported petitioners at rates considerably higher than that of the Ninth Circuit's own judges. Only 9 visiting circuit judges, participating in 11 immigration appeals, gave two-fifths of their votes to petitioners, while 33 out-of-circuit district judges, several of whom participated in 6 or 7 cases although many took part in only one or two, gave less support, but at 28.8% that support was twice that given by the Ninth Circuit judges. The 32 in-circuit district judges, none of whom sat in more than 5 cases, supported petitioners one-fifth of the time (20.8%).

Unpublished Rulings Overall. During the full period examined, the Ninth Circuit decided almost 10,000 immigration appeals disposed of with non-precedential dispositions. The Ninth Circuit's own appellate judges decided the equivalent of 9,600 such cases. "Other" judges cast 3.4% of the votes, and by themselves would have constituted panels deciding 340 cases. For Ninth Circuit judges who each decided more than a few immigration appeals, the cumulative support for petitioners was12.4%. That support decreased over time, but individual judges varied considerably in the support they manifested for immigrants' appeals.

Despite the small proportion of the votes "other" judges cast, their overall support for petitioners considerably exceeded that of Ninth Circuit appellate judges. Judges from outside the circuit, whether appeals court or district judges, were supportive of petitioner almost one-third of the time (31.2% each), while Ninth Circuit district judges showed less support (27.7%), a level still almost twice that of their circuit's appellate judges.

Of the visitors, judges from Sixth and Eighth Circuits sat in the largest number of Ninth Circuit immigration appeals (46 each), and those judges supported petitioners at a high rate (42.3% and 38.0%, respectively). At the other extreme, none of three visitors from the Fifth Circuit voted for petitioner in 9 cases, with Judge Thomas Reavley having a 0-7 score. Support by a single circuit's judges usually masked variation among them, something also seen when several judges from the same district partici-pated. Among 8 visiting circuit judges who heard 10 or more cases, Judge Eugene Siler (6th Cir.), with 25, voted for petitioner 30% of the time, the norm for visiting circuit judges; his Sixth Circuit colleague Ronald Gilman voted to grant one-third of the petitions he reviewed (34.4%, 16 cases); and Third Circuit Judges Robert Cowen and Jane Roth supported petitioner in 44.1% and 41.7% of their 17 and 12 cases, respectively. Unlike the situation with some Ninth Circuit judges, an increase from participa-tion in only a few cases to a larger number did not lead to lower support, but these out-of-circuit judges did not sit on screening panels, participa-tion in which lowered Ninth Circuit judges' rate of support.

The 65 out-of-circuit district judges who sat in these Ninth Circuit immigration appeals supported petitioners slightly more than did visiting circuit judges, but they, too, varied both individually as well as when grouped by home circuit and district. The Ninth Circuit borrowed 15 district judges from the Second Circuit, two less than from the Sixth Circuit, but the Second Circuit visitors decided twice as many cases—125, half of which were heard by judges from the Eastern District of New York. Another 60 cases were decided by 9 Southern District of New York judges, with Judge Kevin Duffy in two-thirds (39 cases) and providing support marginally higher than that given by his colleagues (18.8% v. 15.8%). The other out-of-circuit district judges were scattered across the circuits. Six Eighth Circuit district judges heard 15 cases and voted to grant not a single petition, while 5 Fifth Circuit judges heard 27 immigration appeals. Seventeen Sixth Circuit district judges participated in 51 Ninth Circuit immigration appeals, none in more than 7. Ten Seventh Circuit district judges heard 67 cases and overall supported petitioner in 43.4% of the cases, but the 7 Northern District of Illinois judges gave only 29.5% support; among these, Judge Suzanne Conlon heard 20 cases, in which she provided 32.5% support. Judge Jane Restani from the Court of International Trade also sat in 20 cases. The greatest individual participation was by former state appellate Judge Richard Mills (C.D. Illinois), who took part in 30 immigration appeals and supported petitioner one-third of the time.

Eighty-one Ninth Circuit district judges participated in these immigration appeals. Half took part in only 3 or fewer cases; only 14 sat in 10 or more cases each; and none heard more than the 18 in which Judge Ronald Leighton of Western Washington participated. Those giving higher-than-average support to petitioners were Judges Leighton, at 44.4%; Claudia Wilken of Northern California, 65%; David Ezra of Hawai'i, 31.8%; and James Singleton of Alaska, 35.7%. Among the relatively more frequent participants, the lowest support for petitioners was by Senior Judge Samuel King from Hawaii, only 5.9% in 17 cases.

The district judges from within the circuit who participated in these cases were from all the circuit's districts except Guam and the Northern Mariana Islands. Only one District of Idaho judge and two from the District of Montana participated in a total of 7 cases. Exhibiting the lowest support from any Ninth Circuit district—10.9%—were 3 Eastern Washington judges, one of whom sat in only one case; Judge Edward Shea, hearing 10 petitions, supported not a single one. By comparison, 5 cross-state Western Washington colleagues, sitting in 30 cases, had the highest support, 38.4%, largely resulting from Judge Leighton's votes. Four district judges each from Hawaii and Oregon supported petitioners at a level below the norm. For Hawaii's judges, with 17.7% support, Judge King's low support more than offset Judge Ezra's relatively high score. The 18.4% support by District of Oregon judges came largely from Judge Michael Hogan's 15% support in ten cases. On the strength of Judge Singleton's votes, the five Alaska district judges hearing 46 of these appeals supported petitioners at a 22.8% level, about at the in-circuit district judge norm. Ten District of Arizona judges had an overall above-average support of 29.2%, and Judge Raner Collins heard twelve cases (20.8% support).

California's four judicial districts contributed 37 judges to hear immigration appeals resulting in non-precedential rulings—only 4 from the Eastern District and only in 10 cases, but 9 judges from Southern California, 10 from Northern California, and 14 from Central California, the Ninth Circuit district with the largest number of judges. The judges from the California districts together heard 169 cases and supported petitioners at the norm for all Ninth Circuit district judges sitting in these cases (23.0%). There was relatively little variation in support shown by judges of each district, with Central California (20.6%) and Southern California (21.6%) lower than the norm and Eastern California (25%) and Northern California (26.3%) higher.

8
AND NOW THE SENIORS

The focus thus far has been on courts of appeals' use of two types of "non-regular" judges, those about whose participation the greatest concern has been expressed: judges visiting from other circuits and in-circuit district judges. Of lesser concern but still troubling to some is the use of courts of appeals' own senior judges, which are now added to this study. The lesser concern stems from the fact these judges have been members of the court and have moved, usually without a hitch, to senior status.[1] A few judges who never "go senior" and some judges who do not elect to do so when eligible, perhaps because they are unwilling to give up the rights to vote on whether the court should rehear a case en banc and to sit on en banc courts when they were on the panel,[2] may have been on the court much longer than colleagues who accepted senior status as soon as eligible or shortly thereafter.

Some words are in order about who senior judges are. As a technical matter, they are judges who have become eligible in terms of years of service and age—under the Rule of 80, the combination of age and length of federal court service adding to that number, e.g., 70 and 10 or 65 and 15—and have opted to take senior status. That vacates the judgeship they held, and the president may then fill it by nomination if the Senate confirms. Senior judges are no longer in active service but are neither "retired" nor have they "resigned," either of which would terminate their service on the court. The decision to take senior status is the eligible judge's choice, but technically, for a judge to maintain chambers and staff, the circuit chief judge must designate that judge as "willing and able" to work. It might be said that senior judges are "semi-retired," although many in fact work nearly full-time, but they do not *have* to do so. As former Chief Judge Wilfred Feinberg of the Second Circuit put it, "A senior federal judge is a judge who remains on the federal bench but is no

---

[1] For the occasional judge who is placed on senior status prior to eligibility because of disability, the change may be more abrupt.

[2] This has been quite obvious in the Ninth Circuit, where several of President Carter's appointees remained in active status long after being eligible for senior status. Judge Harry Pregerson "went senior" only at the end of 2015 at the age of 93, not long before his death, and Judge Stephen Reinhardt has not yet done so.

longer expected to work full time."[3] Rather than being "retired," they are, in the language of 28 U.S.C. § 371(b), only "retired from regular, active service." As noted immediately above, the only "privilege" they lose is that they may not vote on whether a case should be heard en banc; only active judges may participate in that decision. Yet if a senior judge was a member of the panel that decided the case for which en banc rehearing is granted, any senior judge(s) from the panel may, at the judge's option, participate in the en banc court. In the Ninth Circuit, which has a limited (or "short") en banc panel (LEB), whose members are drawn by lot, a senior judge on the panel in a case that is to be reheard en banc may opt to have his or her name placed in the draw for selection of the LEB.

Many panels including a senior judge look much like panels that existed before the judge assumed senior status. Indeed, in some courts of appeals, senior judges are not indicated as such in the judge listing at the beginning of an opinion, although other circuits do so indicate. There is no "Senior Judge Badge." Perhaps not indicating a judge's senior status is a way of showing that senior judges are considered full members of the court, but seen less charitably, it might be done so that it would not be clear to readers the large proportion of judge-participations for which they account. However, when a judge has moved to senior status during the pendency of a case, e.g., after oral argument, that fact may be so noted in a footnote, just as is done at times when there is a change in status between panel participation and en banc rehearing of a case. By contrast, visiting judges and in-circuit district judges are always indicated with an asterisk showing their court of origin, and their senior status is often also indicated.

Among the judges of the court, it might not matter whether a colleague on a panel is a senior judge. However, an active judge is expected to preside, although some panels have the most senior (longest-serving) judge preside, regardless of official status, and one judge made a point of saying senior judges should preside, because "we have stripped them enough when they go senior."[4] Put differently, among the judges, it is likely that a judge is a judge is a judge. That would be quite likely as to those who have only recently taken senior status. However, when a judge has been in senior status for some years, the other judges' awareness of the judge's status will be greater, at least as much for the judge's age and overall seniority on the court as from the judge's official status.

---

[3] Wilfred Feinberg, "Senior Judges: A National Resource," 56 Brooklyn Law Review 409, 410 (1990).

[4] Interview with Judge J. Clifford Wallace, March 1 and 9, 1977, San Diego.

There are, however, some matters as to which a senior judge's status as such does affect the court's work. One is that a senior judge's presence on a panel decreases those eligible to vote on petition for rehearing en banc, because a senior judge on a panel, although that judge may vote on a panel rehearing request (PFR), may only *recommend*, not *vote*, on a petition for rehearing en banc (PFREB). However, a senior judge can, and does, participate in the panel's response when an off-panel judge has suggested revisions in an opinion absent which an en banc call would be made.

There is no question that, as will be borne out below, senior judges are frequent participants in the work of the courts of appeals. Judge Feinberg pointed out that in 1989, they participated in 14% of appeals,[5] and some scholars found that, for the 1977-2008 period, the proportion of cases in which they participated rose so that it exceeded 15% after 2000.[6] Whatever the numbers, their presence is thought crucial, particularly when—as this is written—since 1991 there has not been a major judgeship bill, that is, one adding judgeships. As a former circuit chief judge who had taken senior status after his chief judgeship ended said, "The system would collapse if not for the work of a lot of the senior judges." They worked, he said, out of a sense of teamwork, in which younger judges worked with older judges (some of them senior judges), and now the senior judges could give back, both to junior colleagues and to the court as a whole.[7] In short, there is more to their participation than "filling a spot," although Judge Feinberg pointed to their crucial role when they "take up the inevitable slack caused by vacancies" created by death and actual retirement[8]—vacancies which are often not quickly filled, particularly with partisan rancor in the Senate.

These senior judges are a regular part of the court's work; indeed, they are an important and essential part if the court is to keep pace with its docket. Yet when a court of appeals has many senior judges participating in deciding cases, their participation may make the panels on which they sit unrepresentative of "the court." Certainly senior circuit judges' regular activity means that for all a president's efforts to place his own

---

5 Feinberg, "Senior Judges: A National Resource," at 412.

6 Lisa M. Holmes, Rorie Spill Solberg, and Susan Haire, "Neither Gone Nor Forgotten: Evaluating the Potential Impact of Senior Status Judges on the U.S. Courts of Appeals," 95 Judicature 227, 231 (2012).

7 The judge is Alfred T. Goodwin of the Ninth Circuit. See Pamela A. MacLean, "Vacancy Debate Focuses on Senior Judges: Is There a 'Crisis' or Are They Filling the Void?" Daily Journal, February 13, 1998.

8 Feinberg, "Senior Judges: A National Resource," at 412.

judges on a court to fill several vacancies, some time will pass before the new appointees significantly displace senior judges on panels. Further, when a panel is composed of only one active circuit judge, a senior judge, and either a visitor or in-circuit district judge, it calls into play the concerns, discussed earlier, as to who is making the law of the circuit—the court's "own" judges or others.

Before data are presented on senior circuit judges' participation in several courts of appeals, an initial foray into the subject comes from Ninth Circuit judges' earlier-stated views about senior circuit judges' participation. This is followed by data on senior circuit judges' participation in the work of the Ninth Circuit Court of Appeals and the First Circuit, and then, for some comparison, data on senior judges' participation in the most recent work of the Sixth and Eleventh Circuits. Although the D.C. Circuit has not been included thus far in the study because it does not use visiting or district judges, it is introduced because its recent history can tell something about the effect of senior judges on the addition of new members to the court.

Ninth Circuit Judges' Views

As might be expected, Ninth Circuit judges expressed fewer concerns about having the court's own senior judges sit on cases than was true with respect to out-of-circuit visitors or in-circuit district judges. Some judges said, however, that one had to look at differences among the senior judges. "Not all seniors should be considered alike," said one,[9] largely a matter of their level of energy or possible enfeeblement, but one senior district judge went so far as to say he saw no difference between active and senior circuit judges.[10] And a senior circuit judge said there was the "same variation in viewpoints as among active judges."[11]

The judges praised the senior judge system, with one going so far as to say that "one of the finest things Congress did was to create senior status";[12] senior judges were the "best reservoir of additional manpower" for the courts of appeals.[13] At least one chief judge had "worked hard" to have those eligible take senior status, and a colleague said that when a

---

[9] Interview with Judge James R. Browning, February 2 and 3, 1977, San Francisco, Cal.

[10] Interview with Judge Gus Solomon (D. Oregon), May 3, 1977, Portland, Ore.

[11] Interview with Judge James Carter, March 1, 1977, San Diego, Cal.

[12] Interview with Judge J. Blaine Anderson, February 10, 1977, San Francisco.

[13] Interview with Judge J. Edward Lumbard (2d Cir.), May 2, 1977, Portland, Ore.

judge took senior status, one had that judge's service and that of the judge's replacement, so one "gets 1 1/3 to 1 1/2 for one."[14]

The most basic advantage in using senior circuit judges was their assistance with the caseload: a senior judge was a "warm body to share the work," someone who "spreads the work."[15] But it wasn't simply *some* assistance: the service that seniors provided was crucial for the court's dealing with its caseload, as made clear in comments that the court "couldn't survive without them" or "couldn't function" without their help.[16] A district judge who often sat with the court said he didn't know "what the court would do without them."[17] Senior judges, by sitting on screening panels (which may contain two or even three senior judges), help particularly with docket-clearing, especially of less complex cases.

Yet senior judges provide far more than warm bodies to clear cases. They "know a lot, have followed trends, know about procedures, and know how to be innovative about procedures"; "sometimes they will recall what others don't remember."[18] They are "obviously familiar with traditions in the circuit, legal thinking, and the court's recent opinions," but they also know something about the circuit's district judges whose cases are coming before the court.[19] Their accumulated experience was "priceless to younger circuit judges, as in providing unwritten methods of handling cases."[20] Moreover, their "primary loyalty was here" (to this court of appeals) and they "have pride in the court."[21] Beyond that, their attitude was said to be more easy-going. That was not to say they were lazy, but their reduced load "gave them abundant time to crank out first-rate product," and it was "amazing" that they were willing to take hard cases.[22] Because "they have twice as much time as we [the active judges] do and they know it and thus are willing to take and work on more difficult cases," one judge said they would take "the most difficult case on

---

[14] Interview with Judge Charles Merrill, February 11, 1977, San Francisco. He said that by and large a senior was equal to one-third to one-half an active judge.

[15] Interview with former Chief Judge Richard Chambers, May 20, 1977, San Francisco; interview with Judge Stanley Barnes, March 2, 1977, Los Angeles; Merrill interview.

[16] Anderson interview; interview with Judge Shirley Hufstedler, February 28, 1977, Los Angeles.

[17] Interview with Judge Charles Renfrew (N.D. Cal.), February 17, 1977, San Francisco.

[18] Interview with Judge Joseph Sneed, March 2, 1977, San Francisco; interview with Judge Eugene A. Wright, April 12, 1977, San Francisco.

[19] Lumbard interview.

[20] Interview with Judge Anthony Kennedy, March 7, 1977, San Francisco.

[21] Hufstedler interview; Lumbard interview.

[22] Kennedy interview.

the calendar," although the judge conceded that some wanted the easiest cases.[23]

These positive aspects do not mean the absence of problems. Like participation by "non-regular" judges, their presence increased the number of people with whom one had to deal. "The bigger the court, the more difficult it was to arrive at consensus," said one judge, adding, "With many people, you don't have a court—[you] have many courts."[24] One type of problem was "administrative," in that it was "not always clear when senior judges would sit,"[25] and they were "not as available" because they "work short hours or a few days a week," so that one was "not sure when one can reach them to communicate."[26] (Another administrative aspect, mentioned above, was whether a senior judge should preside over a panel.)

The aging process created other problems, seen indirectly in the comment that using seniors was a "disadvantage only when they are enfeebled" and in the remark, "You don't want to argue a case to a person who is going to sleep,"[27] although the latter comment was countered by the observation that "some are just as alert as they ever were." There was, however, "some slowing down in the sense [of the judges] not feeling under pressure, so they couldn't be hurried or given orders."[28] "There comes a time," observed another, "when they don't get work out as rapidly—but this can be handled."[29]

Another aspect of the aging process directly relates to development of legal doctrine. A senior judge's precepts, observed one who was himself a senior, "may be fairly well frozen. Convincing him to see the light of new or different legislation or new themes by the Supreme Court is more difficult," such that a senior judge would be "more inclined to dissent from a departure" from the past.[30] Another observer agreed: "If a judge is

---

[23] Interview with Judge Ozell Trask, April 11, 1977, San Francisco.

[24] Interview with Judge Harry Pregerson (then C.D. Cal.), March 1, 1977, Los Angeles.

[25] Kennedy interview.

[26] Wright interview. This statement was made before the court's acquisition of an internal e-mail system.

[27] Interview with Judge Walter Ely, March 1, 1977, Los Angeles; interview with Judge Alfred Sulmonetti (Circuit Court, Multnomah County; member of Hruska Commission), February 8, 1977, Portland, Ore.; Ely interview. Judge Ely continued, "There comes a time when a senior judge ought to quit," with "gentle ways . . . used on a judge approaching senility" who was "moved to less important work."

[28] Wright interview.

[29] Lumbard interview.

[30] Interview with Judge John Kilkenny, May 3, 1977, Portland, Ore.

fixed or static, it will be a problem to the court."[31] This theme was more fully developed by another judge, still in active service, who said the problem was "subtle." As he explained:

> Every man in his career is painting a picture—a career unfolds, one takes one position after another, trying to maintain jurisprudential consistency. The longer you are there, the more complete the picture. Senior status is no time for a new canvas; all you are doing is touching it up. One comes to a case with a "mental set" (not closed-mindedness) that is going to dictate what you do. All of us have conceptions, but it is more pronounced [with seniors].[32]

Bringing it back to "who writes the law," he concluded by saying that "in terms of litigants' perception," this was only an issue if there is only one active judge on the panel. Indeed, this matter of who was writing the circuit's law was put most directly by the judge who said that "lawyers want two active members of the court on a panel," as he went on to say that Chief Judge Warren Burger had raised the question of the Supreme Court's view of a case with only one active judge—"'Is it Ninth Circuit law?'"[33]

In the Circuits

Extent of Seniors' Participation. Before a look at actual participation by senior circuit judges in the work of their courts, the number of senior judges, and the proportion of the court of appeals judges they constitute, should be noted. For this purpose, May 2017 was chosen, although it is after the end of the primary study period and before some judges took senior status as the Obama administration ended. The difference in time does not lead to significant differences in relative numbers of senior and active-duty judges, although numbers do vary somewhat over time as judges opt for senior status and time elapses before that judge's position is filled.

The theme of variation, emphasized throughout the volume, reappears here as variation across the circuits in the number and proportion of senior judges and thus in the extent of their role. As has been observed about senior judges for the 1977-2008 period, "the effect of their presence varies dramatically across the circuits," as they make up only a small

---

[31] Sulmonetti interview.

[32] Sneed interview. He also observed that some people say, "That's another description of wisdom."

[33] Browning interview.

proportion of the circuit judges in some courts of appeals, while in others, they come close to outnumbering the active judges.[34]

The number of senior judges in a court of appeals varies, not only because some die, but also because judges take senior status, even if not all do so immediately as soon as eligible. The number also increases because a number of vacancies appear on the courts of appeals in the last year of a president's term, especially a second term, a time when the confirmation of new judges slows or stops completely; thus the number of senior judges has increased while the number of active-duty judges has decreased, at least for some time into the new Congress.

In late 2017, there was one court of appeals with only a couple of senior judges—the Fourth Circuit, with 2 senior judges to 14 active-status judges. At the other end of the spectrum, a couple of circuits had almost as many seniors as active-status judges, for example, the Third Circuit, with 12 active-status judges and 10 senior judges. And the First Circuit had 6 active judges but also 4 senior judges (one of whom is not able to sit, a situation true of some senior judges in other circuits), plus retired Supreme Court Justice David Souter, who now sits regularly and who could be treated as a senior judge of the circuit. In the Second Circuit, the number of active judges and senior judges was also equal, with 11 of each. Courts of appeals in which the seniors were only slightly outnumbered by their active colleagues include the Fifth Circuit (13 active, 9 senior judges), the Sixth Circuit (14 and 8), and the Eleventh and Federal Circuits, each with 11 active judges and 7 seniors. In the Seventh Circuit, the number of active judges was precisely double the number of seniors (8 and 4). In the largest court, the Ninth Circuit, there were 26 judges, plus 3 vacancies, and 17 senior judges.

The focus in this chapter is primarily on the Ninth Circuit, the circuit with which this study began, because of its large number of senior circuit judges. Particular emphasis is given to data for cases with published opinions beginning with mid-June, 2013 (720 F.3d), and extending into 2016, and for cases resulting in non-precedential dispositions for roughly the same period, starting in January, 2013, with 510 Fed. Appx. Other courts of appeals given attention for the same period are those for the First and D.C. Circuits, the latter of which allows a look at possible effects of adding several new active-duty judges to the court in a short span, which resulted from Senate Democrats using the "nuclear option" to break the filibuster of nominations to fill vacancies there. The Sixth and Eleventh Circuits are also examined, but only for 2015-2016. In this data,

---

[34] Holmes, Spill Solberg, and Haire, "Neither Gone Nor Forgotten," at 230.

for convenience, someone is counted as a senior judge if one at the time an opinion is filed, even if that judge may not have yet taken senior status when assigned the case or when it was argued.[35] As suggested earlier, this may lead to a slight over-count of senior judges' participation, but looking at judges this way is appropriate in terms of how others look at panel composition as of the time a case was decided and later: what they *see* is a senior judge, with whatever effects their perception of the case might produce in terms of "who has made the law of the circuit."

Ninth Circuit Data. Participation by Ninth Circuit senior judges in their court's work is both considerable and much greater than that by out-of-circuit visitors and the circuit's own district judges. In cases that resulted in published opinions, the proportion of those cases in which at least one senior judge was a member of the panel ranged from somewhat less than half (41.9% in 749-764 F.3d and 48.6% in the preceding set, 720-735 F.3d) through three-fifths (59.6%, 488-500 F.3d, and 60.9%, 358-376 F.3d), all the way to three-fourths (74.3%, in the 765-783 F.3d case set). However, in the two most recent case sets, the proportions were much lower, at or under one-third (only 29.6% in 784-800 F.3d). While most panels have only one senior judge, two sat on the same panel in roughly 5% of all cases, ranging from 3.5% in the 736-748 F.3d set of cases up to 6.5% in cases in 765-783 F.3d and to 14.1% of the earlier 358-376 F.3d cases; the proportion was half that in 488-500 F.3d cases (7.7%) and below 6% thereafter. (See Table IV.Part I, in Appendix A, for greater detail.)

Another way to look at senior judges' participation is to calculate the proportion of "judge-spaces" or judge-participations (three per panel) they occupy. They accounted for one-fourth (25.1%) in the first case set because of their especially heavy participation at that time, but for several case sets, the proportion decreased to somewhat over one-sixth (16.0% to 18.5%); then, reflecting their lesser participation in the most recent case sets studied, this proportion was only somewhat above 10% (11.2% and 11.6%).

The senior judges varied widely in the number of cases in which each participated, and, likewise, there was considerable variation in the number of cases in which they wrote a published opinion for the panel. Overall they wrote in over 300 cases, slightly over one-fourth (26.5%) of those in which they participated. However, 4 of the 25 judges wrote in more than one-third of their cases and 8 more did so in just under one-third (30%+); 6 were authors for the panels less than 20% of the time.

---

35 Determining when a judge was assigned to a case requires court records not accessible.

Making a Difference. Are senior circuit judges' votes determinative in panel decisions? When panels are composed of two circuit judges and one senior circuit judge, the latter's vote is determinative in only a small proportion of cases, the highest being 5.5% (488-500 F.3d), with the median near 3%. However, senior circuit judges' votes are determinative or help play a determinative role in other situations as well. If a court of appeals' senior judges sat only with their active-duty colleagues, concern about their presence would likely be muted, but, in at least 10% of all cases studied, an active circuit judge is joined by both a senior Ninth Circuit judge *and* either an in-circuit district judge or an out-of-circuit visitor, and, in two case sets, the proportion rises to one-sixth (16.5%, 720-735 F.3d) and over one-fifth (20.9%, 488-500 F.3d). A senior judge-visiting judge combination is found more often than a senior circuit judge sitting with a district judge except in one case set. For example, the former takes place in 14.0% of cases in 720-735 F.3d but the latter in only 2.5%.

If a panel contains both a senior circuit judge and either a visiting judge or within-circuit district judge so that only one active-duty judge is present, it means that the former two panel members outnumber the panel's one active judge, making their votes determinative. The proportion of cases in which these alignments take place fluctuates, from a low of 6.5% (749-764 F.3d), to a figure generally close to 10%, and to a maximum of one-fifth (20.9%, 488-500 F.3d). Likewise, the presence of two senior judges makes their votes determinative, whether because they constitute a majority of a unanimous panel or because they vote together over the active judge's dissent. The proportion of these two senior-judge cases reaches 14.4% in the first set of cases (357-376 F.3d) but is quite low in the remaining ones, ranging from 3.5% (736-748 F.3d) to 7.7% (488-500 F.3d). All situations in which senior judges' votes and presence are determinative, combined, account for from under one-sixth of all cases (15.7%, 749-764 F.3d) to over one-third (34.1%, 488-500 F.3d), with the median at 20.2%. There are also some instances of panels of three senior judges, but those cases are usually found among the court's non-precedential rulings, a result of three seniors sitting as a screening panel, as cases sent to those panels almost invariably result in "unpublished," non-precedential dispositions.

What about authorship when a panel contains either two senior circuit judges or one senior circuit judge and either a visitor or in-circuit district judge? Senior judges wrote in two-thirds of the cases in panels of two senior circuit judges and one active circuit judge, exactly the proportion suggested by even sharing of opinion-writing, but when panels include a visitor sitting with a senior circuit judge and an active circuit judge, the picture is different. For all panels with visiting judges (whether circuit or district), not surprisingly the visitors write less than their "share" of opinions—26.8% of their cases, but surprisingly, with those panel alignments, the senior circuit judges write an even smaller proportion, only 25%. This means that the active circuit judges on such panels have responsibility for well more than their expected one-third of the opinion-writing, which they do in almost half the cases (48.2%).

However, when panels with judges from other courts of appeals are separated from those with a visiting district judge, differences are evident. One might expect that visiting circuit judges would receive more opinions than visiting district judges When they sit with a senior circuit judge and an active circuit judge, visiting circuit judges write in only one-fifth (20.8%) of the cases, but visiting district judges write in 29.7% of cases with such colleagues. In the former (visiting circuit judge) situation, the active circuit judge writes over half the time (52.8%) and the resident senior judges write in only 26.4% of the cases, whereas in the latter (visiting district judge) situation, the resident seniors write a smaller proportion of the cases (24.3%), just as do the active circuit judges (45.9%).

When a district judge from within the circuit joined a senior circuit judge and an active circuit judge on a panel, the district judge wrote in only 26.2% of the cases, less often than an even distribution would suggest, while active judges wrote in 34.4%, only slightly over the expected one-third, and the senior circuit judges wrote in 39.3% of the cases. This indicates that the seniors were more likely to pick up the work not carried by the district judges.

"Unpublished" Dispositions. Because of the Ninth Circuit's heavy—indeed, predominant—use of non-precedential dispositions, seeing what role senior judges play in such cases is important; noted earlier was the heavier role senior judges play in the screening panels' high-volume disposition process. Just as with cases that resulted in published opinions, there is variation over time in the extent of senior judge participation in cases resulting in non-precedential dispositions. Only in one case set does senior judges' participation fall below half—48.1% in cases from 560-581 Fed. Appx.—and their participation is right at one-half (50.4%) in a later set (600-622 Fed. Appx.). Otherwise, the proportion of such cases with senior judge participation is at least three-fifths (60.1% in one set) and over two-thirds in three other sets, with the highest proportion, 70.6%, in cases appearing in 541-559 Fed. Appx. (See Table IV.Part II. in Appendix A.)

What is noteworthy, however, is that the proportion of cases with more than one senior judge is far greater in these non-precedential rulings than in cases resulting in published opinions, in large measure because of senior judges' participation in screening panels. This means that one has more panels with two seniors or even three, although only once does the proportion of cases with three senior judges rise above two percent. The proportions of cases with two senior judges swing rather wildly, being as high as over one-third (34.6%) one-time and as low as 3.1% at another time, in the next case set.

First Circuit. Senior judges have been, and are, important actors in the First Circuit Court of Appeals. Whereas only slightly over one-fourth of its panels were composed of three active circuit judges, 70% are composed of all circuit judges, active *and* senior, with a range from the upper 50s (e.g., 56.6%, 482-500 F.3d) to a high exceeding 80 percent (81%, 720-735 F.3d). The court's considerable use of its own senior judges does not result from use of screening panels, which it appears not to use, and in any event it issues very, very few non-precedential rulings, which screening panels would produce in large numbers. The proportion of cases with at least one senior judge ranged from below half (e.g., 46.2%) to over half (e.g., 52% and 54.5% and 54.7%) in various case sets. Senior circuit judges regularly accounted for one-fifth of the court's judge-participations (three judge-slots per panel), although the proportion dipped slightly below that in a couple of case sets. There is also a small percentage of cases—less than 5%—in which a senior First Circuit judge sat with either a visiting judge or a district judge, leaving only one active circuit judge on the panel, just as occurs when two senior judges sit in a case. The proportion of cases with two senior judges at times ran as high as one-eighth but in some case sets was under 10%. (See Table IV.Part I, in Appendix A, for other circuits.)

Understanding the proportions of First Circuit cases with the court's senior judges is made somewhat difficult by the regular presence of retired Justice Souter. Treating him as a First Circuit senior judge obviously would increase the proportion of cases in which senior judges participated, and doing so makes the proportion of published-opinion First Circuit cases (almost all its cases) with a senior judge regularly over half, and at one point it exceeds two-thirds (69.6%). When Souter sits with a First Circuit senior judge, it also increases the number of cases with two senior judges (Souter and a First Circuit senior judge). These cases, along with the few cases in which Souter sat with a district judge, increase the proportion of cases in which such judge-combinations are determinative of the panel's outcomes.

The senior judges also accounted for a large proportion of opinions written in the cases in which they participated. Unlike visiting and district judges, who wrote opinions in less than their share of the cases, the opposite was true for the court's own senior judges. While the seniors who participated in cases in 358-376 F.3d—Levin Campbell, Frank Coffin, Conrad Cyr, and Norman Stahl—wrote opinions in slightly less than one-third of those cases (30.8%), in the next set (488-500 F.3d), without Judge Coffin but now including Judge Bruce Selya, the seniors wrote exactly one-third of the opinions in their cases, a proportion perhaps somewhat understated because of the court's few per curiam rulings, which senior judges may have written even though not so identified.[36] In the cases in 550-562 F.3d, seniors' authorship rose to almost half (49.1%), the level at which it roughly remained thereafter except for one set (736-748 F.3d) in which it reached an amazing 70.6%. In the cases appearing in 749-764 F.3d, the proportion was 48.1%, but if one treats Justice Souter as a senior judge, the proportion rises to over half (55%).

Sixth and Eleventh Circuits. Senior judges' participation in the work of the Sixth and Eleventh Circuits is added for further comparison and to underscore the extent of inter-circuit variation. Used is one recent set of cases with published opinions from 2016, in 801-819 F.3d, and the roughly-parallel set of non-precedential dispositions in 623-640 Fed. Appx. (Details can be found in Appendix A, Table IV.Parts I and II.) Sixth Circuit senior judges took part in almost three-fifths of the cases (58.3%) decided with published opinion, which include a small number of cases in which two senior judges sat; the senior judges accounted for 20% of the sittings on these three-judge panels. They took part in a smaller proportion (only 46.3%) of cases resulting in "unpublished" rulings, 12 percentage points less than in cases with published opinions, and they accounted for 16.7% of the participations in the cases with non-precedential dispositions.

At the same time, by contrast, in the Eleventh Circuit, senior judges participated in a much smaller proportion of cases decided with published opinions, with fewer than one-sixth (15.9%) of the panels containing a senior judge, and those judges accounted for only 5.6% of the judges' participations in these cases. In the court's non-precedential rulings from the same period, however, senior judges sat in one-third of the cases and accounted for 11.7% of the participations, twice the proportion in the published-opinion cases. This higher rate of participation in non-precedential dispositions is likely the result of senior judges' greater par-

---

[36] When two senior judges sit on the same panel, the likelihood that a senior judge will wrote for the panel is increased (also not calculated).

ticipation in cases on non-argument calendars, in which visiting judges do not take part.

D.C. Circuit. The Court of Appeals for the District of Columbia Circuit is examined to allow consideration of whether the recent appointment of four new active-duty judges there led to a decrease in the proportion of cases in which the circuit's senior judges participated. This is done to illustrate limits that senior judges' continuing presence has on the effects of a president's appointments.

Until the mid-1990's, judges from other circuits participated in cases of the D.C. Circuit, just as they did in other U.S. courts of appeals. In 1991, for example, they participated in 16 cases, with Judge Ellsworth Van Graafeiland of the Second Circuit sitting in 5; judges of the Third, Sixth, Seventh, and Federal Circuits also participated, with judges of the Federal Circuit contributing as many sittings as Judge Van Graafeiland; and one panel was composed of three Federal Circuit judges, apparently because all D.C. Circuit judges had recused. Retired Justice Brennan sat in one case. In 1992, in addition to 7 cases in which visiting judges participated, there were another 8 in which Clarence Thomas, after his elevation to the Supreme Court, sat with the court of appeals by designation as Circuit Justice to complete his cases in that court.

The visitors' participation in this earlier period was evident in 27 cases decided in 1994, 14 of which were decided with visiting district judges on the panels, two from the Northern District of Illinois (Judges Milton Shadur and Hubert Will) and one each from the Eastern District of Wisconsin (John Reynolds) and the Court of International Trade (Jane Restani). Two of the three visiting appellate judges came from the First Circuit (Judges Levin Campbell and Frank Coffin) and one from the Second Circuit (James Oakes). These judges also accounted for 7 opinions for the court, one of which drew a dissent from the court's own Judge Harry Edwards.

The court then decided against further use of visiting judges, although some of its own judges, particularly Judges Douglas Ginsburg and David Sentelle once they reached senior status, have sat in other circuits. Now only the court's own judges participate in the court's cases and speak for it, but that leaves open how prominent a role the court's senior judges play. Especially to be noted is whether, once the court received four new judges in 2013-2014, the role of senior judges decreased. Judge Sri Srinivasan joined the court in May, 2013, Judges Patricia Millett and Cornelia Pillard in December, 2014, and Judge Robert Wilkins the following month, the latter three after the Senate Democrats exercised the "nuclear option." It was possible that, with more judges now on the court and several vacancies now filled, the court's senior judges would play a reduced role, although the extent of any such reduction would be a function of how frequently the senior judges chose to sit, which is their own decision; they put in their requests for when they wish to sit,[37] so they are not simply used as "filler" on panels. It has been suggested that "the addition of new judges does not normally influence Seniors on how much to sit,"[38] although one could envisage a situation in which, in a short-handed court, senior judges might take on more cases, and with vacancies filled, they might ease off a bit.

In 2007, in the cases in 488-500 F.3d, before the new judges arrived, senior circuit judges participated in 28.1% of the court's cases and accounted for 10.4% of judges' individual participations. There were only two cases in which two senior judges participated, which by definition made their votes determinative, and in no other cases was a senior judge's vote dispositive, as it would have been in a 2-1 division with a senior judge joining one of the panel's two active judges. The cases in 550-562 F.3d (2008) showed an increase in seniors' participation to over half (53.2%) of the court's decisions, and they individually accounted for 20.6% of judges' participations. There were 7 cases with two circuit judges; in those and 4 other cases, roughly one-eighth (13.1%) of the court's decisions, the seniors' votes were dispositive.

Immediately before the arrival of the last three new judges but with Judge Srinivasan participating, there was a further increase in seniors' participation, as they sat in over three-fifths (62.7%) of the 720-735 F.3d cases and accounted for 23.2% of individual judges' participations. There were 4 cases in which two seniors took part, which, along with 5 other cases where the senior judge's vote was dispositive, meant that senior judges were determinative in almost one-sixth (15.2%) of the cases. Cases in 736-748 F.3d included the first opinion in which Judge Srinivasan participated, with Judge Pillard sitting in a case in the last volume of the set. However, their participation did not decrease the senior judges' share of the court's work, which indeed continued to increase, as senior circuit judges participated in over four-fifths (81.2%) of the decisions, and their presence accounted for 37.2% of judges' individual participations. More significantly, there now were 26 cases (30.6% of the court's decisions) with two senior judges,[39] whose votes therefore

---

[37] Personal communication.

[38] Judge Harry Edwards (D.C. Cir.), personal communication, April 9, 2016.

[39] In the D.C. Circuit, this may result from senior judges selecting when they wish to sit; because "if several senior judges prefer to 'front load' their schedules," panels with two senior judges may result. Senior judges' wishes as to when to sit are usually

could decide the case, in addition to 4 others in which their vote was dispositive, so that their participation was determinative over one-third of the time (35.3%).

When Judges Millett and Wilkins began to sit, senior judges' activity, while declining, remained high. Serving to retard the effect of the new judges' presence, initially they had relatively light schedules.[40] The senior judges participated in 56.2% of the cases in 749-764 F.3d, a decrease of 25 percentage points, and their individual participations showed a similar decrease, to under one-fifth (18.7%). There were 15 cases in which two seniors participated but none in the last six volumes in the set; senior judges' participation or votes were dispositive in 18.1% of the cases. Instead of the new judges' presence leading to continuing diminution of senior judges' role, however, participation by the latter was much greater in the next set of cases (765-783 F.3d), as they sat in two-thirds of the cases and accounted for 28.8% of judge-participations, and in 784-790 F.3d, the most recent case set in this part of the study, their participation was only slightly less, in 63.3% of the cases, where they accounted for 28.6% of judge-participations. Because of the relatively high number of cases in these two case sets with two senior judges, 20 and 11 respectively, their votes were dispositive in, respectively, 20.4% and 26.5% of the cases.

What about senior judges' opinion-writing? In cases with only one senior circuit judge participating, *no* senior judges wrote opinions for the panel in the 13 cases in one case set (488-500 F.3d). However, in cases in 550-561 F.3d, they wrote more than their share—43.8% (14 of 32 cases); excluding three cases in which the senior judge dissented and thus could not have been assigned the opinion, the proportion rises to almost half (48.3%). In the first three of the remaining four case sets, senior judges wrote in slightly less than one-third of their cases (31.3%, 30.8%, and 28.2%), but in the last set (765-783 F.3d), the proportion rose to over one-third—38.3% (40% excluding two cases with seniors' dissents). For those cases in which two senior judges participated, a senior judge wrote in more than three-fifths of all cases combined (61.6%), not far under their two-thirds "fair share." In one case set (736-748 F.3d), however, that level was exceeded (68%), perhaps aided by dissents by the third (active) judge in two cases. At least as reflected in these data, there seems support for a judge's observation that there was "an unspoken 'courtesy factor'"

---

accommodated by the Clerk of Court. Edwards personal communication. See also Levy, "Panel Assignment in the Federal Courts of Appeals," at 85: "[T]he scheduling preferences of the circuit's senior judges are honored."

[40] Edwards personal communication.

that allows a senior judge to decline writing "in a particular arduous case" but said "it does not happen much."[41]

These data on senior judges' participation and opinion-writing suggest that their presence can serve to limit or retard the effect of new active-duty judges. Put somewhat differently, media attention is legitimately focused on confirmation of new circuit judges because these positions become the subject of high partisan contestation, but that attention is not necessarily, or even likely, matched by attention on (lack of) immediate effect when the newly-confirmed judges take the bench. In the D.C. Circuit, where partisan contestation over nominations was high and where several new judges reached the court of appeals at roughly the same time, there is further evidence for the point made more generally on the basis of evidence across the circuits, that "the continuing presence of senior judges on the courts of appeals may serve to moderate the impact of changing partisan control of the executive branch on the composition of the bench."[42] Also relevant is the comment, made with respect to the Ninth Circuit's addition of many new judges as a result of the Omnibus Judgeship Act of 1978, that while an influx of new judges can be a "major factor in reducing the backlog, all new personnel, judges not excepted, need orientation and training, and thus do not reach peak efficiency immediately." Moreover, "[n]ew judges, though very energetic and anxious to address the backlog quickly, are also likely to review all their initial appeals with great deliberation, even those that might appear relatively easy to the veteran."[43] Thus, there are many factors limiting the immediate impact of new judges on a court of appeals, with the presence of senior judges being but one, albeit an important one.

---

[41] Id.

[42] Holmes, Spill Solberg, and Haire, "Neither Gone Nor Forgotten," at 232.

[43] Eric Neisser, "Riding Herd on the Backlog: The Ninth Circuit's Approach," California State Bar Journal (March 1981), 96-97.

9
FURTHER ACTION: EN BANCS
AND SUPREME COURT

By now, the effect of the presence of non-regular judges on the "law of the circuit" has been demonstrated through an examination of such judges' participation in, and writing for, three-judge panels. Yet while the rulings of such panels—whether published opinion or non-precedential dispositions—are almost always the end of a case in the court of appeals, in a small but important number of cases, a court of appeals will sit to rehear a case en banc. And, of course, litigants take their cases to the U.S. Supreme Court, hoping that the justices will grant their certiorari petitions. To carry forward examination of the possible effects of non-regular judges' presence, it is important to see whether that presence might affect the likelihood of a case being reheard en banc or of the Supreme Court's granting review.

This chapter is thus an examination, in turn, of en banc cases in several courts of appeals and of Supreme Court cases taken from those courts. A full examination of what role the presence of such "other" judges plays in en banc rehearing or Supreme Court decision is beyond the scope of this study, but what is portrayed here may at least provide some sense of whether decisions in which such judges have participated are likely to result in en banc rehearings and Supreme Court decisions.

En Bancs

En Banc Rehearing. A somewhat low-visibility effect of the presence of "other" judges on a three-judge panel might be that the court of appeals would be more likely to rehear en banc cases in which such judges participated, so that a larger number of the court's own judges would be speaking for it in a new statement of circuit law. As only the court of appeals' active judges may vote to rehear a case en banc, it is important to know whether other types of judges sat on the panels in cases taken banc, as the presence of those "other" judges might have led the active judges to believe the panel was incorrectly propounding the law of the circuit. If the court's regular judges are displeased that those judges have helped develop circuit precedent, one might expect that in cases reheard en banc, a higher proportion of panels would have contained a non-regular judge than would be true for panels consisting only of circuit judges. The same might also be true for cases resulting in dissents from denials of rehearing en banc, as in such cases there had obviously been a call to rehear the case en banc. Unfortunately, it is difficult to learn from the public record, including courts' websites, when there has been a call for rehearing en banc *unless* the judges' vote to reject the call *and* a judge supporting rehearing wrote a dissent from the denial. Thus the picture here must by needs be incomplete, but it will be more than now available.

This chapter will contain an examination of the data available, not only for the Ninth Circuit but also for the First, Sixth, and Eleventh Circuits. First, a word is necessary about the role of "other" judges who have participated in a case in which en banc rehearing is sought.[1]

When a petition for rehearing (PFR), that is, a panel rehearing, or—usually "and"—a suggestion for rehearing en banc (PFREB) is filed, the panel members, at times after requesting a response from the opposing party, vote on whether to grant the petitions. Only active-duty judges may cast a formal vote as to the petitions for en banc rehearing; other panel members—visiting judges, in-circuit district judges, and the circuit's own senior judges—may only "recommend" the grant or denial of the request. However, most en banc calls result not so much from what appears on the surface, that is, litigants' en banc rehearing suggestions, as from an off-panel judge's registering an objection to a panel's decision and opinion.[2] All members of a panel play some role in responding to those objections. If an off-panel judge has communicated concerns to the panel but perhaps has not yet called for a vote on whether to take the case en banc, the panel will respond to that judge (usually "copying" all the court's judges). All members of the panel—or, if the panel was divided, those in the majority—would participate in developing the response, so a "non-regular" judge might be involved in activity that might lead to an en banc call. Yet such a judge's presence on the panel can pose problems, seen in a message from the court's en banc coordinator to his colleagues: "Because the only active judge on the panel was not the author of the decision, I have extended the time until October 8 for the panel to respond to Judge Fletcher's request for en banc rehearing."[3] It is clear, however, that once

---

[1] For a more complete exposition of en banc procedure, see the primer at Stephen L. Wasby, "The Supreme Court and Courts of Appeals En Bancs," 33 McGeorge Law Review 17, 19-23 (2001).

[2] See Stephen L. Wasby, "Why Go En Banc?," 63 Hastings Law Journal 747 (2012).

[3] Alfred T. Goodwin, memorandum to active judges, June 12, 1981, *re*: United States v. Veatch, 674 F.3d 1217 (9th Cir. 1981) (panel of Judges Sneed [active], and Kilkenny [senior] and Judge Robert Grant (S.D. Ind.)).

an en banc vote has actually been requested, only the court's own members participate in the communication leading up to the vote. And, most definitely, any visiting judge or district judge who served on the panel may not participate in voting, which only the court's active judges may do.

The situation of court of appeals' senior judges is somewhat different. If a senior judge has been on the panel in which en banc rehearing is sought, that judge (if in the panel majority) may—usually, will—participate in the panel's response to requests that it modify its opinion and perhaps even in the response to an en banc. However, some senior judges feel that they ought not participate in those exchanges, and one senior judge went further about not participating in the choice of cases to be heard en banc. While observing that "it would be useful for the court to take a case en banc to clarify the issues left in doubt" by earlier court action, he "prefer[red] not to enter into the discussion of [the particular case] as the chosen instrument." While he stood on his recommendation on the panel as to disposition of the PFREB,

> Because I do not participate in the routine en banc activity of the court, my entering into the consideration of selecting this particular case for en banc treatment would be inconsistent with my assigned role of a bystander on en banc strategy. If an active judge calls [the case] en banc, the active judges can determine for themselves whether that case commends itself to the court for further consideration.[4]

As noted, senior judges may not participate in the vote on whether to rehear a case en banc. However, once en banc rehearing is granted, in all circuits but one, the entire court sits en banc and a senior judge who was on the panel may opt to sit on the en banc court. However, in the Ninth Circuit, which uses a limited en banc (LEB) of 11 judges (the chief judge and 10 others drawn by lot), a senior judge who had been on the panel may opt to have his or her name placed in the pool from which the en banc panel is drawn.

Panel Composition in En Banc Cases. What is reported here is hardly the first discussion of what leads courts of appeals to rehear cases en

---

4 Alfred T. Goodwin, memorandum to panel, November 29, 2007, *re*: Wang v. Gonzales, 186 Fed. Appx. 786 (9th Cir. 2006), revised, 262 Fed. Appx. 798 (9th Cir. 2008). Shortly thereafter, in a memorandum to the panel and other judges, he did state views as to this case: He said the case "may not be the best case upon which to deploy en banc resources, but it is here and ready to be considered. I do not share the view that an intra-circuit conflict on the standard of review of immigration Judges' adverse credibility findings exists. Where such an intra-circuit conflict exists, I believe it is the duty of the court to resolve that conflict as expeditiously as possible." Memorandum, December 19, 2007.

banc. Of the studies bearing on the topic, three in particular seem most relevant. The first is by D.C. Circuit Judge Douglas Ginsburg and co-author Donald Falk, who examined the D.C. Circuit's en banc cases from 1981-1990.[5] (See below for discussion of D.C. Circuit.) The second, by Tracey George, was a study of the Second, Fourth, and Eighth Circuits.[6] And the third was by Pierre Bergeron, who focused on the Sixth Circuit from 1990-2000.[7] (See below for discussion of Sixth Circuit.) Among the factors examined in these studies were dissents in the panel which heard a case then taken en banc (unanimous or split panel decisions); the ideology of the panel members or the ideological direction of the panel ruling; the panel's affirmance or reversal of the district court or agency from which appeal was taken; and, in Bergeron's Sixth Circuit study, the difference between "uniformity cases," that is, those in which the court of appeals reheard a case en banc to stabilize the law of the circuit by re-solving intra-circuit inconsistencies, and "importance cases," those taken because of a case's "exceptional importance."

A methodological caveat is that shown here are only the proportions of cases heard en banc in which the original panel had non-regular judges. Such information can provide only a partial picture of whether non-regular judges' presence "makes a difference," as, to be certain of such possible effects, one would have to compare panel composition in a court of appeals' en banc cases with the panel composition for *all* cases decided in that court. Making that comparison, Bergeron found that in Sixth Circuit en banc cases from 1990-2000, almost one-third (31.6%) of panels in cases taken en banc contained a visiting judge, "almost three times the rate for all cases."[8] Also, comparisons made here can be only very rough because the time periods used for en banc cases are not the same as those used for studying panel composition generally. Also, Bergeron's helpful distinction between "uniformity" and "importance" cases is not applied.

In what follows, data are presented, first, on the composition of panels in cases taken en banc and, then, on whether those panels were unanimous or divided and whether they affirmed or reversed (in whole or in part) the lower court or agency ruling. These elements are examined

---

[5] Douglas H. Ginsburg and Donald Falk, "The Court En Banc: 1981-1990," 59 George Washington Law Review 1008 (1991).

[6] Tracey E. George, "The Dynamics and Determinants of the Decision to Grant En Banc Review," 74 Washington Law Review 213 (1999).

[7] Pierre H. Bergeron, "En Banc Practice in the Sixth Circuit: An Empirical Study, 1990-2000," 68 Tennessee Law Review 771 (2001).

[8] Id., 794. Note that for Bergeron, counter to the usage in this volume, a "visiting judge" is either judge from another circuit or one of the circuit's own visiting judges.

because, as noted above, they have been thought to be cues for whether post-panel action is likely to take place. Certainly, a divided panel would be a cue, both to other judges of the court of appeals and to the justices, of disagreement on an issue that might warrant further examination, and a dissenting panel member might well ask for en banc rehearing or another judge might use that dissent as the basis for an en banc call. In considering whether to rehear en banc, court of appeals judges may not pay particular attention to whether the panel reversed or affirmed as such as much as they would look at the panel outcome and the doctrine the panel announced, unless the panel reversal seemed arbitrary, but earlier studies so suggest that affirmance or reversal is a possible cue for further action.

The Ninth Circuit. In looking at the possible effect of panel composition on en banc rehearing, the Ninth Circuit Court of Appeals, the court that has received primary attention in this study, is examined first. Of all the courts of appeals examined, the Ninth Circuit, in addition to being one of those making considerable use of "other" judges, is by far the largest in number of judges and cases decided, and, as part of its work product, has decided a non-trivial number of cases en banc, indeed 450 from 1969 through 2016. Because of that number, after presentation of some basic information about panel composition and results for the entire period, aspects of the panels are examined for three separate periods—1989-1999, 2000-2009, and 2010-2016—to avoid obscuring possible changes over time. Within each period, analysis is somewhat more fine-grained than for the entire period. (See Table V.Part II in Appendix A.)

Overall View. Because some en banc rulings are "original en bancs," that is, no panel ruling—or at least no published panel ruling—precedes the en banc decisions,[9] and because panel data is unavailable for some cases as the panel ruling was vacated on the granting of en banc rehearing, information on panels is not available for all en banc cases. For 1989-2016, that leaves over 400 Ninth Circuit cases decided en banc for which panel composition information is available. Of these en banc cases, in just under two-thirds, the panel that initially decided the case was composed solely of circuit judges, either all active-duty circuit judges or those judges joined by senior circuit judges; however, only slightly over one-fourth of the panels were composed solely of active-duty circuit judges. Slightly over one-half of the panels contained a senior circuit judge joining either active-duty circuit judges or visiting or district judges; in 10% of the cases,

---

[9] In the Ninth Circuit, even when the court's first ruling is its en banc decision, a panel has usually issued some sort of opinion although that opinion might not be filed. This is quite likely when the panel itself, having begun deliberation in a case, called for en banc consideration. Whether this procedure is used in other circuits is not known.

two senior judges participated. Judges visiting from other circuits and district judges from within the Ninth Circuit early participated in roughly one-sixth of the cases decided by the panels. The panels deciding cases then taken en banc were unanimous 37% of the time and divided 63%, with nine-tenths of the divisions a result of dissent and the remaining one-tenth a result of a panel member's separate concurrence (in the result only).[10] The panels were slightly more likely to affirm the lower court or agency ruling (47.2%) than to reverse in whole or in part (52.8%).

1989-1999. In the first part of the extended period studied, beginning in 1989 and extending through 1999, there were 129 en banc decisions but only 110 for which panel information is available. In this set of en banc cases, the presence of "other" judges on the panels preceding the en banc ruling is quite a bit less frequent than for all the court's cases. This might indicate that presence of a visiting judge or an in-circuit district judge on a panel did not particularly serve as a prompt for the court to take a case en banc, and the high proportion of panels composed solely of active circuit judges reinforces the notion that disputes among the court's own judges account for such rehearing. However, apart from statistics about the proportions of cases with certain panel compositions, and apart from cases most often being called en banc because of disagreement with the panel outcome, the impression conveyed by having the law of the circuit written by a panel majority composed of a visiting judge and a senior circuit judge is that "this just should not happen." However, it is no surprise that when a panel's only active circuit judge dissents, en banc activity is more likely.

The panels in over two-thirds (68.2%) of the en banc cases in this period were composed solely of circuit judges—both active-duty and senior—but only two-fifths (43.6%) were composed solely of active-duty circuit judges. One-third of the panels in these en banc cases contained at least one senior judge, among which were a small number (5% of all cases) with two senior circuit judges, and one case even had three. Almost 10% of the panels contained two non-regular judges (visiting judge, district judge, or senior circuit judge). Unlike the pattern of overall use of visiting and district judges by the Ninth Circuit, with visiting judges used more frequently than in-circuit district judges, in these cases the proportion of panels containing district judges was twice the proportion of panels with a visiting judge (18.2%, 9.1%).

---

[10] A panel is considered divided if not unanimous as to the opinion, so when a judge concurs only in the result, the panel is considered divided; however, most often—here, in all but two of the split panels—division has been the result of a dissent, not a separate concurrence.

On the two other dimensions of interest—affirmance or reversal of the district court or agency from which appeal was taken, and unanimity or division—40% of the panels had affirmed the lower court or agency and 60% had reversed in whole or in part, and slightly less than half (45.2%) of the panels had been unanimous. In the divided panels, a dissent created the division in the vast majority of instances (84.2%), with the other panels divided because a judge concurred only in the judgment or result. When a senior judge was on a panel that divided, the two most frequent patterns were (a) a majority composed of an active judge and a senior judge, with the other circuit judge dissenting, and (b) a senior judge dissenting from the ruling by of a two-active-judge majority.

A closer look at panel unanimity and division reveals that when a panel contained a district judge, a lower proportion of the panels were split than when the panels were composed solely of active circuit judges—50% and 55.6%, respectively. Panels with both active and circuit judges were divided three-fifths of the time. In the smaller number of panels with a visiting judge, the proportion of divided panels is the same as that for those panels with a senior circuit judge. It would seem that panel division is relatively more important than a district judge's presence—or panel composition generally.

The differences in the composition of panels when they affirmed or reversed the court or agency below are more stark than for panel unanimity or division. Just under one-half of cases (48.5%) from panels with a senior judge were reversals, but the rate was much higher (63.6%) for panels composed solely of active circuit judges. Interestingly, decisions by panels that contained a district judge reversed almost three-fourths of the time (72.7%), so reversal combined with presence of a district judge seemed a particular prompt to take a case en banc. However, while one might see panels composed solely of active circuit judges as more representative of the full court of appeals than when "other" judges sat, a panel of all-active-circuit judges was no obstacle to en banc rehearing of a case. When unanimity/division and affirmance/reversal are combined with panel composition—that is, sorting by unanimous/affirm-unanimous/reversal and split/affirm and split/reverse—there are no prominent findings. For example, when panels contain only active circuit judges, among the unanimous rulings, 40% of the cases are affirmances and 60% reversals, the same ratio for decisions when the panels are divided.

2000-2009. In roughly the next decade (2000-2009), the Ninth Circuit decided 177 cases en banc (panel data available for 162). Examination of the composition of the panels that initially decided these cases shows that only one-sixth were composed solely of active circuit judges, a severe decline from the earlier period where the proportion exceeded two-fifths, but that two-thirds were composed of circuit judges (including those with senior judges), down only slightly from the previous period. This is a clear further indication that the court made not only heavy but also greater use of its own senior circuit judges, as they participated in over three-fifths (63.6%) of the panels in these en banc cases, almost a two-fold increase from the one-third of the first period. Indeed, 14.7% of the panels in this set of en banc cases had (at least) two senior judges, a three-fold increase from the first period's 5% low. A few panels were composed solely of seniors despite the rule that there should be at least one active judge on a panel; this proportion, while not of great magnitude, was three times that for the first period. Visiting judges sat on 15.4% of panels in cases taken en banc, an increase from under 10% in the first period, and district judges on 17.9%, roughly the same proportion as in the first period. In over one-fifth of the cases (22.8%), panels had either two senior judges or a senior judge and either a visiting or district judge, that is, two "non-regular" judges, which was more than double the proportion in the first period.

Half the panels had reversed the court or agency below in whole or in part and half had affirmed, a 10-percentage-point shift toward affirmance. When, in en banc cases, the panels had reversed, the highest proportion of such results (over three-fifths) occurred in all-active-circuit-judge panels, but less than half (48.1%) of the panels with a senior judge had reversed. Panels composed of active and senior circuit judges reversed at a rate "in between"—in slightly over half the cases (52.8%). By contrast, panels with either a visiting judge or an in-circuit district judge were more likely to have affirmed than reversed the lower court or agency; those panels with a visiting judge affirmed in almost three-fifths of those cases. Looked at another way, when the pre-en banc panels affirmed, only one-eighth of the panels in cases taken en banc were composed only of active circuit judges, but among the reversing panels, one-fifth were composed of all active circuit judges. Over two-thirds (68.3%) of the affirming panels had a senior judge, but the proportion for reversing panels was several points less (61.7%), an indication that reversal was a more important prompt than was panel composition.

The larger proportion of panels in this set of en banc cases were divided, almost three-fifths (58.8%), a slight increase from the previous period. Such splits were primarily a result of dissent, but in several cases a panel member had concurred only in the judgment. When either a visiting judge or district judge was on the panel in a case that went en banc, the proportion of divided panels was at that same level. However, the proportion exceeded three-fifths for all-circuit-judge panels and approached two-thirds when panels were composed solely of active circuit judges or contained a senior judge. Almost three-fourths of the panels with two senior judges were divided, and those with two "other" judges split only slightly less often. When a divided panel contained one senior circuit judge, by far the most common pattern, in over half the instances, was for the senior judge to join an active circuit judge to form the majority while the other active judge dissented. When two senior judges sat on a panel that divided, the senior judges split—one in the majority, one dissenting— somewhat more often than they formed the panel majority by themselves with the sole active judge in dissent.

In these cases taken en banc, among the unanimous panels, only 13.6% were composed only of active circuit judges, but 18.1% of the divided panels were so composed. Similarly, in unanimous panels, a senior judge was present on 56.1% of the cases but on over two-thirds of the split panels. When a panel contained two senior judges, the difference in proportions was even greater; they sat on 10.6% of unanimous panels and almost twice that proportion (19.1%) of divided panels; panels with two "other" judges (including two senior circuit judges) were 15.2% of unanimous panels but one-fourth of divided ones. Panels with either a visiting judge or district judge accounted for similar proportions of unanimous and divided panels. These data might suggest that interaction between presence of one or more senior (or other) judges and division in a panel would more often lead to en banc rehearing.

When panel unanimity and affirmance or reversal are combined, the panel compositions that occurred most frequently were panels with a senior judge, or those composed of all circuit judges, that were divided and had reversed the lower court; somewhat fewer were unanimous affirming panels with a senior judge or all active circuit judges.

2010-2016. The most recent set of Ninth Circuit en banc cases examined, from 2010 into 2016, contains 127 en banc rulings for which panel information is available (not available for 16 cases). Of the panels in these en banc cases, only one-fourth were comprised solely of active-duty circuit judges, an increase from the previous set's one-sixth. With senior circuit judges added, over three-fifths (62.5%) of the panels were made up solely of the court's own circuit judges, continuing the decline from the previous two periods. Panels containing a senior circuit judge from the court—some of which also contained a visiting judge or a district judge— decided just over half (52.0%) of the panels in this set of en banc rulings, a slight decline, and 10% of all the panels contained two senior circuit judges, a smaller proportion than in the immediately previous set.

Illustrating the court's shift in relative usage of the circuit's own district judges and out-of-circuit visitors, where previously there had been more district judges than visitors, here only 11.8% of the panels had a district judge, while well more than twice that proportion (27.6%) contained a visiting judge.

Only slightly over one-fourth (27.9%) of the panel rulings in these en banc cases were unanimous, a decline, with dissents (rather than separate concurrences) accounting, as before, for almost all panel division. When a senior judge was on a panel, the proportion of unanimous rulings was slightly higher (29.7%), and it was even higher when two senior judges sat—in fact, over one-third (35.7%)—and higher still (41.4%) with two "other" judges (of whatever type) sitting. Panels with a senior judge were 52.8% of unanimous panels but only 48.4% of cases with divided panels, and panels with all circuit judges (active and senior) were closer to being roughly the same proportion of unanimous (58.2%) and split (60.2%) decisions. On divided panels with a single senior judge, the most common pattern was that the senior judge would join one active judge to form the panel majority while the other active judge dissented; there were smaller numbers of cases in which the senior judge dissented from a two active-circuit judge majority. When a district judge was in the panel mix, panel unanimity dropped to one-sixth. From a different angle, panels with a district judge were only 5.6% of unanimous panels but 10.8% of split panels.

Half the panels in these en banc cases had affirmed the lower court or agency, and half had reversed at least in part. Worthy of note is that panels of all active circuit judges were much more likely to have affirmed—three-fifths of the time—than panels containing a senior judge and those of all circuit judges, active and senior, and those with a visiting judge affirmed at about the overall rate, while those on which a district judge sat or on which two senior circuit judges participated had affirmed less, at a proportion closer to two-fifths. From a different perspective, panels of all active-duty judges constituted 30% of the cases panels affirmed but only just under 20% of reversed cases. Panels composed solely of circuit judges were a somewhat larger proportion of cases in which panels affirmed (61.5%) than when panels reversed (57.8%); the same was true for visiting judges—29.2% of affirmances, 26.6% of reversals. By contrast, panels with a senior circuit judge constituted a somewhat smaller proportion of affirmances than reversals (47.7% v. 50%), also true for panels with a district judge (7.8% affirmance, 10.9% reversal).

For panel affirmance and unanimity together, the proportion of all divided active-circuit-judge panels that affirmed is the same as those in which split panels reversed (38.7% each), but for all panels composed only of active and senior circuit judges, almost half (48.5%) were split panels reversing, while less than one-third (31.8%) were divided panels affirming. In panels of that composition, unanimous panels affirming accounted for twice as many cases as those reversing (17.7% v. 8.9%), but all (of the small number) of all-active-circuit-judge panels that affirmed were unanimous. When a senior circuit judge served on a panel, slightly more of the unanimous decisions were affirmances (16.7%) than reversals (15.2%), but for divided panels with a senior circuit judge, there were more reversals than affirmances (379% to 30.3%); this was true as well for panels with a visiting judge (42.4% to 33.3%). One cannot divine much from these data, but the importance of panel reversal to rehearing en banc seems relatively clear and overall of greater effect than panel composition.

Dissents from Rehearing Denial. In addition to decisions rendered in cases heard or reheard en banc, one finds a non-trivial number of instances in which, when en banc rehearing is denied, one or more judges issued a published dissent from that denial. Those cases receive attention here, although not within this purview are the instances when, as is evident in the case reports, rehearing is denied but the panel modifies its original opinion. Also not included are cases in which the court denies rehearing and no judge chooses to issue a public dissent, because courts of appeals seldom make such information (easily) available, although a few courts do reveal vote counts when an en banc call has been made. Rehearing denials are most often not recorded in the published reports. Absence of a published dissent from denial of en banc rehearing does not mean that no judges voted to rehear the case but means only that they chose not to express their disagreement, a task they would have to undertake in addition to their regular allotment of (panel) opinions.

Are there differences in panel composition and result between cases to which rehearing en banc has been granted—explored in the last several pages—and those in which rehearing en banc is denied but one or more judges file a dissent to that denial? In the extended period 1990-2016, in the Ninth Circuit there were over 200 instances in which denial of en banc rehearing was accompanied by a published dissent. In almost three-fourths of these cases (72.7%), the panels were composed only of circuit judges, a higher proportion than for cases taken en banc (65.4%). Likewise, the proportion of cases in which panels were composed only of active circuit judges was higher—by more than 10 percentage points—than in the en banc cases (37.0% v. 26.8%). As one would then be led to expect, the proportion of cases in which a senior circuit judge participated was much higher in cases reheard en banc (two-thirds) than in those where en banc rehearing was denied with a published dissent (only half). These data would tend to suggest, if indirectly, that the presence of a senior judge on a panel made it more likely that en banc rehearing would be granted, even after, and if, a senior circuit judge's presence might have triggered an en banc call.

Cases with two senior circuit judges on a panel constituted a somewhat smaller proportion of these cases with dissents from rehearing denial (8.3%) than those decided en banc (10.5%), but all cases with two non-regular judges are a higher proportion of cases with dissents from en banc denials than cases decided en banc (19.4% v. 15.3%). As to panels with visiting judges and district judges, there is no difference in the proportion of cases in which a district judge sat on the panel, but panels with visiting judges were a somewhat higher proportion of en banc cases than of cases in which en banc was denied with a dissent filed (17.5% v. 14.4%).

When it comes to panel unanimity or division, in half of the cases in which en banc hearing was denied but a judge dissented, the panel was unanimous, a proportion somewhat lower (44%) than in cases actually heard en banc. And as to whether panels had affirmed or reversed the lower court or agency, the proportion of reversals is notably lower in en banc cases than in those not taken en banc but where a judge dissented (52.8% v. 63.1%).

The First Circuit. Having explored possible effects of the presence of out-of-circuit visitors and in-circuit district judges in the Ninth Circuit, with its very considerable use of such judges, it is important to see whether the patterns seen there also appear in other courts of appeals that make such use of "non-regular" judges. First to be examined is the First Circuit Court of Appeals. What follows is *not* an examination of the fate of all First Circuit published opinions—that is, what proportion were reheard en banc—but only of those to which en banc hearing was granted and those where, with en banc rehearing denied, there was a published dissent from the denial. Thus what factors led to en banc calls is not determined here, as the fate of many such calls are not known because not publicly available.

The period examined for this court is 1983-2015, a more extended period than used for study of this circuit's panel composition, nor are identical time periods used for en banc cases and those with dissents from rehearing denial. Because of panel opinions withdrawn and vacated on the granting of en banc rehearing, or because in a few instances the court

210

of appeals appears to have heard a case en banc without a panel opinion having been filed, information on panel composition is available for the relevant period for only 39 First Circuit en banc decisions.

Between one-fifth and one-fourth of the panels in these cases contained either a visiting judge or an in-circuit district judge, or, in one case, both. Senior judges sat on panels in two-fifths of the cases heard en banc, with two senior judges sitting in one-third of those (one-eighth of all en banc cases). Only active-duty circuit judges sat on only one-fifth of the panels in these cases, but judges of the circuit (both active and senior) composed the panels in three-fifths of the cases. In 17.9% of the cases, only one active judge sat, because of combinations of visitors and senior judges or the presence of two senior circuit judges, and it is in these cases that the court's active judges might particularly feel that the en banc court should make the ultimate ruling. (For greater detail for the First and other circuits, see Table V.Part I in Appendix A.)

Another reason for taking a case en banc might be lack of panel unanimity. Three-fifths (59%) of these panels were unanimous and two-fifths (41%) divided. What is significant is that in these 16 divided cases, either a visiting judge or a district judge made up the majority along with a single active circuit judge in 6 cases, and in 4 cases, it was a senior judge joining an active circuit judge. In only one case was the majority a visiting judge and a district judge, with the active circuit judge in dissent, thus leaving only "others" to write the law of the circuit.

Decomposing these data to examine the relationship between panel composition and panel unanimity shows little difference in panel unanimity between panels with a visiting or district judge, but two-thirds of panels with a senior judge were unanimous, as were all cases with two senior circuit judges, perhaps another indication that the court's active judges want to make circuit law themselves regardless of panel unanimity. There also is little difference as to whether the panels in these en banc cases affirmed the district court or agency or instead overturned the lower court in part or whole.

Dissents from Rehearing Denial. What about First Circuit cases in which en banc rehearing was denied but one or more judges published a dissent from that denial, thus showing clearly that the court was internally divided? Examination of some 25 instances in which First Circuit judges dissented from denial of en banc rehearing from 1994-2015 reveals that visiting judges were as likely to have been on the panel as in cases that were taken en banc—in one-fifth of each type of case. However, there were *no* district judges on panels in the cases with dissent from denial of rehearing, compared to one-fourth of those heard en banc. Roughly the same proportion of cases of each type had two non-regular judges. To change the focus, panels in the denial-with-dissent cases were more likely to have been composed of all circuit judges (active and senior combined) than was true in the en banc cases—68% to 59%—and likewise, the panels were more likely to be composed of all active circuit judges in dissent-from-denial than in en banc cases—32% to 23.1%. These findings reinforce at least a tentative conclusion that the presence of "other" judges contributes to the decision to take a case en banc. Cutting in the other direction, however, is unanimity, as panels were more likely, although not by a large margin, to have been unanimous in cases heard en banc (59%) than when en banc was denied with a published dissent (52%). This is counter to the expectation that cases from split panels are more likely than rulings from unanimous panels to be reheard en banc, but the numbers are small. Again, most division in panels was from dissents, not separate concurrences in the judgment.

When en banc rehearing was denied but a dissent was registered, was panel composition related to unanimity? The answer seems to be "No," as panels with visiting judges and those with senior circuit judges divided evenly between unanimity and being split, although those in which the panel was composed solely of active circuit judges were slightly more split than unanimous. (Remember, there are none on which district judges sat.) A comparison of en banc and rehearing-denied-with-dissent cases shows a difference in relative unanimity only for "all active judge" panels, which were more likely to have been unanimous in cases taken en banc but slightly more likely to be split in those where rehearing is denied. As a very high proportion of First Circuit cases decided with published opinions are unanimous, these data suggest that panel division is a prompt at least for an en banc call although slightly less so for actually granting en banc rehearing.

In these cases with dissents from denial of rehearing en banc, the ones in which the panel had a senior judge were evenly divided between those affirming and those reversing the lower court or agency, but those panels composed solely of all active judges were far more likely to have affirmed than reversed by a ratio of 3:1. However, as with panel division, because of the overall propensity of First Circuit panels to affirm lower court rulings, reversal appears to be a cue for en banc calls although less so for granting rehearing en banc.

The Sixth Circuit. Pierre Bergeron, in his examination of the U.S. Court of Appeals for the Sixth Circuit for 1990-2000, questioned whether that court's heavy use of out-of-circuit visitors and in-circuit district judges—"the Sixth Circuit has tapped the resources of visiting judges at a much higher rate than its sister circuits"—led to "results in certain cases that might be out of step with the philosophies" of the circuit's own appellate judges.[11] The statistics he developed on the court's en banc cases were taken as evidence supporting a positive response to his question.

In 57 en banc decisions where a panel had first decided the case, Bergeron's "visiting judges" had been on the panel in almost one-third (31.6%) of the cases. What was most important was that this proportion "was almost three times the rate for all cases" (31.6% v. 12.8%), a finding that Bergeron suggested differed from George's earlier finding, from other courts, of only a 5% difference. Strengthening Bergeron's inference of the effect of visiting-judge presence in prompting en banc rehearing was that the proportion of cases taken en banc when there had been visiting judges on the panel was almost identical for "uniformity cases," those in which the court heard a case en banc to resolve intra-circuit inconsistency, and "importance cases," those taken en banc largely because of the importance of the issue independent of concerns about internal inconsistency. Bergeron had thought the importance cases might be less dependent on panel composition, but he did not discover that, and this similarity in proportions was "not unexpected." There was a clear effect of divided panels, with uniformity en banc cases about evenly divided between those with unanimous and those with divided panels, but those cases reheard en banc because of importance came disproportionately from divided panels. As to whether en banc rehearing was more likely when the panel had reversed the district court or agency, where George had found a panel affirmance rate of less than 40%, Bergeron also found that panels had affirmed less than half the time, but he found further that uniformity cases were much more likely to come from panels that had reversed than was true for "importance" cases.

In the present analysis, "uniformity" and "importance" cases are not distinguished à la Bergeron, but all Sixth Circuit en banc rulings are considered together. As seen earlier, this court makes very high use on its panels of the circuit's own district judges in addition to drawing on visiting judges to a lesser extent. What effect did the presence of these judges, along with the appeals court's own senior judges, appear to have on cases the court reheard en banc? There are 159 such cases from 1989-2016—thus covering but also extending the period Bergeron used—but information is available for only 140.

In the cases taken en banc, the panels in somewhat over half (52.9%) were composed solely of the court's own (active and senior) judges,

---

[11] Bergeron, "En Banc Practice in the Sixth Circuit," at 593-94. It should be remembered that he considers both types of judges under the "visiting judge" category.

although only more than one-third (36.4%) were panels only of active circuit judges. Senior judges took part in one-fourth of the panels; in only two panels were there two senior judges. In only 5% of these en banc cases had visiting judges sat on the panels, but district judges sat in *almost one-third* (32.1%). The panels in these en banc cases were twice as likely to have been divided (66.3%) as unanimous (33.6%), with dissents accounting for most of the division. In roughly half of the cases with divided panels, either a senior circuit judge or an in-circuit district judge was in the majority, with a visiting judge appearing there in two additional cases; in one case, the majority was composed of a district judge and senior circuit judge. And, in two-thirds of the cases taken en banc for which relevant data is available, the lower court or agency in whole or in part two-thirds of the time.

What happens when one puts together panel composition with panel unanimity and panel affirmance or reversal? When cases taken en banc came from panels composed of circuit judges, roughly one-third were unanimous, but the proportion was slightly more (35.6%) when only active circuit judges were panel members. When a senior circuit judge was on the panel in an en banc case, the proportion of divided panels was slightly higher (71%) than when neither they or other non-regular judges are present (67%). When district judges were present, the proportion of split panel rulings was 67.5%, less than when senior judges were on the panel. This is a possible slight indication that district judges' presence may be more likely to prompt en banc rehearing, but the differences in proportions are not large.

Likewise, when panel composition is matched with whether the panel affirmed or reversed, the proportions of affirmance and reversal vary little with aspects of panel composition. However, when panels are composed only of circuit judges, the proportion reversing was only 61.4% but was five points higher when panels had only active circuit judges (66.7%). The figure was the same for panels of senior circuit judges, with the proportion for panels with district judges only slightly behind (65%). There is only a limited indication here that non-regular judges' presence made it more likely that en banc hearing would occur when a panel reversed the lower court.

When, however, unanimity (or division) and affirmance (or reversal) are examined together in relation to panel composition, there is some indication of possible effect of non-regular judges' presence on panels. When panels in en banc cases were unanimous, the absolute numerical differences were small, but panels of all active circuit judges were slightly more likely to have affirmed than when either a senior circuit judge or district judge was on the panel, a (minor) indication that presence of the latter might prompt the court to rehear a case en banc. For split panels, there was some effect of senior circuit judges' presence but not for district judges.

The Eleventh Circuit. The Eleventh Circuit Court of Appeals made considerable use of both out-of-circuit visitors and in-circuit district judges in addition to its own senior circuit judges, and it was not uncommon for a panel to contain more than one non-regular judge. For 1988-2016, the Eleventh Circuit decided 142 cases en banc (panel information unavailable for 16). Given its use overall of non-regular judges, it is not surprising that they sat on many of the panels whose decisions were reheard en banc.

Only 10.3% of these panels were composed solely of active circuit judges; adding senior circuit judges increases the proportion to only one-third composed of the circuit's own appellate judges, active and senior. This suggests that the presence of non-regular judges on a panel, whether or not a prompt to taking a case en banc, certainly cut in favor of en banc hearing being granted. Visiting judges sat on one-third of the panels in cases taken en banc, with a somewhat smaller proportion—over one-fourth (27.8%)—having a district judge on the panel. The court's own senior circuit judges sat on almost half (47.6%) of the cases taken en banc; in 6 cases, two senior judges participated. In over one-fifth (22.2%) of the cases, two non-regular judges had been on the panel, most often a combination of a senior circuit judge and a visiting judge.

Eleventh Circuit cases taken en banc were far more likely to have been ones in which the panel reversed rather than affirmed the district court or agency, with somewhat short of three-fourths (70.1%) of the panels having reversed in whole or in part. Less starkly, unanimous panels predominated over split ones, 3:2, with three-fourths of the divided panel rulings a result of dissents rather than separate concurrences. There is no predominant combination of judge-types in the divided panels, although there are 7 cases each in which either a visiting judge or district judge was in the majority, with one other case each in which a majority contained a district judge or visiting judge, and a senior circuit judge dissented. A district judge's dissent, in 5 cases with active circuit judge majorities and 3 cases with the majority containing a senior judge, would not as likely be the prompt for the en banc hearing so much as was the position of the circuit judge majority; the same would be true in the couple of cases in which the dissenter was a senior circuit judge. In 5 of the panels of which senior circuit judges were members, that judge was in the majority, and in another 3, the senior judge concurred in the result. There were also two in which two senior judges composed the majority.

In these cases taken en banc, examination of panel composition by whether panels were unanimous or divided reveals a mixed picture. Half of the relatively small number of panels composed solely of active circuit judges were unanimous, compared with over three-fifths (63%) of the panels of active and senior circuit judges combined, and the proportion unanimous was almost identical (64.3%) for those with senior judges, an indication that, while one might have expected panel division to be a prompt, the court's judges were not hesitant to take en banc cases from unanimous panels. In cases taken en banc that had been decided by panels containing two non-regular judges, almost three-fourths (73.3%) were unanimous, so panel composition overrode unanimity. When a visiting judge was on the panel, there was a smaller proportion unanimous, just over three-fifths (61.5%), but panels with district judges (sometimes two) were unanimous only half the time, suggesting that presence of a district judge was a cue, just as was panel division.

Differences in panel composition seemed to result in relatively little difference in the proportion of panel decisions affirming or reversing. The highest proportion of panel reversals taken en banc, 77.1%, occurred when a visiting judge was on the panel, but the proportions for panels with district judges or with senior circuit judges was only slightly lower (73.7%, 74.1%); those panels with two non-regular judges issued a reversal 72.2% of the time. When panels were composed of all active circuit judges or active and senior circuit judges combined (68.8%, 67.3%), the proportion of reversals fell below the overall proportion. Despite the small numerical differences, it does appear that presence of non-regular judges on panels which reverse had a slight prompting effect on taking a case en banc, and it also seems to be the case that even when panels of circuit judges had affirmed the lower court, there was a slightly greater likelihood that cases from those panels would be taken en banc.

When panel composition is combined with unanimity/division and affirmance/reversal, some differences appear, but no relationships stand out, an indication that none of these factors—type of judge on panel; panel unanimity; panel reversal of lower court—was a predominant prompt for the court of appeals to take a case en banc. In cases taken en banc, for panels composed only of circuit judges, 40% were unanimous reversals while another 30% were reversals by divided panels. Almost half of the relatively few panels composed solely of active-duty circuit judges were split reversals, with unanimous affirmances following. In these cases taken en banc, when senior circuit judges were on a panel, almost half the panel rulings were unanimous reversals, with another one-fourth-plus split reversals. That pattern is repeated when visiting judges were on such panels, although in the latter configuration, slightly over half were unanimous reversals. When a district judge was a member of a panel in a case taken en banc, slightly more than one-third of the cases were unanimous reversals and the same proportion were split reversals.

A Note on the D.C. Circuit. As the Court of Appeals for the District of Columbia Circuit has for some time used neither visiting judges nor the district judges from the circuit's one district, it is possible to examine only whether inclusion on panels of the court's own senior circuit judges might have led to more frequent taking of cases en banc. In the D.C. Circuit's 42 en banc cases from 1990-2015—with panel composition data for only 37—three-fourths of the panels were composed solely of active circuit judges and only less than one-fifth (18.9%) contained one of the court's senior circuit judges, a proportion less than that for senior circuit judges' presence in the court's published rulings overall. The panels in these en banc cases were predominantly split (70.3%), and, in a smaller proportion of cases (56.8%), the panels had reversed the district court or agency. When unanimity and reversal are combined, panels of all active circuit judges—the predominant type among those in which cases were taken en banc—break out almost the same as to reversal regardless of unanimity or division, but the panels with senior circuit judges are so small in numbers as not to be determinative of much of anything.

Supreme Court Review

If there is some evidence that the presence of non-regular judges on panels of several courts of appeals might be among the prompts for those courts to take cases en banc, do those factors seem to act as prompts (or "cues") for the Supreme Court as the justices consider whether to grant review to rulings of the courts of appeals? Thorough study of that question would require examination of all court of appeals cases in which certiorari was sought, that is, including the vast majority of cases receiving cert denials, in order to compare panel composition for those in which review was granted with those in which certiorari was denied, but that is well beyond the scope of this volume. However, some light can be cast on the subject by examining cases in which certiorari was granted and the Supreme Court decided the case with an opinion, either signed or per curiam, including both per curiams decided after argument and the more frequent instances of per curiams issued without plenary treatment, that is, solely on the certiorari petitions. Also receiving attention are those cases in which the Supreme Court granted certiorari, vacated the court of appeals ruling, and remanded to that court (GVR) in light of a previous ruling in a case usually selected from among numerous petitions posing the same issue.

Examined here are data about the proportions of cases the Supreme Court took from a particular court of appeals in which the panel deciding the case below contained a non-regular judge. It might be thought that the Supreme Court would be more likely to take cases with such "other" judges because their presence might make the case problematic, but that presence also cuts the other way, with the justices perhaps preferring cases with what seems a more complete statement by active (or active and senior) court of appeals judges. It is the latter logic that leads some justices to call upon the courts of appeals, or at least certain ones, to hear cases en banc more often.[12]

As usual, the first court of appeals to be examined is that for the Ninth Circuit, followed by attention to several other circuits. (For details, see Table VI in Appendix A.) Examined are the same factors thought to be potential prompts within a court of appeals for en banc consideration: panel composition, including visiting and district judges and a court's own senior judges; panel affirmance or reversal (in whole or in part) of the ruling from a lower court or agency; and the panel's unanimity or division. Only very basic analysis is presented—only of the "marginals" for panel composition, unanimity, and affirmance/reversal, without further "cross-tab" analysis like that seen earlier. No attention is given to Supreme Court resolution (affirmance or reversal) of the cases to which it has granted review, although the rate at which the Ninth Circuit has been reversed has been a matter of considerable controversy.

Inclusion of panel unanimity or division, and panel affirmance or reversal of the lower court or agency, as possible prompts for Supreme Court review follows from literature on possible "signals" and "cues" which make more likely the granting of certiorari from the thousands of cert petitions that are filed. The most significant factor has repeatedly been shown to be inter-circuit conflict, the situation when various courts of appeals take different positions on an issue. Beyond that, however, cues include disagreement *within* a court of appeals, that is, a divided panel vote, and disagreement *between* levels of the court system, that is, court of appeals reversal of a lower court or agency. Other factors—not exam-

---

[12] See Stephen L. Wasby, "The Supreme Court and Court of Appeals En Bancs," 33 McGeorge Law Review 17 (2002); for a condensed version, see Wasby, "How Do Courts of Appeals En Banc Decisions Fare in the U.S. Supreme Court?," 85 Judicature 182 (#4, 2002).

ined here—also play a part, such as subject matter of a case, e.g., civil liberties, and the identity of a party, e.g., government or business.[13]

As to whether panel composition serves as a cue, the justices—or the clerks preparing "cert pool" memoranda for them—would know whether a court of appeals panel was divided or unanimous, and the presence of visiting and district judges would be evident. However, the justices might not be aware of, or heed, the presence of senior circuit judges on panels, especially in those courts of appeals that did not so identify their senior circuit judges as such in the panel opinions, as many circuits do not. Of course, justices familiar with the lower court judiciary would likely know, for cases coming before the Court, of at least some judges' senior status.

The Ninth Circuit. Examination of panels in Ninth Circuit cases which the Supreme Court decided to review and in which it issued opinions begins with a broad picture covering the entire period starting with October Term 1989 (1989-90) and extending through the most recent Term, O.T. 2016 (2016-17). To see whether that picture varies over this slightly more than 25-year period, three periods are then examined separately.

Overall. From O.T. 1989 through O.T. 2016, 480 cases from the Ninth Circuit were decided by the Supreme Court with opinion, along with 190 cases in which the Court granted certiorari, vacated the lower court ruling, and remanded to the Ninth Circuit for reconsideration in light of an intervening case. (Not included are those cases GVR'd for other reasons, along with rulings on stays, most of which came in death penalty cases.) Of the 480 cases, some 32 had been decided by the Ninth Circuit using its limited en banc (LEB) of 11 judges, leaving 448 Supreme Court decisions with published opinions in cases from three-judge panels. As 8 of the 190 GVR rulings had been Ninth Circuit en banc decisions, there were 182 instances of GVR treatment of rulings from Ninth Circuit panels.

Visiting judges participated in one-eighth (12.7%) of the panels in these cases, while in-circuit district judges sat in almost one-fifth (19.6%). Considering visiting judges, district judges, and the court's own senior circuit judges as "other" judges, 15.6% of the panels in these cases had two non-regular judges. Two-thirds of the panels had been composed of the court of appeals' circuit judges—active-duty and senior—but in only less

---

[13] See the discussion in Stephen L. Wasby, *The Supreme Court in the Federal Judicial System* (4th ed., 1995), pp. 213-15; and, for greater detail, see Doris Marie Provine, *Case Selection in the United States Supreme Court* (University of Chicago Press, 1980); H.W. Perry, Jr., *Deciding to Decide: Agenda Setting in the United States Supreme Court* (Harvard University Press, 1991); and Joseph Tanenhaus, Marvin Schick, Matthew Muraskin, and Daniel Rosen, "The Supreme Court's Jurisdiction: Cue Theory," *Judicial Decision-Making*, ed. Glendon Schubert (Free Press, 1963).

than one-third (30.1%) did three active-duty circuit judges compose the panel. Senior circuit judges sat on panels in slightly over half the cases (51.1%), with two senior circuit judges in 7.4% of all the panels.

Cases given GVR treatment showed somewhat different patterns. Panels in those cases were more likely to have contained a visiting judge than were cases with published opinions, but the reverse was true for cases on which an in-circuit district judge sat—a smaller proportion of such GVR than of published opinion cases. Panels with two non-regular judges were slightly more frequent in the Supreme Court's published opinions than in those receiving GVR treatment. The three-fifths proportion of panels composed solely of the Ninth Circuit's own circuit judges was less than for cases to which the justices had given full treatment, and the same was true for panels on which only active-duty circuit judges served (less than one-fourth—23.1%). Likewise, Ninth Circuit cases in which senior circuit judges participated constituted a smaller proportion of all GVR cases than was true of cases in which the justices wrote opinions (42.3% v. 51.1%), but the proportion of cases with two senior judges on a panel was the same for both case types.

The panels in these Ninth Circuit Supreme Court cases were more likely to have reversed than affirmed the lower court or agency whose decision was being considered, by a ratio of 3:2 for published opinion Supreme Court cases and slightly less (55:45) for GVR rulings. The Ninth Circuit panels deciding cases that in turn the Supreme Court decided with opinion were very likely to have been unanimous (69.3%), and even more panels in cases given GVR treatment had been so (78.8%). Most division in the panels was from a dissent, with only 10.2% having a separate concurrence, but that proportion was higher for panels in the GVR cases (18.2%). When panels with senior circuit judges divided, the predominant pattern (62.3%) was a split between two active circuit judges, with the senior circuit judge joining one to form the majority.

O.T. 1989-1999. In the period from October Term 1989 through O.T. 1999, the Supreme Court handed down opinions in 187 Ninth Circuit cases and GVR'd another 28. In 9 of the former, the court of appeals had heard the cases en banc, and in all but two of those, the en banc division had been close—6-5, 7-4, or 8-3—with one case decided 9-2 and 10-1. Three of the GVR cases had been en banc rulings—two by an 8-3 vote and one unanimous.

In addition to these cases decided en banc in the court of appeals, there were others in which, while the Supreme Court reviewed a three-judge panel ruling, there had been a published dissent to the Ninth Circuit's denial of en banc rehearing. There were only 5 such cases in this period, fewer than in the following ones. In all 5 cases, the panel had been unanimous and 2 of the panels had affirmed the lower court. Examination of the composition of the sets of judges—ranging from 3 to 7—issuing dissents from denial of en banc rehearing reveals that three of the five sets were composed entirely of conservative judges, one of liberal judges, and one was ideologically mixed. In addition, in one case that had been heard en banc, 5 judges, all conservatives, filed an unusual dissent to the court's decision to *take* the case en banc.

Of the 178 Supreme Court published rulings in cases decided by three-judge Ninth Circuit panels, visiting judges served on only 7.9% of the panels, but the court's own district judges were present in one-fifth—a reversal of the court's overall use of more visiting judges than district judges. The presence of two non-regular judges (including two senior judges) was found in fewer than 10% of the cases (8.4%). Of the panels, 70.8% had been composed of the court's own judges, active and senior, but only 43.4% were panels of active-duty circuit judges only. Only two-fifths (41.0%) of the panels contained a senior circuit judge, with only a few (3.3% of the total) having two senior circuit judges. For cases receiving GVR treatment, there were much smaller proportions of panels with all circuit judges (51.8% v. 70.8%); only active circuit judges (29.4% v. 43.5%); and at least one senior judge (29.4% v. 41.0%); on the other hand, there were more panels with visiting judges (12.9% v. 7.9%).

In the cases the Supreme Court decided with published opinions, in three-fifths the court of appeals had reversed the lower court, perhaps indicating that such reversals were a prompt to the justices to take the cases. In cases receiving GVR treatment, affirmances and reversals were evenly split, indicating that reversal was more of a cue in the cases to which full treatment was given but less important when a case was sent back to the lower court for further consideration.

A similar difference can be seen in courts of appeals' unanimity or division in cases in which the Supreme Court ruled. Over two-thirds (69.4%) of the panels in the Supreme Court's published rulings from Ninth Circuit cases had been unanimous, with the decisions divided in less than one-third (30.6%), a result of dissent in all but only the couple of cases in which a judge wrote a separate concurrence. In the GVR cases, by contrast, far more panel rulings were unanimous than had been true in the justices' published rulings (81.3% v. 69.4%), and, correspondingly, far fewer were divided (18.7% v. 30.6%). This was a further indication that divided panels were at least something of a prompt for further action by the Supreme Court, as suggested in the literature. When one senior judge participated in a split panel decision, most frequently that judge joined one active circuit judge for the majority, with the other "active" dissenting. In two instances, the senior judge dissented to the ruling by a panel majority of an active circuit judge and an in-circuit district judge.

O.T. 2000-O.T. 2009. In the ten Supreme Court terms O.T. 2000-2009, the justices decided with published opinion almost the same number of cases from the Ninth Circuit as in the immediately previous period—182. Of those, the Ninth Circuit had decided 13 en banc, leaving 169 decided by three-judge panels. The picture for Ninth Circuit cases receiving GVR treatment is more complicated because two Supreme Court cases accounted for a large number of these GVRs—*Zadyvas v. Davis*,[14] which accounted for 12 Ninth Circuit GVRs in O.T. 2000, and particularly the *Booker* sentencing case,[15] which accounted for 66 GVR treatments of Ninth Circuit cases in O.T. 2004 (and 3 more in O.T. 2005). Arbitrarily counting these two sets of GVRs as only one case each to avoid their "overinflating" the numbers, there were 69 GVR rulings in Ninth Circuit cases in this period, less than in the earlier ones, and only two were Ninth Circuit en banc rulings.

Of the 13 en banc rulings resulting in Supreme Court published rulings, three had been decided by decisive margins: 9-2, 11-4, and 12-3, the latter two falling in the period in which the Ninth Circuit had experimented with a 15-judge, rather than its usual 11-judge, LEB; however, most en banc decisions were by closer margins: 6-5 (3), 7-4 (5), and 8-3 (2). One of the two en banc rulings receiving GVR treatment had been decided 6-5, the other 8-3. The closer division in most of the en banc cases might have indicated to the Supreme Court that the judges' disagreement on the law indicated the importance of the issue in a case, thus warranting its review beyond the fact that a court of appeals en banc decision was itself an indication of case importance. Certainly, given en banc decisions' *relative* rarity, it is clear that proportionately more en banc rulings were taken by the Supreme Court than were panel rulings, despite the far greater number of the latter. This picture bears on the calls by some justices for the Ninth Circuit to decide more cases en banc, purportedly to provide the Supreme Court with a broader range of the court of appeals' thinking; however, it appears that, of Ninth Circuit rulings reviewed by the Supreme Court, those from panels fared better than did those from en banc decisions.[16]

---

[14] 533 U.S. 678 (2001).

[15] Booker v. United States, 543 U.S. 220 (2005).

[16] See Wasby, "The Supreme Court and Court of Appeals En Bancs."

In addition to the en banc cases the justices reviewed, there were 16 panel rulings in which sets of judges published a dissent from denial of en banc rehearing, many more than in the previous period. More of the panels in those cases were split than unanimous (10:6). More striking is that in all but two, the panel had reversed the lower court or agency. Combining unanimity/division with affirmance/reversal, the predominant pattern (in 10 of the 16) is a split panel that reversed. But most striking is that in all but three of the cases, the sets of dissenting judges— ranging from 3 judges all the way to 9 (median between 5 and 6)—were solidly conservative, and in another case, in which two separate dissenting opinions were filed, the larger set was of conservative judges while the other was a mix of judges of liberal and moderate ideologies. These data provide support for the argument that judges filing such dissents are doing so to speak directly to the Supreme Court, writing what amount to cert petitions, with conservative Ninth Circuit judges receiving a favorable reception for those opinions from a largely conservative set of justices.

The composition of panels whose decisions were taken by the Supreme Court in this period shows some noticeable differences from the patterns of O.T. 1989-1999. The proportions of panels with visiting judges and district judges were almost identical, a shift from the presence of more cases in which district judges than visitors participated. Visiting judges sat on roughly one-sixth (15.3%) of the panels in these Supreme Court cases, double the earlier proportion, but the proportion of cases with in-circuit district judges, also roughly one-sixth (16.0%), was a decline from the earlier one-fifth. Likewise, panels with two non-regular judges constituted over one-fifth (22.5%) of all cases, more than twice that earlier. The proportion of cases from panels composed solely of active-duty circuit judges was only one-fifth (19.5%), compared to over two-fifths earlier, but the proportion of cases by all circuit judges (active and senior) was only slightly lower—two-thirds (66.2%) compared to the earlier 70.8%. Filling out this picture is the much larger proportion of panels with senior judges; over three-fifths (62.7%) contained at least one senior judge, an increase from the earlier two-fifths (41.0%), and the proportion of panels with two senior judges was more than three times that of the earlier period—11.8% compared to 3.3%. Perhaps this increase should not surprise, because some of the judges who had joined the Ninth Circuit from 1977-1980, including ten filling new positions created by the Omnibus Judgeship Act of 1978 (the "Carter judges"), had begun to take senior status.

In cases receiving GVR treatment from the justices at this time, the proportion of panels composed of only active-duty circuit judges was even less than in cases with Supreme Court published opinions (13.4% v. 19.5%), but otherwise the proportions of panels with various types or combinations of judges were roughly the same as for panels in cases receiving full published Supreme Court opinion treatment.

As to how, in cases taken by the Supreme Court that resulted in published opinions, the lower court or agency had been treated, the panels had reversed in whole or in part in over two-thirds of the cases (62.1%), a higher proportion than the even affirm/reverse split seen earlier. For GVR cases, the proportion of reversals was similar but slightly slower (58.2%). The proportion of cases in which the panels had been unanimous was exactly the same as earlier (69.2%), with dissents accounting for all but 5.7% of panel divisions. Among the GVR cases, the proportion of unanimous panels was somewhat higher than for cases resulting in published opinions. In the split panel decisions from panels with one senior judge, two basic patterns accounted for all but a few cases: the panel's senior judge joined one active circuit judge to form the majority, with the other active circuit judge dissenting (13 instances), or the two active circuit judges formed the majority and the senior circuit dissented (8 cases).

OT 2010-2016. In the most recent period examined, covering O.T. 2010-O.T. 2016, the Supreme Court issued published opinions in 111 cases from the Ninth Circuit. Of those, 10 had been decided en banc, with all but one having significant numbers of dissenters (6-5, 7-4, 8-3). Of the 33 Ninth Circuit cases receiving GVR treatment, 3 had been en banc rulings (6-5 or 8-3). In this period, the number of cases to which the justices gave plenary treatment where the panel ruling had led to a published dissent of the denial of en banc rehearing was roughly on track with the total for the previous period; while fewer than ten terms are included, the number was double that from OT 1989-1999. In such cases, panels were evenly divided between unanimous and divided outcomes, but strangely, the panels in all these cases had reversed the lower court or agency. The sets of judges dissenting from rehearing denial ranged in size from 5 through 8, and 8 judges joined in dissent in 7 of the 10 cases, and *all* the sets were composed of conservative judges. (One case prompted a 7-judge opinion concurring in the rehearing denial, with another such opinion by two judges.[17])

The proportion of panels with visiting judges (one-sixth) remained at roughly the same level as in the previous ten terms, while the proportion of panels with an in-circuit district doubled (from 15.3% to 29.8%), paralleling the court of appeals' increasing use of its own district judges

---

[17] Nelson v. NASA, 568 F.3d 1028 (9th Cir. 2009), rev'd, 562 U.S. 134 (2011).

and its use of them more than visiting judges. However, in the GVR cases in this period, in only one was a district judge on the panel, but visiting judges participated in a higher proportion of cases than those the justices decided with published opinion. Panels with two non-regular judges (including senior circuit judges) constituted one-sixth of the panels in cases resulting in published Supreme Court opinions, a decrease from the more than one-fifth (22.3%) of the previous period.

One-fourth (24.85%) of the panels were composed solely of active-duty circuit judges, a proportion slightly higher than in the O.T. 2000-2009 period, and almost two-thirds (64.3%) were decided by panels of active and senior judges, roughly the same proportion as in the immediately preceding period. Senior judges participated in half the panels in these cases, a decrease from the preceding ten years, and the proportion of cases with two senior judges as panel members, small as before, was also lower. The pattern for senior judge participation was similar in GVR cases.

Of the 101 cases decided by Ninth Circuit three-judge panels, in almost two-thirds (64.3%) the result had been a reversal (in whole or in part) of the lower court or agency, roughly the same as before, and 70% of the panels had been unanimous, also the same as before; almost all split panels likewise resulted from dissents rather than opinions concurring separately (in the judgment). When a senior judge was on a divided panel, the most common pattern was for that judge to join one active circuit judge to form the majority. As to cases in which the Supreme Court's action was to GVR, a higher proportion of panels had been unanimous than in the Court's published cases. This was a further indication of the role of split panel rulings as a prompt for a grant of certiorari. Likewise, a somewhat higher proportion of panels whose rulings were to be GVR'd had affirmed the ruling before them than was true for cases resulting in the justices' published opinions, showing that reversal was a somewhat greater cue for the granting of cert for plenary treatment.

Other Circuits: First Circuit. As the circuit with the smallest number of circuit judges and without a massive caseload, the First Circuit has not provided a large number of cases resulting in Supreme Court decisions. For the Supreme Court's 1991-2015 Terms, there were only 50 such cases, two of which had been decided by the en banc First Circuit in divided rulings (3-2, 4-2). Although the First Circuit had made at least moderate use of visiting judges and in-circuit district judges, such judges sat on a relatively small portion of the remaining 47 cases taken from that circuit that had been decided by three-judge panels (no panel information for one). District judges participated in only one-sixth (17.0%) and visiting judges even less, only one-eighth (12.8%), which is also the proportion of cases with two non-regular judges, half of which contained a senior circuit judge-district judge combination. Fewer than one-fourth (23.4%) of the panels were composed solely of active circuit judges, but senior and/or active circuit judges made up over three-fifths (63.8%); the proportion of cases with a senior judge was only slightly lower (59.6%). (Four panels with a senior circuit judge had two such judges.)

The suggestion that division in the U.S. court of appeals is a cue for the Supreme Court to agree to review a case is not borne out by these First Circuit cases. Apart from the already-noted en banc rulings the justices reviewed, First Circuit panels had decided 83% of these cases unanimously. Likewise, in two-thirds of the cases, the panel had affirmed the lower court or agency, making lower court reversal not a significant cue for cases from this court of appeals.

Sixth Circuit. As a court of appeals certainly larger than that for the First Circuit and with a number of judges like that of a number of other courts of appeals, the Sixth Circuit had more of its cases decided by the Supreme Court—136 in the 1991 through 2015 Terms.[18] Eleven of these cases (8.1%) had been decided by the Sixth Circuit Court of Appeals sitting en banc, and in all but one of those, the en banc court had been divided, with half receiving four or more dissenting votes. Of the 124 cases decided by a three-judge panel (no available information for one), in only a very small proportion (3.2%) did a visiting judge sit, but district judges sat on two-fifths of the panels, a reflection of this court's frequent use of its own in-circuit district judges. And 8.5% of the panels had two non-regular judges, either two senior judges or, more often, a combination of senior circuit judge and a district judge. One-fourth of the cases had been decided by all-active-circuit judge panels, and over half (51.6%) by panels of senior and/or active judges. Senior circuit judges sat in over two-fifths (43.5%) of the panels, some of which had two.

In the Supreme Court's Sixth Circuit cases, the proportion of unanimous panel decisions was less than in the First Circuit cases—only somewhat over one-half (53.2%). The composition of panels that were split (three-fourths by dissent, one-fourth by separate concurrence) varied widely. The most frequent combination (10 cases) was a majority formed by an active circuit judge and a district judge, with the other active circuit judge dissenting; in fewer cases, a senior circuit judge dissented from an opinion by a majority of two active circuit judges. A smaller number had a senior circuit judge in the majority, with the two active circuit judges

---

[18] The Supreme Court consolidated some Sixth Circuit cases into a single decision but here those cases are counted separately.

divided; and a number equal to that had two senior circuit judges on opposite sides of the case.

Of the cases that went to the Supreme Court from panels, somewhat over half (53.5%) were reversals in whole or in part. That over half—even if only slightly over half—of the panel actions are reversals suggests that the court of appeals' action reversing a district court or agency has been at least in a part a cue for the justices in considering taking a Sixth Circuit case.

Eleventh Circuit. Of the courts of appeals that used considerable numbers of "other" judges, the Eleventh Circuit had 136 of its cases decided by the Supreme Court in the 1991-2015 Terms. That number fell between that for the First Circuit and for the Sixth Circuit. Unlike cases from the Sixth Circuit, there were only 3 Eleventh Circuit en banc decisions on which the justices ruled, two of which had resulted in relatively close votes but one of which was a 13-0 ruling. Excluding those en banc cases and others for which no panel information is available, basic data exist for panels in 124 published Supreme Court rulings.

The proportions of cases with either a visiting judge or a district judge were somewhat close, with visiting judges sitting in over one-fourth (27.4%) of these cases and district judges in one-fifth, the direction the reverse of that in the First Circuit and quite different from the Sixth Circuit's situation of minimal visiting judge participation and two-fifths of panels containing a district judge. The proportion of panels with two non-regular judges was in the same range as for the First and Sixth Circuits, with an almost equal number of pairings of visiting judge with senior circuit judge and district judge with senior circuit judge. As with the other circuits examined, all-active-judge panels accounted for only a relatively small portion of all cases, slightly over one-fifth (22.6%). Panels composed of circuit judges, whether active or senior, were roughly double that proportion (43.5%), but that is less than the proportion in Sixth Circuit cases and only about two-thirds the proportion in First Circuit cases. A senior circuit judge sat in two-fifths of the panels, roughly the same proportion as in the Sixth Circuit but less than the First Circuit's three-fifths.

It is noteworthy that in Eleventh Circuit cases going to the Supreme Court, division in the court of appeals does not seem to have been a major Supreme Court cue. Almost four-fifths (78.8%) of the panels in these cases were unanimous, slightly less than the proportion in the First Circuit and well above the proportion in the Sixth Circuit; as elsewhere, panel division is predominantly the result of dissent. The panel alignments in the split cases follow no pattern, with a wide variety of judge combinations. While reversal seems to have been only a slight cue for the Supreme Court to take in Sixth Circuit cases, in the Eleventh Circuit, like the First, it seems to have been even less so, as in over three-fifths (63.5%) of the Eleventh Circuit cases the Supreme Court took, the panel had affirmed the lower court or agency and thus reversed in only 36% of the cases.

10
CONCLUSION: WHAT WE HAVE SEEN

This study has shown, clearly, that borrowed judges—judges visiting from other circuits and in-circuit district judges—play a significant role in the U.S. courts of appeals, as do those courts' own senior judges. It should also be clear that the view that all cases are decided by three judges from a circuit's court of appeals is incomplete. Put differently, in a number of circuits the court of appeals' active-duty judges play a more limited, or perhaps one should say a less complete, role than many tend to assume. Thus, the reality portrayed here is definitely not the same as the picture many lawyers and other observers carry in their heads.

There is considerable variation among circuits, and there is also change over time, another form of variation. Indeed, *variation* is a central theme throughout this study. A number of dimensions of variation are obvious, so one may say that, if in real estate it is all about "location, location, location," in the courts of appeals' borrowing of judges, it is all about "variation, variation, variation."

Among the many types of variation seen here are:

- across time, on all dimensions;

- across circuits in the use of "other" judges;

- the relative use of visitors and in-circuit district judges;

- among visitors, the relative use of visiting circuit judges and visiting district judges;

- among visitors, the circuits and districts from which they are drawn;

- within a circuit, in districts' contributions of judges;

- within any circuit, in use of senior judges;

- across circuits, effects of cues, including "other" judges' presence, on rehearing cases en banc; and

- across circuits, effects of cues, including "other" judges' presence, on the Supreme Court's taking cases.

Of all these elements of variation, perhaps the most important is that some U.S. courts of appeals utilize visiting judges while others do not.

Those courts borrowing judges from other circuits use them to assist with their caseloads, which have grown substantially without any increase in judgeships. This means that a court's own judges, including its senior judges, cannot fully handle the growing docket and thus need assistance from elsewhere. It is significant, however, that some courts of appeals, while also facing increased dockets, make little or no use of visitors, although some do draw on the circuit's district judges. Perhaps some courts which do not borrow other circuits' judges either have not experienced major caseload increases or their judges simply work harder to stay current.

Some of these courts appear to abjure use of visitors as a matter of practice, but others—specifically, the Seventh and District of Columbia Courts of Appeals—do so as a matter of policy. According to a judge of the D.C. Circuit, its policy, adopted during efforts to increase collegiality within the court, "took into account the culture and needs of our court and facilitated decision making." The goal of the policy was "to ensure expeditious issuance of our decisions, balanced work assignments among our judges, and coherence in the law of the circuit."[1] Even if one does not believe that borrowed judges negatively affect those last elements, the concerns expressed about the court's culture and decision making likely have been considered by other "non-using" courts and could serve as a warning to those courts which, even if under pressure of caseload, do make use of borrowed judges.

It is clear that visiting judges and in-circuit district judges significantly assist some courts of appeals in processing their caseload, presumably the purpose for which they are borrowed from the courts on which they usually sit. Of greater interest and importance is that visiting judges and in-circuit district judges may actually play a somewhat larger role in developing the law of the circuit through their participation in published opinions than in helping dispose of less significant cases. While they participate in cases resulting in non-precedential ("unpublished") dispositions, such participation is lessened as a result of court of appeals' use of the screening panels, on which these "other" judges do not serve but which contribute much to docket-clearing; senior judges play a larger role on such panels.

Also important is that some judges—almost always, senior judges—sit frequently in multiple other circuits in addition to their own "home" duties on a court of appeals or district court. A function of this activity, one not necessarily explicitly intended, is to tie the nation's federal

---

[1] Harry T. Edwards, "Collegial Decision Making in the US Courts of Appeals," lecture, All Souls College, Oxford University, July 20, 2017, at 28.

judiciary together. These frequently-visiting judges are not in any formal way the "flying squadron" of judges envisioned by Chief Justice Taft, but their frequent visiting is sufficiently regular, and generally sufficiently distinctive in its frequency from others' visiting, that one can identify them as a cadre serving Taft's purpose, even if in not quite the same manner. If the cadre of frequent visitors helps tie the nation's judiciary together, the variation across circuits in their use of visitors and in-circuit district judges reinforces the notion that the U.S. courts of appeals remain regional bodies, at least partly autonomous within the larger national judicial system.

What one takes from the picture presented here is in large measure a function of one's perspective. How one evaluates courts' borrowing of judges is affected by whether one is a *visiting* judge, a *visited* judge, or a non-judicial observer. *Visiting* judges, while acknowledging some diffi-culties, are quite positive about having visited in other circuits. By con-trast, judges on *visited* courts of appeals, while seeing advantages to—and even the necessity of—the use of visiting judges and in-circuit district judges, are far more likely to identify and focus on problems in such use. Non-judicial observers are, on balance, more likely to be critical than positive, in large measure because of their expectations of what court of appeals panels should be.

Some will be pleased to know that many circuits make minimal or no use of visiting judges and relatively little use of their own district judges. Others, perhaps more pragmatic, are not thrilled by some circuits' extensive use of "other" judges but recognize that such use is essential to the courts of appeals being able to stay reasonably current with their dockets; for these observers, the balance tilts at least somewhat more towards "getting the cases out" than to "let's do it ourselves." Moreover, the use of in-circuit district judges, especially shortly after their appoint-ment to the bench, is seen as performing a valuable socialization function which serves to make the district judges "better" from the appellate court's perspective, although the Second Circuit's significant use of district judges in cases from their own districts is alarming.

However, those who would have all U.S. court of appeals cases decid-ed by those courts' own judges are likely to find troubling the stories told here concerning the First, Sixth, Ninth, and Eleventh Circuits, which exhibit considerable use of visiting judges from other circuits and in-circuit district judges. The concern of this set of observers would not be allayed even though the proportion of cases in which these "other" judges' votes are determinative is quite small, as "quite small" is not "none." In short, at least for these circuits which make non-trivial use of "other" judges, concerns about "who makes the law of the circuit?" are, based on the numbers, real.

From data presented, there should also be greater appreciation of the role played by court of appeals' senior circuit judges, even though they are not "borrowed" but are continuing members of the court on which they sit. Like judges visiting from other circuits or judges borrowed from districts within the circuit, they obviously assist substantially in helping with the docket. Indeed, because they are more likely to sit on the screening panels which handle high volumes of cases, they play an especially important role in docket-clearing. Less obvious but quite important, especially to presidents making judicial appointments, is that senior judges' continuing presence serves to limit the effect of newly-appointed judges, because without the senior judges' participation, the new judges would more completely dominate three-judge panels hearing cases.

* * *

The data presented here say much about the frequency and importance of non-regular judges' participation in the U.S. courts of appeals' work. Yet whatever those data say about that frequency and importance and about what borrowed judges' separate opinions may reveal about their role, far more is needed for a more complete picture of what really takes place when a judge visits another circuit or when a district judge sits on that judge's own circuit court of appeals. More must be asked, for example, about whether a visitor's flight bag contains the law of that judge's circuit, with the judge attempting to inflict it upon the host circuit, thus perhaps prompting changes in that circuit's precedent, or whether the visitor instead follows the host circuit's precedent even if raising questions about it. To identify whether visiting judges cite the visited or home circuit's cases, a much closer look at the borrowed judges' opinions would be required, both their opinions for the panel and their separate opinions, to determine if the doctrine of those cases is closer to that of their own circuits.[2] This would aid knowledge of the effect of "other" judges on development of a circuit's substantive law, as would exploration of the related question of whether opinions by visiting judges and district judges sitting by designation are given as much weight by other judges and observers as those by regular judges.[3]

---

[2] The high usage of "unpublished" rulings makes this difficult because in most circuits, no such dispositions are signed, preventing identification of the authors.

[3] Shepard's Citation system can be used to determine whether cases decided by visiting judges were later cited more or less positively than those decided by a court of appeals' own judges. See Budziak, "The Effect of Visiting Judges on the Treatment of Legal

It would also be helpful to determine, if one could, whether visitors decide cases just as do the host circuit's judges, perhaps injecting views to the extent they would "at home," or whether at times they are simply ciphers occupying the third place on a panel and following the preferences of the panel's two "home circuit" judges, particularly when the latter write the panel's disposition. That visitors are not necessarily timid is apparent even in pre-argument communication.

A more complete picture would also require further investigation of whether cases in which "other" judges participate affect whether courts of appeals rehear cases en banc or whether the Supreme Court chooses cases to review based on their presence on panels, as well as whether that presence affects the justices' treatment of cases to which they have granted plenary consideration. Determining the effects of lower court judges' opinions on the Justices would be difficult, however, given the Justices' relatively infrequent mention or stated analysis of the lower court opinions they review and lack of access to the Court's internal decision-making.

This study has provided the first thorough, albeit in some ways incomplete because exploratory, examination of the role in the U.S. courts of appeals of judges borrowed to assist in those courts' work. Also presented has been a first look at another heretofore understudied aspect of the U.S. courts of appeals: those courts' use of their own senior circuit judges, whose participation clearly is needed for these courts to function effectively. It is quite evident that borrowed judges definitely play a significant part, certainly so in numbers of judges used and also in terms of effects on the development of circuit law, although the full extent of the latter remains less clear. Moreover, of significance for the federal judiciary as a whole is the role of frequent visitors in creating a cadre of judges whose work aids in holding the nation's judiciary together.

Policy in the U.S. Courts of Appeals."

Table I.A. Part I. Participation by Judge Type in Published Opinions (F.3d)

Circuit	Type	358-376		488-500		550-562		720-735		736-748	
		n	%	n	%	n	%	n	%	n	%
D.C.		No visitors or district judges, by policy									
First	VCJ	12	7.4	24	18.8	30	21.9	15	12.4	22	15.1
	VDJ	4	2.6	10	7.8	3	2.2	0	0.0	0	0.0
	VIS	16	9.9	34	26.6	33	24.1	15	12.4	22	15.1
	DJ	16	9.9	14	10.9	23	16.8	8	6.7	7	4.8
	ANR	32	19.6	48	37.5	55	40.1	18*	14.9	29	20
	n	163		128		137		121		145	
Second	VCJ	12	6.3	6	4.9	7	5.7	5	3.6	1	0.8
	VDJ	2	1.0	8	6.5	6	4.9	6	4.3	0	0.0
	VIS	14	7.3	14	11.4	13	10.7	11	7.4	1	0.8
	DJ	35	18.3	25	20.3	33	27.0	30	20.6	13	10.8
	ANR	49	25.7	39	31.7	46	37.7	52	29.4	14	11.7
	n	191		123		122		139		120	

VCJ: cases with visiting judges
VDJ: cases with visiting district judges
VIS: all cases with visitors

DJ: cases with in-circuit district judges
ANR: all cases with non-regular judges
n: number of cases

Judge Type, Published Opinions

Circuit	Type	358-376		488-500		550-562		720-735		736-748	
		n	%	n	%	n	%	n	%	n	%
Third	VCJ	12	9.4	17	30.4	11	15.3	0	0.0	8	3.7
	VDJ	7	5.5	3	5.4	5	6.9	5	5.7	1	0.5
	VIS	19	14.8	20	35.7	16	22.2	5	5.7	9	4.2
	DJ	4	24	24	42.9	16	22.2	3	3.4	1	0.5
	ANR	23	44	44	78.6	32	44.4	8	9.2	10	4.7
	n	128		56		72		87		215	
Fourth	VCJ	9	7.2	0	0.0	6	6.8	2	2.7	0	0.0
	VDJ	0	0.0	0	0.0	0	0.0	0	0.0	0	0.0
	VIS	9	7.2	0	0.0	6	6.8	2	2.7	0	0.0
	DJ	7	5.6	12	21.4	31	35.2	10	3.7	11	10.0
	ANR	16	12.8	12	21.4	37	42.6	12	16.4	11	10.0
	n	125		56		88		73		110	

Judge Type, Published Opinions

Circuit	Type	358-376 n	358-376 %	488-500 n	488-500 %	550-562 n	550-562 %	720-735 n	720-735 %	736-748 n	736-748 %
Fifth	VCJ	4	2.3	0	0.0	0	0.0	0	0.0	0	0.0
	VDJ	1	0.6	0	0.0	0	0.0	0	0.0	0	0.0
	VIS	5	2.9	0	0.0	0	0.0	0	0.0	0	0.0
	DJ	8	4.6	0	0.0	18	14.3	18	14.3	16	10.8
	ANR	8	4.6	0	0.0	18	14.3	18	14.3	16	10.8
	n	174		159		126		148		150	
Sixth	VCJ	10	5.6	0	0.0	1	0.7	2	1.1	1	1.0
	VDJ	24	13.6	13	8.3	7	4.6	1	0.6	11	10.7
	VIS	34	19.2	13	8.3	8	5.3	3	1.7	12	11.7
	DJ	63	35.6	76	51.7	25	16.4	50	27.9	34	33.0
	ANR	97	54.8	89	60.5	33	21.7	53	29.6	46	44.7
	n	177		147		152		179		103	
Seventh	DJ	None, by policy		No visitors by policy		7	3.2	39	15.1	35	14.0
	ANR	284		227		220		258		250	

237

Judge Type, Published Opinions

Circuit	Type	358-376		488-500		550-562		720-735		736-748	
		n	%	n	%	n	%	n	%	n	%
Eighth	VCJ	2	0.5	2	0.9	4	1.6	0	0.0	0	0.0
	VDJ	3	0.7	2	0.9	5	2.0	0	0.0	0	0.0
	VIS	5	1.5	4	1.8	9	3.6	0	0.0	0	0.0
	DJ	18	5.5	10	4.5	35	14.7	13	8.3	3	1.6
	ANR	23	7	14	6.4	44	17.1	13	8.3	3	1.6
	n	330		220		248		156		188	
Ninth	VCJ	28	7.6	21	9.5	4	1.6	15	5.4	11	4.8
	VDJ	29	6.5	18	8.2	5	2.0	64	23.0	35	15.2
	VIS	52	14.1	39	17.7	9	3.6	79	28.4	46	20.0
	DJ	29	7.8	39	17.7	35	14.1	34	12.2	16	7.0
	ANR	81	22.0	78	35.5	44	17.7	113	40.6	62	27.0
	n	369		220		248		278		230	

Judge Type, Published Opinions

Circuit	Type	358-376		488-500		550-562		720-735		736-748	
		n	%	n	%	n	%	n	%	n	%
Tenth	VCJ	0	0.0	2	1.7	0	0.0	0	0.0	0	0.0
	VDJ	1	0.5	0	0.0	0	0.0	1	1.0	0	0.0
	VIS	1	0.5	2	1.7	0	0.0	1	1.0	0	0.0
	DJ	7	4.8	9	7.5	9	6.9	1	1.0	6	6.8
	ANR	8	5.5	11	9.2	9	6.9	2	2.0	6	6.8
	n	14		120		131		98		88	
Eleventh	VCJ	28	16.0	30	25.8	5	4.4	12	6.0	13	12.1
	VDJ	32	18.3	24	20.7	30	26.5	7	9.3	17†	15.9
	VIS	60	34.3	54	46.6	35	31.0	19	25.3	30	28.0
	DJ	24	13.7	19	12.1	12	10.6	32	42.7	35†	32.7
	ANR	84	48.0	68	58.6	47	41.5	51	68.0	65	60.7
	n	175		116		113		75		107	

Judge Type, Published Opinions

Circuit	Type	358-376		488-500		550-562		720-735		736-748	
		n	%	n	%	n	%	n	%	n	%
Federal	VCJ	0	0.0	0	0.0	0	0	0	0.0	0	0.0
	VDJ	0	0.0	8	9.0	15	18.1	12	14.0	0	0.0
	VIS	0	0.0	8	9.0	15	18.1	12	14.0	0	0.0
	DJ					None					
	ANR	0	0.0	8	9.0	15	18.1	12	14.0	0	0.0
	n	129		89		83		86		86	

* case, not participation (where two non-regular in same case)
† One case with both visiting district judge and in-circuit district judge.

Table I.A.Part II. Participation by Judge Type in Published Opinions, continued

Circuit	Type	749-764		765-783		784-800		801-819		820-839	
		n	%	n	%	n	%	n	%	n	%
First	VCJ	17	11.5	28	14.3	5	8.1	20	9.8	4	2.6
	VDJ	0	0.0	0	0.0	0	0.0	0	0.0	0	0.0
	Souter	0	0.0	11	5.6	4	6.5	6	2.9	13	18.5
	VIS	17	11.5	39	19.9	9	14.5	26	12.7	17	11.1
	DJ	22	14.9	13	6.6	3	4.8	32	15.7	15	9.8
	ANR	39	26.3	52	26.5	12	19.4	53	28.4	32	20.9
	n	148		196		62		204		153	
Second	VCJ	2	1.3	0	0.0	Not Coded					
	VDJ	2	1.3	0	0.0						
	VIS	4	2.7	0	0.0						
	DJ	16	10.7	20	13.0						
	ANR	20	13.3	20	13.0						
	n	150		134							

VCJ: cases with visiting judges
VDJ: cases with visiting district judges
VIS: all cases with visitors
DJ: cases with in-circuit district judges
ANR: all cases with non-regular judges
n: number of cases

Judge Type, Published Decisions

Circuit	Type	749-764		765-783		784-800		801-819		820-839	
		n	%	n	%	n	%	n	%	n	%
Sixth	VCJ	4	3.0	4	2.4	1	1.2	1	0.6	11	6.7
	VDJ	3	2.3	4	2.4	1	1.2	1	0.6	4	2.4
	VIS	7	5.3	8	4.7	2	2.4	2	1.3	15	9.1
	DJ	37	28.0	42	24.9	21	24.7	47	29.9	21	12.7
	ANR	44	33.3	50	29.6	25	29.4	49	31.2	36	21.8
	n	132		169		85		157		165	
Ninth	VCJ	10	4.3	15	5.1	23	5.8	12	4.9	21	7.1
	VDJ	45	17.3	64	21.8	68	17.2	66	24.2	42	14.2
	VIS	53	21.4	79	27.0	91	23.0	78	28.6	63	21.4
	DJ	33	13.3	26	8.9	24	6.1	35	12.8	41	13.9
	ANR	86	34.7	105	35.8	115	29.0	114	41.8	104	35.3
	n	248		293		395		273		295	

Judge Type, Published Decisions

Circuit	Type	749-764		765-783		784-800		801-819		820-839	
		n	%	n	%	n	%	n	%	n	%
Eleventh	VCJ	25	19.8	29	16.3	22	23.7	25	16.4	37	23.7
	VDJ	16	12.7	35	18.5	13	14.0	35	23.0	29	18.6
	VIS	41	32.3	59	33.1	35	32.6	60	39.5	66	42.3
	DJ	34	27.0	55	29.7	32	34.4	30	19.7	40	25.6
	ANR	75	59.5	114	64.0	67	72.0	90	59.2	106	67.9
	n	126		178		93		152		156	

Table I.B. Participation by Judge Type in Unpublished Dispositions (Fed. Appx.)

	510-525		526-540		541-559		560-581		582-599		600-622		623-640	
	n	%	n	%	n	%	n	%	n	%	n	%	n	%
D.C.							No visitors by policy							
First														
VCJ	0	0.0	0	0.0	3	20.0	0	0.0	0	0.0	0	0.0	2	6.7
VDJ	0	0.0	0	0.0	0	0.0	0	0.0	0	0.0	0	0.0	0	0.0
Souter	0	0.0	5	50.0	1	6.7	8	50.0	1	14.3	3	12.0	2	6.7
VIS	0	0.0	5	50.0	4	26.7	8	50.0	1	14.3	0	0.0	4	13.3
DJ	0	0.0	4	40.0	0	0.0	0	0.0	0	0.0	0	0.0	1	3.3
ANR	0	0.0	9	90.0	4	26.7	8	50.0	1	14.3	3	12.0	5	16.7
n	2		10		15		16		7		25		30	

VCJ:	cases with visiting judges	
VDJ:	cases with visiting district judges	
VIS:	all cases with visitors	
DJ:	cases with in-circuit district judges	
ANR:	all cases with non-regular judges	
n:	number of cases	

Judge Type, Unpublished Dispositions

	510-525 n	%	526-540 n	%	541-559 n	%	560-581 n	%	582-599 n	%	600-622 n	%	623-640 n	%
Second														
VCJ	15	3.0	1	0.2	0	0.0	0	0.0	0	0.0	6	1.2		
VDJ	26	5.1	3	0.6	1	0.2	6	0.9	0	0.0	0	0.0		
VIS	41	8.1	5*	1.0	1	0.2	6	0.9	0	0.0	6	1.2	X	
DJ	155	30.5	44	9.0	67	12.0	84	13.1	47	10.4	54	9.6		
ANR	196	38.5	53	10.9	68	12.2	90	14.0	47	10.4	60	10.7		
n	598		488		559		641		430		501			
Third														
VCJ	6	1.1	4	0.1	5	1.0								
VDJ	0	0.0	13	2.4	1	0.2								
VIS	6	1.1	17	3.2	17†	3.5	X		X		X		X	
DJ	16	3.0	0	0.0	11	2.3								
ANR	22	4.1	17	3.2	28	5.8								
n	532		536		479									

Judge Type, Unpublished Dispositions

	510-525 n	%	526-540 n	%	541-559 n	%	560-581 n	%	582-599 n	%	600-622 n	%	623-640 n	%
Fourth														
VCJ	0	0.0	0	0.0	1	0.1								
VDJ	0	0.0	0	0.0	0	0.0								
VIS	0	0.0	4‡	0.4	1	0.1	X		X		X		X	
DJ	14	1.3	13	1.3	13	1.2								
ANR	14	1.3	17	1.7	14	1.2								
n	1038		1010		1172									
Fifth														
VCJ	0	0.0	0	0.0	0	0.0								
VDJ	0	0.0	0	0.0	0	0.0								
VIS	0	0.0	0	0.0	0	0.0	X		X		X		X	
DJ	2	0.3	11	1.1	7	0.4								
ANR	2	0.3	11	1.1	7	0.4								
n	669		991		1478									

Judge Type, Unpublished Dispositions

	510-525		526-540		541-559		560-581		582-599		600-622		623-640	
	n	%	n	%	n	%	n	%	n	%	n	%	n	%
Sixth														
VCJ	14	3.0	13	3.3	6	1.6	19	3.7	3	0.9	1	0.2	5	1.5
VDJ	8	1.7	11	2.8	22	5.8	21	4.1	17	5.0	7	1.6	8	2.4
VIS	22	4.8	24	6.2	24	7.4	40	7.8	20	5.9	8	1.8	13	3.9
DJ	199	43.0	173	44.4	120	31.6	162	31.8	123	36.1	54	36.7	114	34.2
ANR	221	47.7	197	50.5	148	38.9	202	39.5	153	44.9	60	38.4	127	38.1
n	463		390		380		512		341		450		333	
Seventh														
DJ	3	2.1	3	2.3	2	0.9	No visitors by policy	X		X		X		X	
n	146		128		229									

Judge Type, Unpublished Dispositions

	510-525		526-540		541-559		560-581		582-599		600-622		623-640	
	n	%	n	%	n	%	n	%	n	%	n	%	n	%
Eighth														
VCJ	0	0.0	0	0.0										
VDJ	0	0.0	0	0.0										
VIS	0	0.0	0	0.0	X		X		X		X		X	
DJ	2	1.9	0	0.0										
ANR	2	1.9	0	0.0										
n	106		102											
Ninth														
VCJ	9	1.1	39	5.9	17	1.1	44	3.9	60	2.7	72	4.0	55	4.5
VDJ	116	14.2	131	13.0	153	10.8	160	14.3	147	6.6	253	14.4	129	10.9
VIS	125	15.3	170	16.3	173	12.2	204	18.3	207	9.2	324	18.5	184	15.0
DJ	65	8.0	74	7.3	100	7.1	70	6.2	143	6.4	152	8.7	102	8.3
ANR	180	22.1	244	24.2	273	19.3	274	24.6	255	15.8	476	27.1	286	23.3
N	815		1010		1418		1116		2243		1755		1230	

Judge Type, Unpublished Dispositions

	510-525 n	510-525 %	526-540 n	526-540 %	541-559 n	541-559 %	560-581 n	560-581 %	582-599 n	582-599 %	600-622 n	600-622 %	623-640 n	623-640 %
Tenth														
VCJ	0	0.0	0	0.0	0	0.0								
VDJ	0	0.0	0	0.0	0	0.0								
VIS	0	0.0	0	0.0	0	0.0	X		X		X		X	
DJ	4	1.0	5	1.4	3	0.7								
ANR	4	1.0	5	1.4	3	0.7								
n	393		346		430									
Eleventh														
VCJ	32	5.5	12	3.6	13	1.9	37	3.8	10	1.7	32	3.7	10	1.7
VDJ	15	1.6	5	1.5	23	3.3	28	2.9	16	2.7	36	4.1	15	2.5
VIS	49[§]	5.3	17	5.0	36	5.2	65	6.7	26	4.4	68	7.8	25	4.2
DJ	47	5.1	29	8.6	45	6.6	49	5.1	27	4.6	42	4.8	24	4.1
ANR	96	10.5	46	13.6	81	11.8	114	11.7	53	9.0	110	12.6	49	8.3
n	917		338		687		972		589		876		592	

Judge Type, Unpublished Dispositions

	510-525		526-540		541-559		560-581		582-599		600-622		623-640	
	n	%	n	%	n	%	n	%	n	%	n	%	n	%
Federal														
VCJ	0	0.0	0	0.0	0	0.0								
VDJ	3	2.6	0	0.0	0	0.0								
VIS	3	2.6	0	0.0	0	0.0	X		X		X		X	
DJ	0	0.0	0	0.0	0	0.0								
ANR	3	2.6	0	0.0	0	0.0								
n	116		125		268									

* Including 11 Supreme Court (ret.)   X = not coded
‡ Including 4 Supreme Court (ret.)
§ Including 2 Supreme Court (ret.)

Table II. "Non-Regular" Judges, 2013-2016 (720 F.3d on; 510 Fed. Appx. on)

	Visitors			Dist. JJ	Total	Circuit JJ		
	Circuit	District	Total			Active	Senior	Total
D.C.	None by Policy					11	6	17
First	7	0	7	15	22	6	4	10
Second	1	5*	6	61	67	11	11	22
Third	0	0	0	5	5	12	10	22
Fourth	1	0	1	22	23	14	2	16
Fifth	0	0	0	9	9	13	9	22
Sixth	4	10	14	59	63	14	8	22
Seventh	None by Policy			25	25	8	4	12
Eighth	0	0	0	8	8	9	5	14
Ninth	19	61	80	80	160	26	17	43
Tenth	0	1	1	6	7	11	7	18
Eleventh	21	20	41	50	91	11	7	18
Federal	None							

*All CIT

Table III. Part I. District Judge Participation in Published Decisions (F.3d)

Circuit	358-376	488-500	550-562	720-735	736-748
D.C.	No district judges, by policy				
First	5 JJ – 16	6 JJ – 14 Mass 3 (8)	6 JJ - 23 P.R. 5 (16)	4 JJ - 8	2 JJ - 7
Second	24 JJ – 35 SDNY 13 (15) EDNY 5 (9)	14 JJ – 25 SDNY 7 (16) EDNY 4 (6)	18 JJ – 33 SDNY 9 (10) EDNY 4 (10)	12 JJ - 28 SDNY 12 (21) EDNY 2 (4)	13 JJ – 13 SDNY 10 (10) EDNY 3 (3)
Third	2 JJ – 4	13 JJ – 24 EDPa 8 (16)	6 JJ – 16 NJ 4 (10)	1 J – 3	1 J -3
Fourth	6 JJ – 8	7 JJ – 12	9 JJ – 31	8 JJ – 10	6 JJ – 11
Fifth	6 JJ – 8	0	8 JJ – 18	4 JJ – 16	4 JJ – 12

District Judge Participation, Published Decisions

Circuit	358-376	488-500	550-562	720-735	736-748
Sixth	25 JJ – 63 EDKy 5 (12) EDMi 8 (17) NDOh 4 (8) SDOh 3 (8)	31 JJ – 76 EDKy 5 (12) EDMi 6 (19) NDOh 8 (17) SDOh 5 (12) EDTn 4 (10)	15 JJ – 25 NDOh 5 (9)	15 JJ – 50 EDMI 8 (14) NDOh 6 (10) SDOh 7 (22)	19 JJ – 34 EDMi 5 (9) NDOh 5 (8)
Seventh		None by policy	3 JJ – 7 NDIl (7)	12 JJ – 39 NDIl 5 (13)	11 JJ – 35 EDWi 3 (13)
Eighth	3 JJ – 18	2 JJ -10	7 JJ – 35	4 JJ – 13	2 JJ - 3
Ninth	13 JJ – 29	26 JJ – 39 NDCal 4 (8) CDCal 5 (7) SDCal 4 (5)	20 JJ – 31 NDCal 5 (5) CDCal 5 (9)	23 JJ – 35 AK 4 (9) CACal 5 (8)	10 JJ – 13

District Judge Participation, Published Decisions

Circuit	358-376	488-500	550-562	720-735	736-748
Tenth	4 JJ – 7	7 JJ – 9	4 JJ – 9	1 J – 1	2 JJ – 6
Eleventh	9 JJ – 24	11 JJ – 14	9 JJ – 13	14 JJ – 27 MDFl 5 (6)	23 JJ – 39 MDFl 5 (11) SDFl 4 (8)

District Judge Participation, Published Decisions

Table III.Part II. Participation by District Judges, Published Opinions, continued

Circuit	749 -764	765 – 783	794 – 800	801 – 819	820 – 839
D.C.	No district judges, by policy				
First	9 JJ - 19 RI 3 (8)	7 JJ	2 JJ – 2	3 JJ – 4	5 JJ – 14
Second	9 JJ – 15 SDNY 8 (14)	14 JJ – 19 SDNY 4 (12) EDNY 3 (3)	X	X	X
Third	4 JJ – 7	X	X	X	X
Fourth	4 JJ – 7	X	X	X	X
Fifth	4 JJ – 10	X	X	X	X

District Judge Participation, Published Decisions

Circuit	749-764	765 – 783	794 – 800	801 – 819	820 – 839
Sixth	19 JJ – 32 EDMI 6 (14) NDOh 6 (9)	25 JJ – 41 EDKy 3 (6) EDMi 6 (12) SDOh 6 (8)	17 JJ – 26 EDMi 7 (9) SDOh 3 (6)	21 JJ – 33 EDKy 4 (7) NDOh 4 (5) SDOh 8 (15)	12 JJ – 19 EDMi 5 (9) SDOh 3 (3)
Seventh	14 JJ – 51 SDIn 3 (11) NDIl 6 (30)	1 J – 1	X	X	X
Eighth	4 JJ – 13	X	X	X	X
Ninth	18 JJ – 27 Nev 4 (5)	19 JJ – 22 NDCal 4 (4)	17 JJ – 21 SDCal 4 (6)	23 JJ – 33 NDCal 4 (5) SDCal 3 (5)	23 JJ – 34 Ariz 3 (4) SDCal 4 (6) Haw 3 (5) EDwa 3 (6)

District Judge Participation, Published Decisions

Circuit	749 -764	765 – 783	794 – 800	801 – 819	820 – 839
Tenth	1 J – 3	X	X	X	X
Eleventh	23 – JJ 51	22 JJ – 55	17 JJ – 24	13 JJ – 27	19 JJ – 35
	MDAl 4 (10)	NDGa 4 (8)	MDFl 5 (7)	MDFl 6 (10)	NDA13 (8)
	MDFL 5 (13)	NDFl 4 (15)			MDFl 4 (6)
	SDFl 6 (12)	MDFl 4 (13)			SDFl 6 (8)
		SDFl 6 (11)			

X = not coded

Table III. Part II. District Judge Participation in Unpublished Dispositions (Fed. Appx.)

Circuit	510 – 525	526 – 540	541 – 564	560 – 581	582 – 599	600 – 622
D.C.	X	X	X	X	X	X
First	0	1 JJ	0	0	0	0
Second	25 JJ – 85 SDNY 17(76)	17 JJ – 44 SDNY 13(36)	18 JJ – 39 SDNY 13(27)	24 JJ – 76 SDNY 16(54)	21 JJ – 48 SDNY 16(54)	26 JJ – 52 SDNY 11(14)
Third	2 JJ – 12	0	2 JJ – 11	X	X	X
Fourth	6 JJ – 7	6 JJ – 13	7 JJ – 11	X	X	X
Fifth	1 JJ	4 JJ (10)	5 JJ (7)	X	X	X

District Judge Participation, Unpublished Dispositions

Circuit	510 – 525	526 – 540	541 – 564	560 – 581	582 – 599	600 – 622
Sixth	39 JJ – 192 EDKy 5 (65) EDMi 8 (38) NDOh 9 (28) SDOh 7 (19)	33 JJ – 149 EDKy 3 (11) EDMi 11 (39) NDOh 8 (45) SDOh 7 (30) EDTn 3 (9)	28 JJ – 106 EDmi 9 (26) NDOh 6 (32)	30 JJ – 150 EdMi 9 (53) NDOh 6 (13) SDOh 7 (48)	28 JJ – 106 EDMi 7 (25) NDOh 8 (34)	32 JJ – 142 EDKy 4 (24) EDMi 9 (44) NDOh 6 (20) SDOh 6 (22) EDTn 3 (18)
Seventh	3 JJ	2 JJ	1 J	X	X	X
Eighth	1 J	0	0	X	X	X
Ninth	19 JJ – 63	26 JJ – 62 Al 5 (17) CDCal 5 (15)	24 JJ – 85 Al 3 (18)	22 JJ – 54	35 JJ – 125 Al 4 (35) NDCal 5 (12)	40 JJ – 152 Ariz 4 (20) NDCal 6 (18) CDCal 4 (8) SDCal 4 (18) EDWa 4 (17) WDWa 4 (14)

District Judge Participation, Unpublished Dispositions

Circuit	510 – 525	526 – 540	541 – 564	560 – 581	582 – 599	600 – 622
Tenth	3 JJ	3 JJ – 6	2 JJ – 5	X	X	X
Eleventh	12 JJ – 18 MDFl 4 (7)	10 JJ – 28	13 JJ – 50 MDFl 7 (19) SDFl 6 (14)	24 JJ – 66 MDFl 5 (11)	13 JJ – 25	18 JJ – 36 NDFl 4 (8) MDFl 4 (12)

X = not coded

Table IV.Part I. Senior Circuit Judge Participation in Published Decisions (Selected Circuits)

Circuit	720-735		736-748		749-764		765-783		784-800		801-819	
	n	%	n	%	n	%	n	%	n	%	n	%
D.C.												
1 SCJ	33	55.9	43	50.6	49	41.9	51	49.5	49	44.1	49	44.1
2 SCJ	4	6.8	26	30.6	15	14.3	20	19.4	21	18.9	21	18.9
cases	37	62.7	69	81.2	64	63.9	71	69.8	70	63.1	70	63.1
partic.	41	23.2	95	37.3	74	23.5	91	29.4	99	21.6	91	27.5
N	59		85		105		103		143		111	
First												
1 SCJ	31	42.1	48	33.1	62	41.9	87	44.4	58	41.7	82	40.2
2 SCJ	15*	12.4	8	3.5	17†	11.5	18	9.2	10	7.2	24	11.8
cases	36	46.6	56	46.7	81	54.7	105	53.6	68	48.9	106	52.0
partic.	81	18.5	116	16.8	102	23.0	123	20.9	78	18.7	130	21.3
n	121		145		148		196		139		204	

Senior Judge Participation, Published Opinions

Circuit	720-735		736-748		749-764		765-783		784-800		801-819	
	n	%	n	%	n	%	n	%	n	%	n	%
Sixth												
1 SCJ											88	56.4
2 SCJ	X		X		X		X		X		3	1.9
cases											91	58.3
partic.											94	20.0
n	278		230		248		183		273		156	
Ninth												
1 SCJ	118	42.4	97	42.2	89	35.8	117	63.9	76	28.8	76	27.8
2 SCJ	17‡	6.1	8	3.5	15	6.0	19	6.5	16	5.9	16	5.9
cases	136	48.6	105	45.7	104	41.9	136	74.3	92	44.6	92	33.6
partic.	154	18.5	116	16.0	114	16.0	133	11.2	108	13.1	108	13.1
n	278		230		248		183		273		273	

Senior Judge Participation, Published Opinions

Circuit	720-735 n	720-735 %	736-748 n	736-748 %	749-764 n	749-764 %	765-783 n	765-783 %	784-800 n	784-800 %	801-819 n	801-819 %
Eleventh												
1 SCJ	X										76	27.8
2 SCJ			X		X		X		X		16	5.9
cases											92	33.6
partic.											108	13.1
n											151	

X = not coded

* (+ 3 SCJ - 1)
† (+ 2 SCJ – 3)
‡ (+ 1 SCJ – 3)

263

Table IV. Part II. Senior Circuit Judge Participation in Unpublished Dispositions (Selected Circuits)

Circuit	510-525		526-540		541-559		560-581		582-599		600-622		623-640	
	n	%	n	%	n	%	n	%	n	%	n	%	n	%
D.C.														
1 SCJ	6	26.1	5	17.8	21	40.4	21	56.8	31	47.0	31	43.1	29	60.4
2 SCJ	2	8.7	5	17.8	6	11.5	2	5.4	6	9.1	9	12.5	4	8.3
cases	8	34.8	10	35.7	27	51.9	23	62.6	37	56.1	40	56.1	33	68.8
partic.	10	14.5	15	17.9	33	21.2	25	27.5	43	24.1	49	22.7	33	25.7
n	23		28		52		37		66		72		48	
First														
1 SCJ	5	62.5	4	40.0	8	53.3	11	68.8	5	71.4	9	36.0	13	43.3
2 SCJ	1	12.5	0	0.0	0*	0.0	2	12.5	0	0.0	7	28.0	1	3.3
cases	6	75.0	4	40.0	9	60.0	13	81.2	5	71.4	16	64.0	14	46.7
partic.	7	29.2	4	13.3	10	22.2	15	31.3	5	23.8	23	23.0	15	16.7
n	8		10		15		16		7		25		30	

Senior Judge Participation, Unpublished Dispositions

Circuit	510-525		526-540		541-559		560-581		582-599		600-622		623-640	
	n	%	n	%	n	%	n	%	n	%	n	%	n	%
Sixth														
1 SCJ													144	43.2
2 SCJ													11	3.3
cases	X		X		X		X		X		X		155	46.5
partic.													166	16.7
n													333	
Ninth														
1 SCJ	426	52.3	425	42.1	494	34.8	495	44.4	744	33.2	800	45.6	520	42.2
2 SCJ	108	13.3	17	1.7	490	34.6	35	3.1	582	25.9	51	2.9	313	23.9
3 SCJ	23	2.8	21	2.1	51	1.2	7	0.6	23	1.1	33	1.9	9	0.7
cases	551	67.6	463	45.8	1001	70.6	537	48.1	1349	60.1	884	50.4	892	68.5
partic.	771	29.1	987	32.6	1525	35.8	586	17.5	1979	29.4	1001	19.0	1173	31.7
n	815		1010		1418		1116		2243		1755		1230	

Senior Judge Participation, Unpublished Dispositions

Circuit	510-525		526-540		541-559		560-581		582-599		600-622		623-640	
	n	%	n	%	n	%	n	%	n	%	n	%	n	%
Eleventh														
1 SCJ	X												193	32.6
2 SCJ			X		X		X		X		X		7	1.2
cases													200	33.8
partic.													207	11.7
n													592	

* (+ 3 SCJ - 1)   X = not coded

Table V.Part I. En Bancs (Various Circuits)

	First Circuit 1988-2015		Sixth Circuit 1989-2016	Eleventh Circuit 1988-2016
	Cases En Banc	Dissent/Denial	Cases En Banc	Cases En Banc
Panel Comp.				
n	59	25	155	142
info available	38	25	140	126
All Circuit JJ	60.5%	68%	52.9%	33.3%
All Active Cir JJ	21.1	32	36.4	10.3
SCJ on Panel	39.5	56	24.3	47.6
2 SCJ	13.2	0	1.4	4.8
VJ on Panel	21.1	20	5.0	33.3
DJ on Panel	23.7	0	32.1	27.8
2 non-reg JJ	18.4	20	2.9	22.2

En Bancs

	First Circuit 1988-2015		Sixth Circuit 1989-2016	Eleventh Circuit 1988-2016
	Cases En Banc	Dissent from Denial	Cases En Banc	Cases En Banc
Unanimous	60.5	68.0	33.6	59.0
Divided	39.5	32.0	66.3	41.0
Dissent	86.7	83.3	87.0	76.0
Sep. Conc.	13.3	16.7	13.0	24.0
Affirm	39.5	64.0	33.9	29.9
Reverse/Vacate	60.5	36.0	66.1	70.1

Table V.Part II. En Bancs (Ninth Circuit)

	1989 – 1999	2000 – 2009	2010 – 2016	Total	Dissent/Denial
Panel Comp.					
n	129	177	143	449	216
Info available	110	162	127	339	
All Circuit JJ	68.2%	66.0%	62.2%	65.4%	72.7%
All Active Cir JJ	43.6	16.7	25.2	26.8	37.0
SCJ on Panel	33.6	63.6	52.0	51.6	49.5
2 SCJ	5.0	14.2	10.2	10.5	8.3
VJ on Panel	9.1	15.4	27.6	17.5	14.4
DJ on Panel	18.2	17.9	11.8	16.0	16.2
2 non-reg JJ	9.1	22.8	11.0	15.3	19.4

En Bancs (Ninth Circuit, cont.)

	1989 – 1999	2000 – 2009	2010 – 2016	Total	Dissent/Denial
Unanimous	45.2	41.3	27.9	37.1	50.0
Divided	54.8	58.8	72.1	62.9	50.0
Dissent	84.2	92.6	93.5	91.0	91.9
Sep. Conc.	15.8	7.4	6.5	9.0	8.1
Affirm	40.0	49.4	50.4	47.2	36.9
Reverse/vacate	60.0	50.6	49.6	52.8	63.1

Table VI. Supreme Court Review (Various Circuits)

Circuit	First 1991-2005	Sixth 1991-2005	Eleventh 1991-2005		Ninth 1989-1999	2000-2009	2010-2016	Total
n/pub	50	136	136	n	275	229	144	648
				Pub	187	162	111	460
				GVR	88	67	33	188
En Banc	2	11	3	pub	9	13	10	32
				GVR	3	2	3	8
Panel w/info	47	124	124	pub	178	169	101	448
				GVR	85	67	30	182
All Cir. JJ	63.8%	51.6%	43.5%	pub	70.8%	66.2%	64.3%	67.6%
				GVR	51.8	67.2	66.7	59.9
All Active Cir. JJ	23.4	25.0	22.6	pub	43.4	19.5	24.8	30.1
				GVR	29.4	13.2	26.7	23.1

Supreme Court

Circuit	First 1991-2005	Sixth 1991-2005	Eleventh 1991-2005		Ninth 1989-1999	Ninth 2000-2009	Ninth 2010-2016	Total
SCJ on Panel	59.6	43.5	40.3	pub	41.0	62.7	49.5	51.1
				GVR	29.0	13.2	26.7	23.1
2 SCJ	8.5	8.1	2.4	pub	3.3	11.8	6.9	7.4
				GVR	3.5	13.4	6.7	7.7
VJ on Panel	12.8	3.2	27.4	pub	7.9	15.3	16.8	12.7
				GVR	12.9	14.9	23.3	15.4
DJ on Panel	17.0	41.1	20.2	pub	20.7	16.0	29.8	19.6
				GVR	21.2	17.9	3.3	17.0
2 non-reg JJ†	12.8	19.5	14.5	pub	8.4	22.5	16.8	15.6
				GVR	9.4	16.4	20.0	13.7

† Includes panels with 2 SCJ

272

Supreme Court

Circuit	First 1991-2005	Sixth 1991-2005	Eleventh 1991-2005		1989-1999	Ninth 2000-2009	2010-2016	Total
Unan. – pub op	83.0	53.2	78.8	pub	59.4	69.2	69.3	69.3
				GVR	9.4	16.4	20.0	13.7
Divided – pub op	17.0	46.8	21.2		30.6	30.8	30.7	30.7
Dissent	75.0	72.4	70.8		89.3	94.2	82.8	89.8
Sep. Conc.	25.0	27.6	29.2		10.7	5.7	17.2	10.2
Divided – GVR					18.7	25.3	17.9	21.2
Dissent					69.2	88.2	100.0	81.3
Sep. Conc.					30.8	11.8	0.0	18.2
Affirm	66.0	47.6	64.3	pub	40.5	37.9	35.6	39.3
				GVR	49.3	41.8	42.9	45.2
Reverse/Vacate	34.0	52.4	35.6	pub	59.5	62.1	64.3	60.7
				GVR	50.7	58.2	57.1	54.8

APPENDIX B: DATA SOURCES

Both quantitative, albeit non-statistical, and qualitative methods of analysis are used in this volume to cast light on previously unknown dimensions of non-regular judges' participation in the work of the U.S. courts of appeals. Two principal types of data have been used as the basis for the analysis presented here: case counts and interviews.

Case Counts. For the material at the core of this book, data were developed for a continuing study of participation by visiting judges and in-circuit district judges in the courts of appeals. The case-count data are the source of information on the frequency of judges' participation, their votes, and their authorship of opinions. Cases in volumes of the *Federal Reporter*, for published opinions, and the *Federal Appendix*, for "unpublished," non-precedential rulings, were recorded. Use of those case reports means that cases are counted on the basis of when a disposition was filed, not when an appeal was initiated or oral argument held. Full counts of cases are used, not a sample, because sampling was thought not to identify enough instances of "other" judges' participation, especially in courts which make lesser use of them. There may be a slight over-count of cases, especially for the Ninth Circuit, because a case was counted each time a disposition was filed, and at times a panel filed an amended opinion.

The case sets are consecutive volumes of *Federal Reporter Third Series* and of *Federal Appendix,* not chosen based on specific starting and ending dates, although, of course, those volumes are in chronological order based the dates dispositions are filed. How many volumes would be included in a case set, with each set spanning part of a year, was chosen somewhat arbitrarily, limited by concerns about manageability of numbers. Some sets that originally were shorter than others were consolidated to produce case sets of roughly equal number of volumes—13 to 19 volumes of F.3d (although one set has only 11 volumes) and 18 to 23 Fed. Appx. volumes.

Because of the way the project developed, with attention initially limited to cases with published opinions, data about "unpublished" dispositions begin later. The first three sets of published cases were non-continuous: 358-376 F.3d (2004), 488-500 F.3d (2005), and 550-562 F.3d (2008-2009). Published-opinion case data were then collected continuously starting with 720 F.3d, extending through 839 F.3d. After some consolidation, the case sets were as follows: 720-735 F.3d (2012-2013);

736-748 F.3d (2013-2014); 749-764 F.3d (2014); 765-783 (2014-2015); 784-800 F.3d (all from 2015); 801-819 F.3d (2015-2016); and 820-839 F.3d (2016). Data collection for "unpublished" dispositions began with 510 Fed. Appx. and continued straight through 640 Fed. Appx. The case sets for these unpublished dispositions, again after some consolidation, are: 510-525 Fed. Appx. and 526-540 Fed. Appx. (all 2013); 541-559 Fed. Appx. (2013-2014); 560-581 Fed. Appx. (all 2014); 582-599 Fed. Appx. (2014-2015); 600-622 Fed. Appx. (all 2015); and 623-640 Fed. Appx. (2015-2016). In order to show possible changes within the ten-year period covered, no overall (total) case set was created for published or "unpublished" cases.

Data are generally reported separately for each set of cases. Although volumes of F.3d and Fed. Appx. appear simultaneously, and some advance sheet books contain cases from both, the dates do not map exactly on each other. (Indeed, the dates of cases published in a single volume are not identical across circuits.) Despite this lack of exactitude, F.3d case sets and those from Fed. Appx. were paired where possible, as can be seen in the accompanying table (see next page).

Initially, cases for all circuits, including the Federal Circuit, were coded. However, once it was determined that certain circuits made little or no use of "other" judges, coding was limited to the First, Second, Sixth, Ninth, and Eleventh Circuits. For cases with published opinions, coding for the Second Circuit was discontinued after 765-783 F.3d, although some later cases were noted in connection with the "Second Circuit Problem" (in Chapter 6). For non-precedential rulings, starting with 623-640 Fed. Appx. coding was undertaken only for the District of Columbia, First, Sixth, Ninth, and Eleventh Circuits. Cases from the D.C. Circuit, which uses neither visitors nor in-circuit district judges, were coded only for the court's own senior judges. Cases were initially coded for senior judge participation only for the D.C., First, and Ninth Circuits, but to provide some comparison, this was extended to the Sixth and Eleventh Circuits, especially for later case sets—801-819 and 820-839 F.3d and 623-640 Fed. Appx. A judge was coded as a senior judge if in senior status *when a disposition was filed*, although in some instances that judge may have been in active status when the case was argued and submitted. Although in that situation, the judge was not likely a senior judge when panels were constructed, the concern about "who makes the law of the circuit" makes it important to know if they were senior judges at the time the opinion was filed.

Volume sets and matches

Fed. Third		*Fed. Appx.*

358-376 (19) Feb - Sept 2004
488-500 (13) May - Sept 2007
550-562 (13) Nov 2008 - Nov 2009

= = =

510-516 (7) Jan - March 2013
517-525 (9) March - May 2013
And if combined:
510-525 (16) Jan - May 2013

720-735 (16) June - Nov 2013   =====   526-540   (15) May - Oct 2013
*541 -553 (13) (Oct 2013 - Feb 2014
*554-559 (6)   Feb - March 2014
* If combined:
736-748 (13) Nov 2013 - April 2014   =====   541-559 (19) Oct 2013 - Mar 2014

^^560-573 (14) March - July 2014
^^574-581 (8) July - Oct 2014
^^ If combined:
749-764 (16) April - August 2014   =====   560-581 (22) March - Oct 2014

765-783 (19) Aug 2014 - April 2015   =====   582-599 (18) Oct 2014 - April 2015

**784-790 (7) April - June 2015   #600-613 (14) April - June 2015
**791-800 (11) June - Sept 2015   #614-622 (9) June - Nov 2015
** If combined: # If combined:
784-800 (18)   April - Sept 2015   =====   600-622 (23) April - Nov 2015

++801-807 (7) Sept - Dec 2015
++808-819 (12) Dec 2015 - Feb 2016
++ If combined:
801-819 (19) Sept 2015 - Feb. 2016   =====   623-640 (18) Nov 2015 - March 2016

Cases were not coded by subject area or issue, but data from a separate study of immigration appeals in the Second and Ninth Circuits were utilized to demonstrate some possible effects of the presence of "other" judges in a particular policy area, with 2007-2012 utilized for Ninth Circuit immigration appeals. Cases resulting in published opinions were drawn from 488-688 F.3d, and those resulting in "unpublished" disposition began with 31-49 Fed. Appx. (2002), then for 135-164 Fed. Appx. (2005-2006) and 180-211 Fed. Appx. (2006). Data were then drawn continuously from 212-481 Fed. Appx., extending from 2006 through 2011, thus ending before conclusion of data-gathering for cases used in the principal portions of this study.

For exploration of the relationship between panels with "other" judges and en banc rehearing, data maintained by the author on Ninth Circuit en banc cases, including the composition of the original panel, were used, and comparable data were constructed for the First, Sixth, and Eleventh Circuits as well as for the D.C. Circuit. For the possible relationship between the courts of appeals and the Supreme Court, the author's data set for Ninth Circuit cases heard by the Supreme Court was utilized, and comparable data for several other circuits were collected.

Updates to the data presented in this volume may be prepared, to be available at http://quidprolaw.com/?p=7392.

Interviews. The interviews used include those of Ninth Circuit judges in 1977 and 1986, by the author while in residence in San Francisco and Pasadena, respectively. Their focus was communication among judges, but questions about advantages and problems in the use of visiting, district, and senior circuit judges were included. In 1977, almost all of the then 13 active-duty Ninth Circuit judges and some senior judges, plus some district judges who sat frequently with the court of appeals, were interviewed. Relatedly, some judges' views of having "other" judges sit with the courts of appeals were obtained from their statements in the hearings of the Hruska Commission (Commission on Revision of the Federal Appellate Courts). In 1986, when the earlier interview-based study was extended once the court had begun to utilize an internal e-mail system, almost all the Ninth Circuit's now many more judges were interviewed, including re-interviews of those on the court in 1977.

To obtain the views of *visiting* judges rather than judges on *visited* courts, in 2016, a small study of judges who had visited was undertaken using a survey instrument and telephone interviews. Questions were limited to visiting judges' experiences. Requests were initially sent to 37 judges, a much smaller number than all those identified as having visited most frequently. When it became clear that most of those responding were judges with whom the author had either previous or indirect contact, with returns slim from others, further contact was not attempted. The initial intent to survey district judges who sat most frequently "by designation" with their own circuit was also not pursued.

Only ten interviews or surveys were completed, a response rate of 27%, but two other judges who declined nonetheless added helpful comments. That the "n" is low is not a problem as no statistical analysis had been anticipated, and the responses received provided a sufficient basis for exploration and demonstrated both important commonality of responses and some variation. A selection effect is likely, as judges willing to serve as visitors, and particularly if seeking to do so, are unlikely to be a random collection of even senior judges, the ones most likely to visit.

Communication Among Judges. Another, although less central, data source that helped provide judges' perspectives on how visiting judges are selected and on their visiting in other circuits was communications among Ninth Circuit judges who sat on panels containing visitors and communications by one senior judge who sat frequently outside his own circuit. The author was granted access to the case files of Senior Ninth Circuit Judge Alfred T. Goodwin, whom the author has served as archivist. Those files, which have served as the basis for the author's previous writing about the functioning of the U.S. courts of appeals,[1] provided some material about visiting judges' perspectives on their role, which was also provided by internal communications between resident circuit judges with whom the visitors sat and those visitors, although in many cases the communication was only perfunctory.

---

[1] See, for example, Stephen L. Wasby, "'Watchdog for the Good of the Order': The Ninth Circuit's En Banc Coordinator," 12 Journal of Appellate Practice & Process 91 (2011); Wasby, "Why Go En Banc?," 63 Hastings Law Journal 747 (2012); Wasby, "Goodwin on Judging," 93 Oregon Law Review Online 1 (2014).

INDEX

ABOUT THE AUTHOR

Stephen L. Wasby is emeritus professor of political science at the University at Albany–SUNY. He received his B.A. from Antioch College and his M.A. and Ph.D. from the University of Oregon. He held a Russell Sage Post-Doctoral Residency in Law and Social Science at the University of Wisconsin–Madison.

He served on the faculty of Southern Illinois University at Carbondale from 1966 through 1978. He has been a visiting professor at the University of Wisconsin–Milwaukee; the Faculty of Law, University of Victoria (B.C.); U.S. Naval Academy, as Secretary of the Navy Fellow; and University of Toronto, as Bissell-Fulbright Chair in Canadian-American Relations. From 2006-2010, he was a Visiting Scholar at the University of Massachusetts–Dartmouth. He has served as director of the Law and Social Science Program at the National Science Foundation.

His research has focused primarily on the federal courts, especially decision-making in the U.S. Court of Appeals for the Ninth Circuit. He is the author of several books, including *The Supreme Court in the Federal Judicial System* (4th ed. 1995) and *Race Relations Litigation in an Age of Complexity* (1995), as well as articles in social science journals and law reviews. He recently self-published *A Life in Judging: Ted Goodwin of Oregon.*

He was a member of the editorial board of *Justice System Journal* for 35 years and was its Editor-in-Chief from 2005-2007. He has also served on editorial boards of *American Politics Quarterly, Polity, Law and Society Review, Western Legal History, Law & Politics Book Review,* and *Communal Studies.* He has also served as the Director of the Heritage Grants Program of the National Railway Historical Society.

He resides in Eastham, Massachusetts, with several cats, and he serves on the Zoning Board of Appeals there. He can be contacted at swasby@albany.edu.

Visit us at *www.quidprobooks.com.*

Printed in the USA
CPSIA information can be obtained
at www.ICGtesting.com
JSHW021029160923
48161JS00003B/152